# RECLAIMING AND RE-FORMING BAPTIST IDENTITY

## COOPERATIVE BAPTIST FELLOWSHIP

*Elisa,*
*Blessings on*
*your spiritual*
*journey!,*
*Terry Maples*

**TERRY MAPLES** AND **GENE WILDER**

© 2017

Published in the United States by Nurturing Faith Inc., Macon GA,

www.nurturingfaith.net.

Library of Congress Cataloging-in-Publication Data is available.

ISBN 978-1-63528-024-1

# Endorsements

"A powerful tool to review Baptist history, understand our present situation as Baptists, and guide us into the future as people of God. Personal, transparent and authentic insights to be shared, understood and embraced as we take next steps in local congregations and among believers in a 21st century world."

Edward Hammett, Author of *Reaching People Under 30 While Keeping People Over 60* and Church and Clergy Coach for Cooperative Baptist Fellowship of North Carolina

"Here is a compilation of history and formative aspects of the Fellowship. And, here also is a set of spiritual practices to enhance your prayerful support for our faith community. This is a wonderful resource for engaging our past, praying for our present and anticipating a rich future."

Bo Prosser, Coordinator of Organizational Relationships, Cooperative Baptist Fellowship, Atlanta, GA

"This book is a treasure of information and insights, offering a mix of story-telling, history, and contemporary cultural challenges, while bringing together some of the best thinkers in spiritual formation to offer practical steps in our way forward. I look forward to sharing this book with small groups who want to better understand our Baptist identity and to reshape and deepen the way we understand discipleship, helping us become more aware of the practices that form us together into the people God is calling us to become. If you are like me and need to re-claim and own the faith we have inherited and to be encouraged to set off on a renewed adventure with God, this book is one I highly recommend."

Tommy Bratton, Minister of Christian Formation, First Baptist Church, Asheville, NC

"Taking readers on a deep dive into the richness of our story as a community of Cooperative Baptists, Terry Maples weaves history with hope. His gifts for seeing the spiritual dimensions in the story of our Fellowship's life together ought not to be missed. He is awake to what matters most in the life of faith. This book is an invitation to us all to do the same: to see and to sense that the Christ who has brought us safe thus far in our first 25 years is the same Christ who is leading us still."

Stephen Cook, Pastor, Second Baptist Church, Memphis, TN

"Terry and Gene have cast a vision for the still-unfolding story of CBF that takes seriously the "formation" part of Forming Together. It is a practical call – complete with some helpful guidance – to move beyond business as usual toward a renewed church culture where the emphasis is on spiritual practices that help followers live in the way of Jesus so that they become agents of healing and transformation for God's world. That's a movement I want to be a part of!"

Johnny Sears, Director, The Academy for Spiritual Formation
& Emerging Ministries, The Upper Room, Nashville, TN

"Terry Maples and Gene Wilder provide an insightful history of the events, controversies, and divisions that led to the birth of the Cooperative Baptist Fellowship. More importantly the authors share the stories of freedom-loving Baptists who helped shape our identity. It's an identity shaped by the understanding that "Jesus is Lord" and that he is the lens through which we interpret scripture and interact with one another. CBF is about fellowship, missions, cooperating, community, forming, partnering, conversion, and so much more. This book challenges us to continue the process of conversion and notes the importance of our 'forming together' as we seek to become more like Jesus in all that we do."

David Turner, Pastor, Central Baptist Church, Richmond, VA

"At this 25th anniversary of the founding of the Cooperative Baptist Fellowship, Terry Maples, a Baptist education minister and denomi-network leader, takes us on his personal journey of growing up Southern Baptist and being formed into a Cooperative Baptist. With the help of Baptist pastor Dr. Gene Wilder, this resource presents a detailed narrative of the takeover of the Southern Baptist Convention and the formation of CBF. This book is an excellent resource to help unpack the various flavors of Baptists through the centuries and the opportunities for CBF Baptists to keep alive an historic Baptist narrative and be the presence of Christ in the rapidly changing land-scape of Christianity in America."

Ray Higgins, Coordinator, Cooperative Baptist Fellowship of Arkansas

# Table of Contents

Foreword .......................................................................................... ix

Preface ........................................................................................... xvii

Appreciation .................................................................................. xxi

**Part 1: A Brief History of Baptist Traditions** ............................. 1

    Introduction ................................................................................. 2

    Chapter 1: The Regular Baptist Tradition ................................. 3

    Chapter 2: The Separate Baptist Tradition ................................ 7

    Chapter 3: The Southern Orthodox Tradition ....................... 13

    Chapter 4: The Landmark Tradition ...................................... 19

    Chapter 5: The Southwestern Tradition .................................. 24

    Conclusion ................................................................................ 30

**Part 2: Factors Influencing the Formation of the**
**Cooperative Baptist Fellowship** ................................................. 31

    Chapter 6: Early Indicators of Denominational Conflict ...... 32

    Chapter 7: An Overview of the Southern Baptist Convention
      Controversy, 1980–1992 ....................................................... 38

    Afterword .................................................................................. 43

**Part 3: Forming and Shaping the Cooperative Baptist Fellowship** ........ 45

    Chapter 8: Birthing the Cooperative Baptist Fellowship ...... 46

    Chapter 9: Shaping CBF Identity—The Early Years ............. 53

    Chapter 10: Reshaping the Cooperative Baptist Fellowship—
      2012 Task Force ...................................................................... 58

    Chapter 11: Impact of CBF Executive Coordinators ............ 68

    Chapter 12: CBF—Shaped by the Stories We Tell ............... 91

    Chapter 13: What We Learned in the First 25 Years! ........... 94

**Part 4: What Inspires the CBF's Future?** ................................ 103

    Chapter 14: Forming ............................................................. 104

    Chapter 15: Forming Together ............................................... 146

    Chapter 16: Partner in Renewing God's World ................... 197

    Epilogue ................................................................................. 215

**Questions for Your Reflection** ................................................. 219

**Appendix** ................................................................................... 222

# Foreword

*by Terry Maples*

I am not the same person I was as a teenager. That should go without saying since I am now 59 years old. Other than the obvious changes in my physical appearance, I know a lot more than I did as a teenager because of attending college and grad school and reading hundreds of books. I've been married for 36 years, and my relationship with Joan has changed me in incalculable ways. Our two children have tremendously impacted who I am and how I look at the world—unconditional love has that kind of impact. Serving three congregations has helped shape and form who I am today. Being invited into people's lives and spiritual journeys is sacred work. Relationships mediate formation—pastor to people and people to pastor.

Through all of life's experiences God has sought to shape and form me into what is best for me and those around me. I have often failed to allow the shaping forces to change me for the better. There have been times, however, when I have keenly sensed Spirit nudges and responded in faith. Those kinds of mystical experiences can't help but change you!

My faith journey and epiphanies may not be entirely unique, but they have molded me nonetheless. Those who consider themselves "recovering fundamentalists" will resonate with my struggles and ongoing realizations that "we don't live in Kansas anymore." God can and will do a new thing. I am happy the Cooperative Baptist Fellowship (CBF) is on the cutting edge of the movement that encourages a journey toward owned faith.

I begin this book talking about my faith journey and the dynamic ways in which God continues to shape and form me. I would have no integrity as an author if I write a book advocating staying awake to God while I'm still stuck with the faith of my teenage years. My transformation is still underway, and my struggle to be who God intends will not end until my death. So I tell you a bit of my story to give the context for this book.

### *Inherited Faith*

I was born in 1957 and grew up in north Alabama. My parents grew up outside of Huntsville, Alabama. They married each other at very young ages, and most of their lives were spent within a brief drive from where they were born. Dad was a self-taught, often bivocational Southern Baptist preacher. Mother stayed at home and raised twelve children (it's hard for me to believe too!). I'm the tenth born.

The small towns in which I grew up were close-knit communities. We could play outside for hours without our parents having to worry for our safety because we virtually never heard of any crimes being committed, almost everyone went to church, and our public school teachers led us in prayer every morning—which wasn't questioned because everyone in class was the product of a Christian family. In fact, I sometimes had the same teachers in school and Sunday school.

Life was difficult at times because small rural congregations expected the pastor to be poor—that's why they gave us "poundings" at Christmas each year. To my parents' credit, we never knew we were poor because life was rich in many ways. My siblings and I were happy children, we excelled in school, and we didn't get into too much trouble. The rules were simple: read your Bible and pray every day, obey your parents, get along with your brothers and sisters, and don't do anything to embarrass the family.

Life was simple in church too—or so it seemed. Scripture was interpreted literally (i.e., the Bible says it, so that settles it!). There was no liturgical calendar to follow, we never saw symbols or icons, and we never heard of Lent and Advent (which we thought were only for Catholics). Simple faith expressed by trusting in God through Jesus Christ was highly valued. A good church member was defined by showing up (every time the church doors opened!), giving, and participating in worship and Bible study.

High value was placed on conversion or, as we called it, "being saved." Giving folks opportunity to place faith and trust in Christ was the reason the church existed. Our churches scheduled at least one revival every year primarily for that reason. Revival was the main time of the year to bring people who needed to be converted into the church building to hear the gospel, and it was a prime time to call church members to repent and "get right with God."

Churches that nurtured my faith emphasized the importance of a one-time experience of becoming a Christian (except during revivals when one might question his/her salvation and need to have a "legitimate" encounter and recommit to Jesus). Certainly, we were expected to continue growing in Christ through prayer and Bible study, but I cannot remember anyone talking about the need for ongoing conversions along the way of my spiritual journey.

I placed my trust in Christ when I was nine years old. At the close of Vacation Bible School, my dad shared a simple plan of salvation, and I sensed the Spirit's convicting power. My conscious spiritual journey began. I was baptized by immersion—a deeply spiritual experience for me. I incorporated spiritual disciplines of Bible reading, daily devotions, prayer, and giving into my life. What I desired more than anything was to please God. For these instilled values I am deeply grateful.j

### Owned Faith

Not until I left home to attend the University of Alabama did I begin thinking differently about my relationship with Christ. I became very involved in a church near the university campus and began building relationships with strong believers my age. I started growing exponentially and am certain that lively context began to nurture my calling into vocational ministry. In retrospect I would call my experiences at the University of Alabama an additional awakening or conversion. Encountering various perspectives and faith frameworks in college allowed me to better reflect upon the faith I experienced in my home of origin even though in many ways they weren't hugely different.

I majored in accounting at Alabama because two of my older siblings majored in accounting, I recognized an aptitude for that type work, and accounting could provide me a good living. After graduation I moved to Nashville, Tennessee, to be an auditor for the state of Tennessee. I soon joined Haywood Hills Baptist Church. Haywood Hills continued to nudge me along the path toward ministry. Three months into my new position, I sensed powerful confirmation of God's call to serve as a congregational minister. I drove back to Alabama to share the news with my parents over dinner—but they already knew it (my dad was quite mystical that way). I shared my sense of calling with Haywood Hills the next Sunday and started making plans to attend seminary. Instead of preparing for the CPA exam, I started preaching!

Another significant change occurred while attending Haywood Hills. I met Joan Barbara Weinbender, who was only weeks away from attending seminary herself. Joan and I spent time together in the singles group. Very crucial for both of us was time we spent assisting a mission team from our church. We enjoyed each other's company all day long then sat on a curb outside Joan's apartment talking all night long. For an introvert like me, talking for that long was unexpected and quite shocking. I had never spent more than a few minutes talking to anyone in my whole life (that happens when you are one of twelve children!). I was intrigued by Joan's German heritage and her Wisconsin roots—Wisconsin seemed like another world for a boy from the Deep South!

Joan's theological perspective was significantly different from mine, having grown up in the home of a progressive, social gospel Baptist. Joan's dad was educated at Northern Baptist Seminary in Rochester, New York, and called himself a Rauschenbusch disciple—a far cry from my very conservative Southern Baptist leanings. Joan started Southern Baptist Theological Seminary (SBTS) two months after we met. We married after a ten-month, long-distance courtship. Immediately following our honeymoon, we moved to Louisville, Kentucky, to attend seminary together.

The decision to attend SBTS was another departure from my inherited faith. My parents were thrilled with my calling to vocational ministry, but my dad preferred I attend a more conservative school. Based on what he had heard about SBTS, it was much too "liberal," and Dad feared the faith he instilled in me would be challenged or destroyed.

One reason I opted for SBTS was because the vocational ministers on staff of Haywood Hills Baptist Church were alumni. I appreciated them, their passion for the gospel, and their theological perspectives, so SBTS seemed a wise choice to me. To be honest I had very little awareness of the difference in seminaries or their theological perspectives at that point in my life. Another motivating factor, of course, was the fact that Joan was already attending SBTS. It made sense that we would share our theological education.

The faith certitude I learned in my home quickly bumped into my wife's perspective of what it means to be Christian. While at SBTS, Joan and I took several classes together. Our discussions about what we read and learned in class were lively and often heated. In fact, we can honestly say the only thing we "fought" about in the first five years of marriage was theology. Apart from our spiritual heritage, our upbringing and life values were very compatible. Being married to Joan and desiring to know her fully caused me to explore perspectives and interpretations outside my comfort zone. This liminal time in my life confronted me with the necessity of additional awakening or conversion.

I must confess that seminary was difficult for me at first. The transition from business school to divinity school was in many ways painful. In seminary I was exposed to diverse interpretations and understandings of the Bible, faith, and theology. These quickly collided with more rigid and carefully constructed parameters around my beliefs. I was awakened, challenged, frustrated, and energized at the same time. I was inspired by deeply spiritual and brilliant professors. Opening myself to the very things about which my dad expressed concern scared me to death. Change was inevitable, but change was a dirty word for a novice like me who was taught that doubts and questions are threats to one's relationship with Christ. I was in the midst of an incredible faith crisis that would shift my life and ministry paths.

After seminary graduation I accepted a call to be the associate pastor for education and administration for a traditional Southern Baptist congregation in Florida. Inexperienced and "green," I was excited about sharing what I learned in graduate school with my new faith community. Unfortunately, change truly was a dirty word in this heavily senior adult context. The congregational mantra was, "Let's keep doing things the way we've always done them in order to keep the members happy!" I was very unhappy trying to serve faithfully in a rigid context that was unwilling to explore new ways to form and shape faith. These were good, well-intentioned people, but they simply could not tolerate change or threats to their homeostasis. Our first ministry role out of seminary was a poor fit for us, but my experiences there inspired renewed understandings of what it means to be church. The most difficult part of the experience was the feeling of frustration that crept into my being when before that assignment I had felt successful in every job I ever had. In my first ministry role, I was perceived as a failure—by them and by me. My success-driven ego had trouble dealing with that reality. In hindsight, I can see God needed to teach me humility. I learned a lot about myself during those three painful years, and my ministry "chops" improved.

Following what I perceived as "failure" in my first full-time ministry position, I felt the need to do career counseling. I wondered if I had misread my vocational calling. I knew I was a good accountant, and I knew I could run a hardware store (which I did in high school and college), so why was ministry so difficult? I contracted to work with Ben Curtis in Nashville, Tennessee. Ben's wisdom encouraged me on my journey. I'll never forget a couple things he said to me: (1) *You don't live at that address anymore* (i.e., let go of your childhood perspectives on life, faith, and church), and (2) *You can effectively serve another church or go back and be an accountant or run the hardware store—God can bless any of these paths.* Looking back, I realize my fundamental thinking about the nature of God's call was bumping into new understandings that were emerging. I viewed God's plan for my life as a rigid, linear path. Ben awakened my consciousness that God is more concerned with faithfulness where one is than the details of where one serves. This realization allowed me to engage the search process for a different congregation to serve.

After a fairly brief search, I was called to serve Westwood Baptist Church in Springfield, Virginia. God knew exactly what I needed following my shaky first ministry experience. Westwood was a breath of fresh air. There was a progressive feel at Westwood, and members were open to change and experimentation. They were sponges—ready to learn from *me*—and they were prepared to teach me too. In fact, I'll never forget a comment one member made to me: "We don't want your book learning; we want to know what *you* think!" That statement was a shock to my system, but it gave me the courage to start living into my understanding of the faith journey. I was transformed by serving alongside hospitable, loving people. I found my voice and courage to live into inner convictions that began to emerge. I was permitted to try new and different approaches. Innovation was highly valued. I am forever grateful to the members of Westwood for their investment in me and my family and for the ways in which they participated in my journey of becoming a congregational educator.

After almost five years in Springfield, I accepted a call to serve on staff at Huguenot Road Baptist Church in Richmond, Virginia. Westwood is where I found my voice, but Huguenot Road is where I developed the confidence to trust my instincts about Christian education and to flesh out how congregations form faith in Jesus. I served Huguenot Road for almost 20 years and experienced many conversions along the way—as did the congregation.

Two other essential components in my formation as a church educator cannot be ignored. Shortly after moving to Richmond, I helped start a peer-learning group—Greater Richmond Area Christian Educators (GRACE)—for like-minded folks engaged in Christian education ministries. I was privileged to learn from and stand on the shoulders of bright and gifted colleagues. I learned so much from reading cutting-edge books, and we stretched each other during lively discussions. I have no doubt in my mind that I am the educator I am today because of journeying with GRACE.

When GRACE first started, many participated in a twice-yearly Family Systems Retreat at Lost River Retreat Center in West Virginia. Soon my GRACE colleagues helped me recognize the value of working on myself (doing family of origin work) and gaining new perspectives on self-defined and self-differentiated leadership. I am deeply indebted to Larry Matthews and others who invested in me through these retreats. A systems approach influences all I think, write, and do today.

## My Journey Now

After 27 years in local church ministry, I was called to guide the work of CBF in Tennessee. I served in that role for almost six years before assuming the same type of position with CBF in Virginia. While I no longer guide local-church educational ministry, I am very much invested in helping churches nurture deeper, more mature faith.

I'm privileged as part of my work to visit different churches, to spend time talking to staff ministers and lay leaders, and to coach around faith formation. One thing is clear: many congregations are stuck doing Christian education in the same ways they have for decades. Innovation is not highly valued. Even when leaders have conviction that different approaches are better, resistance comes because change makes folks uncomfortable.

Local-church educators often teasingly refer to themselves as "the splinter on the banister of the local church" because educators are often the change agents. They recognize the need for change and work diligently to help nudge the congregation in the direction of spiritual growth. Their efforts are not always appreciated, but they serve a vital role for a faith community.

I'm wired to look for gaps in the life and ministry of a congregation. My INTJ Meyers-Briggs-type motto is, "There is always room for improvement." My analytical perspective is not negative; rather, I am simply passionate about awakening consciousness and nudging individuals and congregations toward spiritual vitality.

No longer focused on just one congregation, I enjoy a much wider audience these days. Serving as coordinator of CBF in Virginia gives me a vantage point to reflect on the gaps created by institutional thinking, resistance to change, and failure to listen for the Spirit's direction. For congregations to thrive into the future, we must wake up to current reality and learn how to embrace new ways of forming faith together as we partner to renew God's world.

# Preface

## *Why now?*

As a student of family systems theory, I know "why now?" is always a good question to ask when considering a major project. Why now—25 years into the life and work of CBF—write a book about Baptist heritage, values, and convictions that birthed our movement and factors shaping our future? The convergence of the following factors cause me to believe this is the right time for this writing project:

- My journey as an educator in Baptist congregations and my work as a CBF field coordinator in Tennessee and Virginia convince me many folks sitting in the pews of local Baptist congregations know too little about our Baptist heritage and the streams that formed and shaped Baptists. Education about our rich heritage is needed. Even in congregations where folks have been educated about Baptist heritage, a lack of knowledge and understanding persists. I see this book as an opportunity to resource Baptists and other Christians and to invite awakening about important life-giving values and convictions we cherish and are convinced must be passed to the next generation.

- If we don't know our heritage, we are destined to repeat mistakes of the past. A review of the issues that prompted the formation of CBF is needed—not to dwell on the past but to celebrate it and learn from it.

- I deeply value my Baptist heritage. Over the past three decades I have observed how our cherished values have been eroded and misunderstood. We stand on the shoulders of early Baptists who suffered and died for their convictions. I believe it is imperative we educate about and preserve these freedoms.

- Many folks still don't understand the difference between a Cooperative Baptist and other Baptist groups in the South. While we share much in common and there is much we can do together for the kingdom of God, we need a resource that helps clarify differences—not to divide us but to foster understanding, empower congregations to self-define, and encourage mutual respect despite differences.

- CBF celebrated 25 years of mission and ministry in 2016. For me, this new resource is a gift to CBF, one that can unpack our heritage, celebrate our faith journey, and anticipate our future together. While CBF's 25th celebration did not focus on the difficult aspects of our birthing story, we provide that story for those who have not heard or need to remember. The focus of CBF is on what God has in store for free and faithful Baptists. A bright future awaits us because of God's grace at work in us, because of our staunch commitment to historic Baptist principles, and because we stay alert to the movement of God's Spirit among us.

### Why me?

I am a lifelong Baptist. My father was a long-time Southern Baptist pastor in Alabama. He loved to tease with this question, "You know what I would be if I wasn't a Southern Baptist?" With a grin on his face, he would respond, "Ashamed!" That remark illustrates my dad's deep commitment to the Southern Baptist way of being Christian. Of course, we know being Christ-followers is more important than our denominational affiliation. However, I feel strongly that our Baptist heritage is rich, unique, and worth passing on to future generations. Unfortunately, the Baptist brand of Christianity has taken a hit in recent decades. Many congregations have removed "Baptist" from their titles and church signs. The time is now to remember and celebrate what is good about being Baptist while acknowledging that the Spirit is also at work in all congregations that trust in God.

I began this writing project with a commitment to first *do no harm*, meaning it is not my intention to display any ill will toward other Baptist groups. Good kingdom work continues through faithful Southern Baptists. Most of my family members are good Southern Baptists. I'm very grateful for the members of Southern Baptist congregations that nurtured and encouraged my faith. Mostly, I appreciate the excellent theological education I received at SBTS. Professors and fellow students opened my eyes to a much bigger world, challenged my limited perspectives on life and faith, awakened my consciousness about difficulties inherent in literal interpretation of Scripture, and enabled me to own my faith rather than simply embrace the one I inherited. For that great investment in my spiritual journey, I am deeply indebted.

I acknowledge the tension between "doing no harm" and being true to my lifelong calling as a Christian educator. Good education includes remembering the history of the Southern Baptist Convention (SBC). In reality the SBC became a new convention driven by different attitudes and perspectives under fundamental-conservative leadership. I do not mean to suggest all Southern Baptists are fundamentalists—they are not! However, this new leadership took the SBC down a different path—one that rejected and left behind key historic Baptist understandings, one that shifted to a top-down organization with a prescriptive approach, and one that closely aligned with a political party to advance an agenda. The fundamentalist mindset believed "the end justifies the means," so the story about the takeover must be told objectively, without glossing over truth about the harm that was done in an attempt to advance the cause.

I ask "why me?" and have come to this conclusion: I am compelled to tell the story of the CBF because I love the Fellowship! My journey began in the Southern Baptist tradition. That tradition left me and many others behind; CBF was there to preserve my Baptist convictions and provide a positive picture of God's kingdom and our place in it. The Fellowship is my home, and I am proud and honored to serve alongside so many thoughtful and gifted people within CBF.

I also sense God's leadership in this writing project. Because of my educational background and ministry experiences, I feel compelled to unpack what it means to form faith, to nurture faith in the context of Christian community, and to partner with others in renewing God's world. These words shaped my ministry, and I believe they can shape the future of the Fellowship if more holistically understood, appropriated, and practiced.

### *How to Read this Book*

Before you begin reading this book, spend some time in prayer, asking the Spirit to speak to you. Perhaps the Spirit will choose to use your interactions with what you read to reshape you and/or your congregation. This is my prayer!

Parts 1 and 2 of this book were written in 1992 by Dr. Gene Wilder as part of his D.Min. project. While visiting Dr. Wilder in his office at First Baptist Church in Jefferson City, Tennessee, I asked Gene about his dissertation. After he described the project, I requested to read it. He not only loaned me a copy of his dissertation but gave me "A Convention of Contention—A Layman's Guide to the Southern Baptist Convention Controversy." In this self-published work Gene attempted to parse his doctoral work into a guide more appropriate for Baptist laypersons. After reading his guide, I envisioned using it to tell the story of what happened within the SBC to set the stage for the formation of CBF. Dr. Wilder was delighted to share his work and encouraged the edits needed to make it more congruent with the focus of this book.

The purpose of Dr. Wilder's dissertation project was to examine diverse Baptist roots (Part 1) and provide a guidebook to examine the issues and events that led to the conflict within the SBC (Part 2). While containing Baptist history, this work is not a history book. According to Dr. Wilder, "One cannot truly understand the events of the present without first understanding the past because we can't know what we've lost until we first know what we had." The chief purpose for this writing project was to help members of the church he served at the time be better informed about denominational matters and become better equipped to make decisions about future denominational partnerships.

Part 3 shows how values and convictions that shaped and formed CBF were put into practice in this new movement of God's Spirit. This section contains historical perspective on CBF (1991–2017) and lifts up the words used to describe the Fellowship during the first 25 years. Rightly so, this section highlights the significant leadership of three executive coordinators: Cecil Sherman, Daniel Vestal, and Suzii Paynter. Part 3 concludes with the significant work of the 2012 Task Force, which strategically shifted the direction and structure of CBF.

Part 4 fleshes out the identity work of the 2014–2015 CBF branding campaign. Specifically, we focus on what it means to shape and form faith in the person of Jesus Christ for the sake of the world. In addition, we unpack key concepts flowing out of the branding process that give shape and form to the future of CBF: "forming together" and "partnering to renew God's world." This section is the heart of this book—making a case for forming faith in the context of Christian community and exploring ways to partner with others in renewing God's creation.

I'm most grateful to the brave souls who dreamed a new dream and birthed the CBF. While moderate Baptists within the SBC did not desire or intend to leave, firm conviction demanded a return to freedom under the lordship of Jesus Christ. With joy I tell the story of the first 25 years of God's work in and through CBF. With excitement I look forward to a future inspired by values, convictions, concern for the poor, an emphasis on justice for all, and the desire to partner—together—with others to advance God's kingdom!

# Appreciation

I owe so much to so many for their contributions to this book. Without the unconditional love, support, and encouragement of my wife, Joan, this book would not exist. I appreciate her editing gifts, her nudging, her capacity to ask good questions, and most of all her ability to make what I write better and clearer. To my children I also express gratitude: Anna Maples Dombo for her assistance with bibliography and footnotes and Andrew Maples for his thoughtful challenges to my myopic thinking.

I express many thanks to Gene Wilder for his excellent foundational contribution to this book. Without his painstaking research I would not have felt comfortable taking on this writing project. I appreciate his willingness to re-edit Parts 1 and 2 and write an afterword.

I'm also grateful to the faith communities in which I was privileged to practice the craft of Christian education and faith formation. I especially appreciate the many experiences I gained while serving Huguenot Road Baptist Church in Richmond, Virginia. Freedom to experiment and innovate for almost 20 years helped shape my understandings and convictions.

I appreciate time spent with the members of the GRACE peer-learning group in Richmond, Virginia. The gifts of each participant are reflected in some way in my philosophy of education and my focus on faith formation. In particular, Israel Galindo, former professor at Baptist Theological Seminary at Richmond and current Associate Dean for Lifelong Learning and Director of Online Education at Columbia Theological Seminary, heavily influenced me through our time together in GRACE, substantive conversations, his writings, and his encouragement of me and my ministry.

I owe a huge debt of gratitude to CBF Tennessee CBF Virginia for calling me to leadership roles within the Fellowship. My role as field coordinator in two state organizations gave me opportunities to immerse myself in the life and ministry of CBF.

I am especially grateful for the privilege of serving alongside two CBF executive coordinators—Daniel Vestal and Suzii Paynter—CBF staff, and state and regional coordinators. I very much value and appreciate my friendship with Bo Prosser, Coordinator of Organizational Relationships for CBF, and for his encouragement and willingness to support this writing project.

Allow me to express thanks to Johnny Pierce for believing in this project and to *Nurturing Faith* for publishing the book.

Finally, thanks to you for reading and engaging the ideas presented in this book. My hope and prayer is that the ideas contained herein will nudge you to deeper faith and greater courage as you consider shifts in attitude, theology, and practice.

**Reclaiming & Re-Forming Baptist Identity**

**Part 1**

# A Brief History of Baptist Traditions

# Introduction

There is no "purebred" Baptist. Instead, each Baptist is a unique combination of a significantly diverse ancestry.

When we look at our family members, it's easy to see how our diverse ancestry culminates in us to produce a unique being. We may have eyes like our grandfather and ears like our mother. Our body build may resemble our mother's, but our hair color may favor our paternal great-grandmother's. We are all unique, born from a wonderful confluence of diverse ancestry.

Each Baptist is also unique, born from a wonderful confluence of denominational traditions. Just as brothers and sisters differ in biological appearance, Baptist brothers and sisters differ in denominational appearance. Many streams of Baptist heritage have shaped us. Denominational identity, like biological identity, is a unique blending of diverse traditions. Various streams of identity give Baptists the denominational personality we have today. Even though we share denominational ancestry, each of us represents a unique composite of those past influences.

Because each Baptist is diverse, we don't look, act, or think identically. Some Baptists worship in a quiet, reserved manner; others prefer more animated and emotional worship. Some Baptists emphasize the pursuit of academic truth; others focus on evangelistic results. Some do everything possible to maintain harmony; others love a good fight. Yes, Baptists are diverse, and historically, Baptists treasured their wonderful diversity. Sadly, over the last half decade, some believed Baptists would be better served by exacting uniformity, by creating an archetype Baptist and requiring all others who wish to wear the Baptist name to think, act, and look like the archetype.

In these next few chapters we will examine the diverse traditions from which we came and gain a better understanding of who we are today. Additionally, our study of these traditions may help us understand why we have, too often, been a denomination embroiled in controversy and why the convention that once held us together ultimately became a convention of contention.

Chapter 1

# The Regular Baptist Tradition

My father was a Baptist pastor, born in the mountains of Tennessee and raised to be suspicious of any minister who led worship in a robe or any clergyman who donned a liturgical collar. I was taught that Catholics and Episcopalians wore robes, Methodists and Presbyterians wore collars, and Baptists were simply clothed in righteousness. Needless to say, I was surprised to discover that my earliest Baptist ancestors, Regular Baptists, were probably more comfortable leading worship in robes than my father ever imagined.

These robe-wearing, liturgical Baptists were known as Regular Baptists, and they were the earliest contributors to our Baptist identity. Regular Baptists were the first Baptists to organize in the South.[1] Their patterns and practices shaped Baptist identity between 1750 and 1800.[2]

William Screven is credited with planting the Regular Baptist tradition in Charleston, South Carolina.[3] Screven, a resident of Kittery, Maine, faced repeated legal and social persecution because he refused to have his children baptized into the state church. In the late 17th century, Screven left Maine in search of religious tolerance. He found the freedom he desired in Charleston, South Carolina.[4] There, Screven established the First Baptist Church and became its pastor in 1696.[5]

By the middle of the 18th century, the Charleston church was flourishing. As the congregation grew and its needs increased, Screven appealed for help from the Baptist Association in Philadelphia, Pennsylvania. Two men, Oliver Hart and John Gano, responded to Screven's appeal, thereby contributing hugely to the establishment of the Regular Baptist tradition in the South.

Oliver Hart was instrumental in strengthening the tradition that Screven began.[6] In 1751 he guided Baptists in the South to greater cooperation by establishing the Charleston Baptist Association, the first Baptist association in the South.[7] Hart, a Baptist who strongly believed in cooperation, eagerly connected with other Baptists and ecumenical groups as well. His ministerial practice provided a Baptist model for cooperation without forfeiting denominational integrity.[8]

John Gano arrived in Charleston in 1755.[9] While Screven established Regular Baptist patterns and Hart practiced them, Gano is credited with expanding Regular Baptist influence. Due largely to Gano's personal missionary activity, Regular Baptist patterns spread rapidly to North Carolina, Virginia, and Kentucky.[10]

During the latter part of the 18th and the early part of the 19th centuries, no greater purveyor of the Regular Baptist identity lived than Richard Furman. Baptist historian Walter Shurden calls him "the most important personality in shaping Southern Baptist tradition."[11] Not only was Furman pastor of the Charleston church for 38 years, but he left an indelible mark on Baptist identity. Furman was driven by a passion for education. Instrumental in beginning the school that bears his name (Furman University), he also influenced the establishment of several other educational institutions, including Mercer University and Rhode Island College.[12] An American patriot, Furman staunchly advocated for religious liberty. So strong was his dissent against English religious oppression that the British offered a bounty for his capture.[13]

The most significant contribution Furman made to Southern Baptist identity was his tireless advocacy for denominational engagement. His service as president of the Triennial Convention and president of the first state Baptist convention demonstrated the importance he placed upon denominational cooperation.[14] No wonder William B. Johnson, first president of the SBC, considered Richard Furman his mentor.

Many Regular Baptist characteristics influenced Southern Baptist identity. The word *order* captures well the influence of Regular Baptists.[15] In fact, to a casual observer today, Regular Baptists might be mistaken for Episcopalians. Their worship was liturgical and formal. Regular Baptist pastors often served as professors, so academic robes were standard attire for both the classroom and the pulpit.[16] Worship was stately and reverent with no evidence of revivalistic emotionalism.[17] Regular Baptist worship was God-centered. Instead of appealing to people for commitment, Regular Baptists viewed worship as an offering to God.[18]

The theological orderliness of Regular Baptists was most clearly seen in their use of confessional statements. In 1767 the Charleston Association adopted the Philadelphia Confession of Faith.[19] The churchly order of Regular Baptists was also evident in their expressions of ecumenism. While adhering to the authority of local congregationalism, Regular Baptists preserved a desire to cooperate with the church universal. Of this ethic Shurden states,

The Charleston tradition represented sort of an early Southern Baptist ecumenism.... They let Presbyterians and even raw Episcopalians come into their churches and preach from their pulpits. They had a sense of ecumenical activity even in the early part of the eighteenth century.[20]

Like all who claimed and understood the Baptist title, Regular Baptists maintained an almost radical adherence to the separation of church and state. An orderly relationship between church and state was non-negotiable for Regular Baptists. Under no circumstance could they tolerate a relationship between church and government that might interfere with their precious understanding of religious liberty.

One of the most enduring traditions passed down to us by Regular Baptists is that of denominational order. Their concern for organized structures of cooperation led not only to the formation of the Triennial Convention but to the establishment of state conventions and Baptist associations. The Regular Baptist model for cooperation was later used in the formation of the SBC.[21]

Regular Baptists also exhibited a devotion to ministerial order, primarily in their passion for clergy education.[22] The list of educational institutions organized or influenced by Regular Baptists points to the importance placed on clergy education and development. Not surprisingly, early founders of SBTS, James Petigru Boyce and Basil Manley Jr., were members of the First Baptist Church of Charleston, Regular Baptists' original southern congregation.[23]

While other traditions also influenced Southern Baptist identity, Regular Baptists established the earliest Baptist tradition in the South. An understanding of the influence of Regular Baptists is imperative for those who wish to understand the Southern Baptist search for identity.

## Notes

[1]Walter B. Shurden, "The Charleston Tradition," lecture presented at The Pastor's School, Mercer University, Macon, GA, recorded 1984.

[2]Ibid.

[3]Walter B. Shurden, "The Southern Baptist Synthesis: Is It Cracking?" *Baptist History and Heritage* 16 (April 1981): 3–4.

[4]William Henry Brackney, *The Baptists* (Westport, CT: Greenwood Press, 1988), 11.

[5]W. R. Estep, "Southern Baptists in Search of an Identity," in *The Lord's Free People in a Free Land: Essays in Baptist History in Honor of Robert A. Baker* (Fort Worth: Evans Press, 1976), 145.

[6]Shurden, "Charleston Tradition."

[7]John Franklin Loftis, "Factors in Southern Baptist Identity as Reflected by Ministerial Role Models, 1750–1925" (PhD diss., The Southern Baptist Theological Seminary, 1987), 56.

[8]Ibid.

[9]Robert A. Baker, *The Southern Baptist Convention and Its People, 1607–1972* (Nashville: Broadman Press, 1974), 43.

[10]Albert McClellan, *Meet Southern Baptists* (Nashville: Broadman Press, 1978), 21.

[11]Shurden, "Charleston Tradition."

[12]Loftis, "Factors," 56.

[13]Robert A. Baker, *A Summary of Christian History* (Nashville: Broadman Press, 1959), 314–315.

[14]McClellan, *Meet Southern Baptists*, 21.

[15]Shurden, "Charleston Tradition."

[16]Winthrop S. Hudson, *Religion in America* (New York: Charles Scribner's Sons, 1973), 122.

[17]Baker, *The Southern Baptist Convention*, 49.

[18]Shurden, "Charleston Tradition."

[19]Ibid.

[20]Ibid.

[21]Ibid.

[22]Hudson, *Religion in America*, 122.

[23]Shurden, "Charleston Tradition."

Chapter 2

# The Separate Baptist Tradition

My family hails from the mountains of east Tennessee. In fact, my father was a whoopin', hollerin', get-red-in-the-face, mountain preacher. When he really got going, his voice ascended to loud and lofty pitches, and guttural grunts of escaping breath punctuated his sentences. Most folks figured my dad hadn't really started preaching until perspiration completely soaked his shirt. Worship was always a "feeling" event. According to our church members, outward displays of emotion always accompanied "real" worship.

My great-uncle loved to tell about his conversion experience. According to Uncle Joe, he was saved during a revival meeting. Here is how I remember his momentous story:

> You all knows I used to be a rough and mischievous man. In fact, I never went to church 'less'n it was to carry on some mischief. One day, me and Buddy decided we'd go up to the church house and mock them folks what was at the revival meetin'. When the people started singin', me and Buddy would stand outside the windows and sing ol' foolish songs. Then when the preacher would git to preachin', me and Buddy would start our own preachin' to see if we could git louder than him.
>
> 'Bout halfway through the preacher's sermon, the Lord got a holt of me and flung me to the ground. I was near scared to death 'cause I thought the Lord was gonna kill me. Then the Holy Ghost lifted me up and pushed me down the aisle of that church and flung me down at the mourner's bench. I started cryin' out to the Lord to forgive my sins and save my soul from the fires of hell. Before long, the Spirit of Jesus hit me like a bolt of lightnin', and I couldn't keep from shoutin'. I know the Lord really saved me that day 'cause I could feel it when he got a holt of my life.

While few Southern Baptists boast of conversion experiences as colorful as Uncle Joe's, many attest to the importance of emotion in conversion and worship. Emotional expressions of faith among Baptists were, however, not original with my Uncle Joe. As early as 1750, a whoopin', hollerin' brand of Baptists began to carve itself into the Baptist identity. This group of emotion-oriented Baptists was known as Separate Baptists.

Between 1725 and 1750 a great revival (later called "the Great Awakening") swept the American colonies. Few, if any, churches in America escaped the impact of this dramatic religious movement. Most affected were Congregationalist churches.[1]

Despite the revival's popularity, not everyone in Congregational churches favored this new expression of Christian faith. Those who endorsed the revival became known as "New Lights" while those who opposed it were labeled "Old Lights."

The main point of disagreement between New Lights and Old Lights was church membership requirement. Before the great revival, Congregationalist churches were very liberal about accepting members. While most members professed faith in Christ, a profession was not required for membership. After the revival, New Lights became adamant about requiring a personal conversion experience prior to church membership.[2]

Within two to three years, the New Lights separated from Congregationalist churches in order to restore the church to what it understood to be primitive purity.[3] These disassociated congregations became known as "Separate" churches.

Separate churches soon recognized they had much in common with New England Baptist theology and polity. Such affinity encouraged Separate churches to become Baptist churches. Hudson summarizes,

> The strong and ultimately overwhelming tendency was for the Separates to become Baptists. The doctrine of believer's baptism, of course, was a fitting expression of the Separates' conception of the church as a community of "experienced" Christians.[4]

The conversion of Separate churches to Baptist churches was remarkable. Garrett comments,

> No religious group profited more from the outburst of revivals than did Baptists. In Massachusetts, for example, there were five Baptist churches before...1740; fifty years later there were 136.... As a result

of the revivals, a new denomination of Baptists came into being called Separate Baptists.[5]

In the mid-18th century, Separate Baptists initiated work in the South. The dominant force in the establishment of Separate Baptist work in the South was a Connecticut farmer-turned-preacher named Shubal Stearns.[6] In 1754 Stearns and fifteen other members of his Connecticut church moved to Opekon, Virginia, to begin a Separate Baptist church. In Virginia, Stearns and his followers encountered considerable opposition. Much of the opposition came from Regular Baptists who had already established churches in that area. Regular Baptists opposed the Separates' overly emotional preaching style, their use of uneducated ministers, their "noisy" meetings, and their extensive use of women in the church's ministry.[7]

In 1755 Stearns received a letter from a friend encouraging him to move his church to an area near present-day Greensboro, North Carolina. Hoping to find a more receptive climate for Separate Baptist ministry, Stearns and his fifteen followers moved to Sandy Creek, North Carolina, and established the Sandy Creek Church.[8]

This rural area of North Carolina was very accepting of Separate Baptists, something far exceeding the hopes of Stearns and his followers. By 1772 the Sandy Creek Church organized 42 Separate Baptist churches and sent out no fewer than 125 Separate Baptist ministers.[9] In 1758 Stearns led these Separate Baptist churches to establish the Sandy Creek Association.[10]

Daniel Marshall and Samuel Harris, two other Separate Baptist ministers, greatly influenced the tradition's expansion. Marshall, Shubal Stearns' brother-in-law, was an active itinerant evangelist. Not only did he spread Separate Baptist practices throughout North Carolina, but he was instrumental in planting them in Georgia.[11] Samuel Harris, a sheriff in Virginia, was one of Shubal Stearns' earliest converts. After his conversion Harris also became an itinerant preacher. He is credited with founding at least 26 Separate Baptist churches in Virginia.

The frontier flavor of rural southern colonies was well suited to Separate Baptists. Loftis states,

> As they moved South, Separates moved to areas that were almost devoid of large populations and established religious groups. Their independent congregationalism fit well with the pragmatic needs of the colonial frontier.[12]

No phrase better describes Separate Baptists than "revivalist emotional-ism." These folks measured the veracity of religious commitment by the degree of one's emotional expression. The linchpin of Separate Baptist beliefs was the conversion experience. Shurden explains, "Separates required an emotionally identifiable religious experience as the sign of conversion."[13]

While Regular Baptists had a penchant for order, Separate Baptists had a passion for feeling. They were pietistic and highly emotional. Winning others to Christ was the primary goal of their worship and ministry. Sensational preaching was delivered to congregations that regularly responded with emotional fervor. Of Shubal Stearns' preaching Brackney comments, "Stearns was an enthusiastic preacher who drew large crowds to his impassioned rheto-ric and flamboyant gestures."[14]

Both Regular and Separate Baptists viewed the Bible as the ultimate source of doctrinal authority, but Separates tended to interpret Scripture more literally. Unlike Regulars, Separates strongly opposed the use of confessional statements, seeing them as human impositions on the authority of God's Word.

Separate Baptists also resisted most ecumenical efforts. Because of their insistence upon a "pure" church, they feared fellowship with other churches, especially congregations from other denominations. Ultimately, their ecclesio-logical focus was the local church, not the church universal.[15]

Separate Baptists would eagerly have supported the sentiments of my well-intentioned friend. For Separates, vocational ministry was characterized by a divine charismatic call. Since God (rather than schools) called minis-ters, Separate Baptists were often strongly anti-intellectual, disdaining both the education and the financial compensation of ministers.[16] Unlike Regular Baptists, Separates freely used lay people, including women, to accomplish church ministry. Interestingly, Shubal Stearns' sister was a Separate Baptist preacher.[17]

While most members of Regular Baptist churches were urban, educated professionals, constituents of Separate Baptist churches were, for the most part, rural, uneducated farmers. Loftis states, "Separates appealed to the inde-pendent and illiterate nature of the frontiersman and were able to mobilize them as a populist movement."[18]

Despite the obvious differences between Regular Baptists and Separate Baptists, the two groups shared some characteristics. Both groups attempted to pattern their congregational church order after the New Testament church.

Both groups practiced believer's baptism. For both groups, religious liberty and the separation of church and state were non-negotiable essentials.[19]

Regular and Separate Baptist traditions functioned independently for less than a century. Hudson comments,

> At first considerable tension existed between the hyper-enthusiastic Separates and the old "regular" Baptist churches.... By 1787, however, this breach had been healed and both groups resolved that henceforth they should be known as "the United Baptist Churches."[20]

These early groups of Baptists in the South soon discovered a truth most Baptists have understood throughout the centuries: more can be accomplished cooperatively than individually as long as all parties respect the diversity of the other. Ultimately, the United Baptist churches impacted the South because they combined the best of both Baptist bodies. To this union Regular Baptists brought organizational and doctrinal stability while Separates contributed the strength and passion of lay ministry and revivalist evangelism.

While the emphasis upon Separate Baptist feeling-based religion is no longer as extreme as it was in the 18th century, Baptist emotionalism is still alive and well today. It's a formidable part of our denominational identity. Yes, for many, tears are still the proof of the Holy Spirit's presence, and passion in the pulpit divinely confirms that the preacher is, indeed, "fired up" by the Spirit of God.

## Notes

[1] Walter B. Shurden, "The Sandy Creek Tradition," lecture presented at The Pastor's School, Mercer University, Macon, GA, recorded August 1984.

[2] Winthrop S. Hudson, *Religion in America* (New York: Charles Scribner's Sons, 1973), 73.

[3] John Franklin Loftis, "Factors in Southern Baptist Identity as Reflected by Ministerial Role Models, 1750–1925" (PhD diss., The Southern Baptist Theological Seminary, 1987), 114.

[4] Hudson, *Religion in America*, 73.

[5] James Leo Garrett, E. Glenn Hinson, James E. Toll, *Are Southern Baptists "Evangelicals"?* (Macon, GA: Mercer University Press, 1983), 3.

[6] Shurden, "Sandy Creek Tradition."

[7] Robert A. Baker, *The Southern Baptist Convention and Its People, 1607–1972* (Nashville: Broadman Press, 1974), 49.

[8] Ibid.

[9] Albert McClellan, *Meet Southern Baptists* (Nashville: Broadman Press, 1978), 16.

[10] William Henry Brackney, *The Baptists* (Westport, CT: Greenwood Press, 1988), 13.

[11] Hudson, *Religion in America*, 75.

[12] Loftis, "Factors," 114.

[13] Shurden, "Sandy Creek Tradition."

[14] Brackney, *The Baptists*, 13.

[15] Ibid.

[16] Shurden, "Sandy Creek Tradition."

[17] Ibid.

[18] Loftis, "Factors," 114.

[19] W. R. Estep, "Southern Baptists in Search of an Identity," in *The Lord's Free People in a Free Land: Essays in Baptist History in Honor of Robert A. Baker* (Fort Worth: Evans Press, 1976), 148.

[20] Hudson, *Religion in America*, 7

### Chapter 3

# The Southern Orthodox Tradition

The messenger's reasoning made sense to me as he presented his motion to the SBC. In a formal but polite manner he proposed, "I move the Executive Committee explore the possibility of changing the name of our denomination to something more geographically inclusive than *Southern* Baptist." Immediately, an agitated roar erupted in the convention center. Obviously, the gentleman's idea was not a popular one.

Seated beside me was a man whose "Deep South" accent immediately betrayed his background. After hearing the motion, he turned to me and protested, "What a stupid idea. We've been the Southern Baptist Convention for years. Why should we change now?"

"I think the motion has some merit," I replied. "You know, the convention isn't just southern anymore. We've got churches in the North, the East, and even in the West."

"Well, that may be so," refuted the man, "but you just don't go around messin' with the name you were born with. You wouldn't want somebody to change your family name, would you? You see, we were 'Southern' by birth, so 'Southern' is the name we still ought to be."

As my fellow conventioneer and I continued to discuss the proposed motion, I realized he and I used the word *southern* in somewhat different ways. To me, *southern* was a word of geographical reference. To him, *southern* reflected a way of life, a way of thinking, and a heritage that should not be ignored.

Loyalty to the southern way of life has characterized the SBC since the early 18th century. As previously stated, Baptist churches of the South owe their 17th-century origins to northern influences. When those northern seeds of denominational tradition were planted in the warm soil of the South, they quickly blossomed into fresh, distinctively southern Baptist representations.

Several events evidenced this shift toward *southern*-ness, but no development was more significant than the establishment of the SBC. The formation of the SBC is best understood by tracing the history of Baptist mission involvement. In the early years of the 19th century, Baptists in America began establishing "societies" as vehicles of support for their mission endeavors. Cecil Ray defines a society as

> an independent organization of individuals who wish to support a specific cause. Societies usually specialize in one type of ministry such as publications, Bible distribution, or foreign missions. Any person who contributes to the society's work is usually considered a member.[1]

The society method of mission funding owes much to the efforts of William Carey, a Baptist missionary to India. Unlike present-day Southern Baptist missionaries, Carey garnered financial support by personally appealing to churches, individuals, and denominational bodies. When Carey's own Baptist association denied his request for mission funding, he enlisted a group of supportive individuals—that is, a mission society—to assist him in raising funds.

Following the urging of missionary Luther Rice, Baptists in America established a national, society-based organization for funding mission work known as the Triennial Convention. The Triennial Convention, begun by Richard Furman in 1814, met every three years to hear reports from various mission societies and to make decisions regarding the funding of mission work.[2] While the Triennial Convention lacked the structure of the SBC, it did represent an early effort to cooperatively fund Baptist mission work.

Few Baptist leaders were as denominationally attractive as Richard Furman. Converted and influenced by the ministry of a Separate Baptist preacher, then serving as pastor of the Charleston Church, Furman embodied the diversity of both Separate and Regular Baptist traditions.[3] During the Revolutionary War, Furman gained the respect of Americans (Baptists and others) for his enthusiastic spirit, his articulate rhetorical expertise, and his outstanding organizational abilities.[4] Because of his skill and popularity, Furman continued to exert primary leadership in the Triennial Convention until his death in 1825.[5]

Around the time of Furman's death, dissension erupted within the ranks of the Triennial Convention. The conflict put great stress upon the relationship between northern and southern Baptists. Several factors contributed to the controversy, but the issue of missionary appointments became the focal point of the dispute. Missionary candidates were examined and appointed by members of the American Baptist Missionary Society. Upon approval by the society, candidates were certified to receive society financial support for their work. As with other societies associated with the Triennial Convention, the American Baptist Missionary Society had constituents from both northern and southern states. While Baptists of the North represented a majority of the society's membership, Baptists of the South generously supported the work with their funds.

Despite their cultural difference, Baptists of the North and South found ways to work together to support mission causes in the early days of the Triennial Convention. Eventually, however, the missionary appointment process came under fire over the issue of slavery. Northern members of the society opposed the appointment of southerners who owned slaves and believed ownership of slaves doctrinally disqualified a missionary candidate. Since a majority of the society's voting members were from the North, missionary exclusion based on slavery became standard practice. As one might expect, Baptists of the South were infuriated at their exclusion. "How can the society justify the acceptance of southern money while rejecting the candidacy of our southern missionaries?" they asked.

While slavery was the presenting issue, the dispute had deeper roots. The ultimate question for the Triennial Convention was, "What is the cohesive foundation upon which denominational fellowship is based?" Was the convention's common denominator one of doctrinal uniformity or cooperative purpose? Regarding the issue of slavery, Baptists of the North insisted on a fellowship dictated by doctrinal uniformity while Baptists of the South deemed missionary purpose the basis for denominational cooperation.

As Civil War tensions mounted, differences in regional philosophies became more and more pronounced. Not only did southerners defend the institution of slavery, but they tenaciously defended every aspect of southern life, using almost every social institution to do so, including the Baptist denomination. Such regionalism quickly cast Baptists of the South as a culturally southern, male-dominated, white denomination.[6]

In 1845 in Augusta, Georgia, southerners established a convention of their own, and the SBC was born. This new convention was birthed not around doctrinal uniformity but around missionary purpose as stated in Article 2 of the convention's constitution: "It shall be the design of this convention to promote foreign and domestic missions and other important objects connected with the Redeemer's Kingdom."[7]

In a break from the Triennial Convention, the SBC rejected the society method of mission funding and adopted a more centralized convention model in which churches contributed funds to a central agency that then disbursed the funds to meet mission needs.

The pragmatism of this new centralized method did not come without a price tag. Loftis states, "In order to sustain this centralization, however, the Southern Orthodox tradition had to recognize theological diversity."[8] The founders of the convention quickly realized that *purpose*, not *theological uniformity*, must be the cement to hold this new denominational structure together.

The Civil War and its aftermath greatly affected the identity of the young denomination. The regionalistic tendencies of Southern Baptists became even more pronounced after the war. Howe states that from 1865 to 1900, "Southern Baptists were defenders of the status quo whose political, social, and economic attitudes coincided with rather than challenged prevailing attitudes of Southern society."[9]

Southerners, who found their cultural identity under constant attack, rallied around their churches and religious leaders in an attempt to retain what was left of their southern traditions. Samuel S. Hill pointed out how religion of southern people and their culture is linked by the tightest bonds. That culture, particularly the moral aspects, could not have survived without the legitimizing impetus provided by religion. Their coexistence enabled southern values and institutions to survive in the face of internal spiritual contradictions and external political pressures.[10]

Despite losing the Civil War, southerners were intent on retaining their identity, and their new denomination was an excellent repository of all that embodied southern heritage. In the early part of the 20th century, the SBC experienced major challenges to its philosophy of doctrinal diversity. These challenges began with the Fundamentalist-Modernist controversy, which was, to an extent, a reaction to the intellectual revolution ushered in by persons like Marx, Freud, and Darwin.[11]

In almost every Christian denomination, division occurred between those open to these new philosophies and those who saw them as a threat to religious faith. Controversy almost always developed around the topic of teaching in Southern Baptist schools.[12]

While division occurred in many mainline denominations, Southern Baptists averted schism partially due to the able leadership of E. Y. Mullins, who served as president of the convention and president of SBTS and was instrumental in leading Southern Baptists to retain their unity amid diversity of theological views. Marsden says of Mullins,

E. Y. Mullins had the rare ability to continue to be esteemed by Fundamentalists...even though his open-mindedness to scientific truth caused them some difficulty with his doctrinal interpretation.[13]

By the time the SBC met in Atlanta in 1924, the controversy had intensified. Several extreme Fundamentalists like C. P. Stealey and R. K. Maiden exerted strong pressure on the convention to adopt a doctrinal statement that would "bring about the death of evolutionary teachings on Baptist campuses."[14] At that convention a special committee was appointed to consider the advisability of issuing a confessional statement on Baptist beliefs. The committee chaired by E. Y. Mullins was to report back to the 1925 convention in Memphis.

In Memphis, the special committee presented its report, which consisted of a Confession of Faith (a revised edition of the older New Hampshire Confession plus ten additional articles), a carefully worded preface on the meaning of confessions of faith, and a closing statement on "Science and Religion." The committee's report was in no way prescriptive and left ample room for wide diversity of interpretation. The preface stated the confession did not contain

> complete statements of our faith, having any quality of finality or infallibility.... [T]hey are statements of religious convictions, drawn from the Scriptures, and are not to be used to hamper freedom of thought or investigation in other realms of life.[15]

By leading the convention to adopt a confessional statement that refused to squelch free interpretation by the individual, Mullins epitomized the very essence of the Southern Orthodox tradition. Howe states,

> Faced with a time of theological transition, ecclesiastical uncertainty, social adjustment, and religious diversity, Mullins emphasized rights under God of the individual, local church, and denomination. The individual was competent, the church autonomous, and denominational relationships totally voluntary.[16]

Between 1845 and 1925 the Southern Orthodox tradition evolved out of a variety of controversies. The characteristics of this tradition were three-fold: (1) Southern Baptists emphasized their regionalism. The "southern" prefix for Southern Baptists was not a statement of geographical reference but defense of a specific cultural orientation; (2) Southern Baptists consolidated commitment to the convention model of organization by rejecting the societal system of the Triennial Convention; (3) Most importantly, Southern Baptists became a people who expressed their denominationalism not in theological uniformity but in voluntary cooperation. As Hewitt stated, "They united around a broad doctrinal statement and a specific missionary and evangelistic purpose."[17]

Recall this chapter's opening story about a motion to change the convention's name. Obviously, the motion failed. Southerners don't take kindly to changes in their traditions, traditions embodying a history of doctrinal inclusiveness immersed in cultural southern-ness.

In light of the controversy that eventually erupted within the SBC in the late 1970s and 1980s, one might ask, "Who's been messin' with the southern-ness of the SBC? Did someone try to alter the principle of doctrinal diversity upon which Southern Baptists cut their teeth?" These comments come back to mind: "You just don't go around messin' with the name you were born with. We were 'Southern' by birth, so 'Southern' is the name we still ought to be."

### Notes

[1] Cecil Ray, Susan Ray, *Cooperation: The Baptist Way to a Lost World* (Nashville: The Stewardship Commission of the Southern Baptist Convention, 1985), 20.

[2] Walter B. Shurden, "The Georgia Tradition," lecture presented at The Pastor's School, Mercer University, Macon, GA, recorded August 1984.

[3] Robert A. Baker, *The Southern Baptist Convention and Its People, 1607–1972* (Nashville: Broadman Press, 1974), 55, 62.

[4] Ibid., 63.

[5] William Henry Brackney, *The Baptists* (Westport, CT: Greenwood Press, 1988), 171.

[6] Shurden, "Georgia Tradition."

[7] Ibid.

[8] John Franklin Loftis, "Factors in Southern Baptist Identity as Reflected by Ministerial Role Models, 1750–1925" (PhD diss., The Southern Baptist Theological Seminary, 1987), 184.

[9] Claude L. Howe Jr., *Glimpses of Baptist Heritage* (Nashville: Broadman Press, 1981), 137.

[10] Samuel S. Hill Jr., "Epilogue," in John L. Eighmy, *Churches in Cultural Captivity* (Knoxville: The University of Tennessee Press, 1976), 202.

[11] Walter B. Shurden, *Not a Silent People—Controversies That Have Shaped Southern Baptists* (Nashville: Broadman Press, 1972), 84.

[12] Ibid., 94–95.

[13] George M. Marsden, *Fundamentalism and American Culture: The Shaping of Twentieth-Century Evangelicalism: 1870–1925* (Oxford: Oxford University Press, Inc., 1980), 217.

[14] Shurden, *Not a Silent People*, 96.

[15] Ibid., 97.

[16] Howe, *Glimpses*, 141.

[17] Glen Hewitt, "Unity and Diversity Among Southern Baptists, " *The Christian Century* 101, June 6–13, 1984, 591.

Chapter 4

# The Landmark Tradition

Grandpa Martin was a model church member. As I was growing up, Grandpa almost never missed a service, and he was active in almost all of the church's activities. He attended Sunday school, Training Union, and only rarely missed a Sunday evening service. When we built the new building, Grandpa was one of those tireless individuals who shoveled dirt, mixed mortar, carried blocks, and painted walls. Often he cut the church lawn, never accepting financial remuneration for his services. Pastors knew Grandpa as the "preacher's friend" because he was quick to compliment and slow to complain. Without a doubt, few who attended my home church were as faithful as my grandfather.

When I was a teenager, I was shocked to discover Grandpa was not a church member. When I asked him why he never joined the church, he replied dryly, "Just never figured I needed to get dunked again. Weren't nothin' wrong with my first baptism, so I couldn't see no reason for being baptized again."

He explained further. As a boy Grandpa accepted Christ during a revival meeting jointly sponsored by the local Methodist and Baptist churches. (In those days the Methodists and Baptists often shared the same building. The Methodist congregation met on the first and third Sundays; Baptists met on the second and fourth.) After the revival, the Methodist preacher took all the new Methodist converts down to the river and baptized them by immersion. A few years later, when Grandpa inquired about becoming a member of a Baptist church, he was told he would have to be re-baptized because the Baptist church did not accept his "alien immersion" (an immersion performed by any minister other than a Baptist one). While he never said so, I think Grandpa was offended at being called an "alien." Because of my home church's baptismal policy, Grandpa opted to be an active alien instead of a twice-dunked Baptist.

Like many others, Grandpa was an innocent victim of a Baptist movement called Landmarkism. Landmarkism, a tradition born among Southern Baptists in the mid-19th century, still influences Baptist thinking today. While the excessively rigid attitudes of the movement are dead or dying, vestiges of Landmarkism still remain in Southern Baptist life.[1]

Simply stated, the Landmark movement was the practice of Baptist exclusivism or, more bluntly, denominational snobbery. Landmarkers believe Baptist churches are the only true churches. According to Landmark doctrine, the "primitive" (or original) church in the New Testament was a Baptist church, and all other denominational groups are ineffectual perversions of the original New Testament church.

While the specific movement can only be traced to the mid-19th century, the spirit of Landmarkism had antecedents in the Separate Baptist tradition. As stated earlier, Separate Baptists and Regular Baptists unified, becoming United Baptists, despite their obvious differences. But not all Separate Baptists favored the union. Those who were strongly independent resisted the unification and eventually moved farther west to frontier territory. There, they kindled the new revivalistic fires of the Second Great Awakening, eventually becoming the spiritual fathers of the Landmark movement.[2]

Much of Landmarkism's hold upon Southern Baptists can be attributed to three of its early leaders: J. R. Graves, J. M. Pendleton, and A. C. Dayton. Baptist historian W. W. Barnes suggests, "Pendleton was the prophet, Graves the warrior, and Dayton the sword-bearer in the new campaign."[3] By far, the strongest personality in the "Great Triumvirate" was J. R. Graves. Originally from Vermont, Graves settled in Nashville, Tennessee, in 1845. In 1846 Graves became assistant editor of the *Tennessee Baptist* and served as the editor from 1848 until 1893.[4] In 1851, during an associational meeting at Cotton Grove, Tennessee, Graves announced the essence of Landmark doctrine. In a stirring address he stated,

> Other churches such as Methodist, Presbyterian, and Episcopalian, all others but Baptist, are not churches, but societies; their ministers should not be recognized as gospel ministers or permitted to preach in Baptist pulpits; and members of all such churches should not be called "brethren."[5]

Without his forceful personality and relentless effort, the Landmark movement would have gained little momentum, but fueled by Graves' dogmatic passion the movement made its mark upon the Baptist denominational landscape. Of Graves, Shurden remarks,

He was a pastor, evangelist, editor, author, publisher, denominational leader; he was many things but most of all he was a controversialist! Possessed with an overdose of charisma and locomotive energy, he drove himself tirelessly.[6]

Graves admitted nothing less. In fact, Graves considered controversy to be the fuel upon which the movement thrived. As editor of the *Tennessee Baptist*, he admitted to deliberately focusing his editorial comments on controversial topics, asserting, "As long as there is conviction about the truth, there must be conflict."[7]

J. M. Pendleton was the theologian of the movement. It was Pendleton's work that gave Landmarkism its name. Estep explains,

> The movement is dated from a gathering of interested Baptists at Cotton Grove, Tennessee, June 24, 1851. The name was derived from a pamphlet written by J. M. Pendleton entitled, *An Old Landmark Re-set*.[8]

The third member of the "Great Triumvirate" was A. C. Dayton. Converted from Presbyterian to Baptist views in 1852, Dayton joined forces with Graves and assumed a writing ministry. He is best remembered as the author of *Theodosia Earnest*, a religious novel that depicts Baptist churches as the only true churches.[9]

Between 1855 and 1893 the leaders of Landmarkism continually attempted to inject the tenets of Landmarkism into the SBC. In 1855 they instigated a heated debated on the floor of the SBC concerning recognition of ministers of other denominations. Until then, the convention's practice had been to invite ministers from other denominations to participate in deliberations. The Landmarkers challenged this practice and forced the debate to a fever pitch.[10]

Landmark's most radical departure from established Southern Baptist practices came in its opposition to the convention's "board method." Regarding the mission boards' authority to examine, appoint, and supervise missionaries, Landmarkers contended Scripture gave such authority to local churches only.[11]

In 1859, at the annual meeting of the SBC in Richmond, Virginia, Graves made several attempts to alter the board structure of the convention. After tense debate, lasting more than a day, the delegates ultimately voted overwhelmingly to retain the convention's board structure.[12]

Graves and the leaders of the Landmark movement were aggressive, determined, and persistent. They did not take "no" for an answer. Estep relates,

> It appeared to some that when Graves' various proposals for altering
> the boards of the Convention were rejected, he attempted to divide
> and conquer by appealing directly and personally to the Baptist
> constituency in a large number of states.[13]

Doctrinally, Landmarkism built its theology around an exclusive view of
the local Baptist church. For them, no other denomination or denominational
body represented the true New Testament church. Not only did this doctrinal
viewpoint cause Landmarkers to viciously attack alien denominations, but it
sensitized them to be highly suspicious of their own. Fearing the denomination would usurp the ultimate authority of the local church, Landmarkers
vigorously opposed all centralized denominational ministries.

The Landmark tradition also applied its distinctive slant to Christian
church history. Landmarkers rewrote church history in order to justify historical church successionism, tracing Baptists through a hodgepodge of religious
groups beginning with Jesus and the disciples and ending with contemporary Baptists. Landmarkers disdained using the word *Protestant* to describe
Baptists. Why should Baptists "protest" if they are a continuation of the primitive church body?

The most popular work outlining Landmark successionism is *The Trail
of Blood* by J. M. Carroll. The subtitle describes clearly the focus of the book:
*Following the Christians Down Through the Centuries or the History of Baptist
Churches from the Time of Christ, Their Founder, to the Present Day.*[14]

The debate over whether or not to embrace the term *Protestant* to clas-
sify Southern Baptists, among other issues, reveals the lasting effect of
Landmarkism upon today's contemporary Southern Baptist identity. Other
debates include questions regarding open versus closed Communion, conflicts
over alien immersion, and the hesitancy of many Southern Baptists to engage
in ecumenical activities. Less identifiable yet pervasive is a sense of denominational arrogance fostered by Southern Baptist leaders of the Landmark
movement. This arrogance has contributed to a belief that Southern Baptists
are "almost exclusively called by God to win the world to Christ."[15]

The following excerpt from a letter to the editor of *The Christian Index*
demonstrates the ongoing influence of Landmarkism upon Baptist thinking:

Would our Lord Jesus be a moderate, a conservative, a liberal, an independent, or a fundamentalist? He would most likely be a fundamentalist. I base that on the principles of fundamentalism…to wit: A God-breathed Bible, the deity of Christ, salvation by faith alone, the premillenial return of Christ, and opposition to modernism in all forms. This could work a hardship on the SBC in that we are not fundamentalists, in spite of what the moderates or liberals claim. Fundamentalists do not tolerate ecumenism and most Southern Baptists do.[16]

While Landmarkers eventually left the SBC to form their own denomination, the American Baptist Association, their influence remains. Some suggest Southern Baptists' 20th-century controversy was little more than a resurgence of Landmarkism. Given the characteristics of the movement, such suggestions seem plausible. Rightly observed, the aggressive, controversial, exclusionary attitudes embodied in 19th-century Landmarkism most certainly have descendants in the SBC of today.

## Notes

[1]Walter B. Shurden, *Not a Silent People—Controversies That Have Shaped Southern Baptists* (Nashville: Broadman Press, 1972), 67.

[2]John Franklin Loftis, "Factors in Southern Baptist Identity as Reflected by Ministerial Role Models, 1750–1925" (PhD diss., The Southern Baptist Theological Seminary, 1987), 117.

[3]W. W. Barnes, *The Southern Baptist Convention, 1845–1953* (Nashville: Broadman Press, 1954), 103.

[4]Shurden, *Not a Silent People*, 68.

[5]Pope A. Duncan, *Our Baptist Story* (Nashville: Convention Press, 1958), 67.

[6]Shurden, *Not a Silent People*, 68.

[7]Robert A. Baker, *The Southern Baptist Convention and Its People, 1607–1972* (Nashville: Broadman Press, 1974), 209.

[8]W. R. Estep, "Southern Baptists in Search of an Identity," in *The Lord's Free People in a Free Land: Essays in Baptist History in Honor of Robert A. Baker* (Fort Worth: Evans Press, 1976), 153.

[9]Shurden, *Not a Silent People*, 70.

[10]Duncan, *Our Baptist Story*, 68.

[11]Shurden, *Not a Silent People*, 75.

[12]Duncan, *Our Baptist Story*, 69.

[13]Estep, "Southern Baptists," 154.

[14]J. M. Carroll, *The Trail of Blood* (Lexington, KY: Ashland Avenue Baptist Church, 1931).

[15]Estep, "Southern Baptists," 154.

[16]Bill Fowler, "The Index Forum," *The Christian Index*, June 18, 1992, 12.

### Chapter 5

# The Southwestern Tradition

If Missouri is known as the "Show Me" state, Texas could be called the "Make Me" state. Texans are proud to be Texans! If you don't believe me, just ask one. When a Texan takes a stand, nothing short of an army will make him change. Remember the Alamo?

I lived in Texas for three years while attending Southwestern Seminary. During those years I served on the staff of a small rural congregation outside Fort Worth. Upon graduation, I accepted a call to pastor a church in another state. I'll never forget the warning I received from a neighboring pastor after he heard about my plans to leave Texas: "What's this I hear 'bout you leavin' Texas?" he asked as he wiped the dust off the toe of his boot.

"I've been called to a church in Baltimore, Maryland, and I'll be moving at the end of July," I answered.

"Baltimore!" he shrieked in disbelief. "Why ya' goin' to Baltimore? Couldn't you find something better here in Texas?"

"Quite honestly, friend, I kept my options open and sent resumes to several states. After talking to the folks in Maryland, I feel called by God to go there."

"Well, son," he replied, "you're a young buck, and there's lots you don't yet understand, but you better think twice 'bout leavin' Texas 'cause once a preacher leaves the state, he may never get the chance to come back."

As my elder friend strode out of the office, I realized his words were not uttered in jest. He was serious—Texas serious. For him, leaving Texas was tantamount to falling from denominational grace.

My friend got his Texas pride honestly. Born out of a struggle for independence and cradled in hostile geography, Texans developed tenacity in defending their stance, regardless of the strength of their adversary. Not only did this stubborn strength enable Texans to win their independence from Mexico, but their "never say uncle" persistence found its way into Texas denominational life.

In the early part of the 20th century, unique Southern Baptist tendencies emerged in the Southwest, with their center of gravity fixed in the state of

Texas[1] The Southwestern tradition borrowed many of its more conservative traits from earlier traditions (Separate Baptists and Landmark Baptists) and blended them with a decidedly frontier pioneer spirit.

One cannot properly understand Southwestern culture without understanding a bit of Texas history. At the turn of the century, the Mexican government encouraged both Mexican and American pioneers to establish colonies in the northern Mexican territory (now called Texas). To the government's surprise, a large number of those who settled the territory were American pioneers who migrated westward from states east of the Mississippi River.

Fearing this large influx of American pioneers might cause the territory to lose its Mexican dominance, the Mexican government launched an effort to "Mexicanize" the territory. As part of this effort, the Mexican government required all new settlers to convert to Catholicism. Many settlers of Baptist heritage were outraged at the prospect of state-coerced religion. Like their colonial forefathers, these Southwestern Baptists deemed religious liberty worth fighting for. Not surprisingly, Baptists were some of the first to use force to procure Texas's independence from Mexico. Leon McBeth states,

> The Texas Declaration of Independence was signed in the blacksmith's shop of a Baptist layman, presided over by another Baptist, Richard Ellis. One of the reasons given for that independence was "that the Mexican government denies us the right of worshipping the Almighty according to the dictates of our own consciences."[2]

In addition to battling the Mexicans, Southwestern appetite for combat was whetted by regular confrontations with Native Americans. These early conflicts with "Indians" and Mexicans developed Baptists who were, "more intent, more aggressive, more conservative...exhibiting a militant spirit of conquest."[3]

The Southwestern tradition was also shaped by the theological diversity of its early Baptist leaders. To an extent, the tradition was a theological hybrid of Landmarkism, Fundamentalism, and Southern Orthodox denominationalism.[4] The spirit of denominational cooperation so dominant in the Southern Orthodox tradition was evident in leaders like Zachariah "Wildcat" Morrow. Morrow, who moved from Tennessee to Texas in 1835, demonstrated a strong commitment to cooperative missions.[5] One of Morrow's most ardent theological opponents was a fundamentalist leader named Daniel Parker. Parker was a strong advocate of the "anti-mission movement," a movement opposing all cooperative, benevolent mission work. In the mid-19th century, Parker led aggressive campaigns throughout the Texas territory opposing all Southern Baptist mission programs. McBeth aptly characterizes this tension between the two traditions:

> The struggle between progressive Missionary Baptists like Morrow and repressive Fundamentalists like Parker continued to shape the spirit of Texas Baptists. Like Sarah in the Old Testament who carried two nations in one womb, Texas has from the first nurtured opposite kinds of Baptists.[6]

While the influence of characters like Morrow and Parker was significant, no one person more strongly impacted the Southwestern tradition than the Mississippi-born Civil War veteran B. H. Carroll. In 1858 Carroll arrived in Texas from Arkansas on a mule. Early descriptions of his recalcitrant personality suggest Carroll was akin to that of his traveling companion! Theologically, Carroll was heavily influenced by Landmarkism. In his lectures at Southwestern Baptist Theological Seminary, he declared Graves, Pendleton, and Dayton the greatest theologians of his day.[7]

Graves' influence was most evident in Carroll's view of Baptist successionism. Like Graves, Carroll tenaciously defended the belief that Baptist history could be traced, in unbroken succession, to the primitive, first-century church. When the president of SBTS dared express a different view of Baptist history, Carroll initiated a denominational controversy, causing "all ecclesiology to break loose in Texas."[8]

In 1880 W. H. Whitsitt, president of SBTS, published a series of articles and a book titled *A Question in Baptist History* in which he asserted Baptists should trace their denominational beginnings to 1614 instead of AD 33. While reaction to Whitsitt's views was mixed across the SBC, no region more strongly expressed opposition to Whitsitt's assertion than Texas, and no person played a greater role in leading the opposition than B. H. Carroll.[9]

In commenting on the controversy, the editor of Virginia's *Religious Herald* stated,

> Does not the history of Texas Baptist affairs for years past reveal a condition of tempestuous and almost ceaseless strife? And has not the

tall form of the distinguished Texan (B. H. Carroll) loomed large in all these conflicts?[10]

Under Carroll's aggressive leadership, the Texas Baptist General Convention and several associations passed resolutions encouraging churches not to send money or students to SBTS until Whitsitt was removed. Finally, in May 1898 Carroll gave notice he would introduce a motion at the 1899 meeting of the SBC asking the convention to dissolve all relations with SBTS. So great was the opposition led by Carroll that Whitsitt announced his resignation on July 13, 1898.[11]

Ultimately, the Whitsitt controversy caused Texans to propose that another seminary be established in order to represent a more orthodox view of church history than the view taught at SBTS. On March 14, 1908, a seminary was chartered with B. H. Carroll as its first president. The school, first located in Waco, Texas, and later in Fort Worth, became known as Southwestern Baptist Theological Seminary.[12] Southwestern Seminary launched an educational process that tended to be more practical than academic. The new seminary used the Bible as its primary text and espoused only fundamental doctrines that focused on evangelism. This more pragmatic approach was well suited to ministers who would attract converts on the expanding southwestern frontier.[13]

No discussion of the Southwestern tradition is complete without mentioning the name J. Frank Norris. Norris was pastor of First Baptist Church of Fort Worth, Texas, from 1909 to 1952. Everything about Norris was sensational, from his pulpit antics to his political and legal recklessness. Norris embodied an aggressive combativeness very characteristic of the Southwestern tradition. Whether in the church, the denomination, or the political arena, Norris loved a fight. Walter Shurden writes, "He was a forceful, dynamic preacher and a rare bird who loved to fly into the fires of the controversy."[14] Norris often attacked city hall, boldly accusing Fort Worth's mayor of corruption, graft, and immorality. On July 17, 1926, D. E. Chipps, a friend of the mayor, came to Norris's study, and an argument ensued. Two hours later, the argument ended with Norris taking a gun from his desk and shooting Chipps. Norris was acquitted of the shooting on the grounds of self-defense.[15]

Charges of institutional heresy were the "bullets" used by Norris to "shoot" the denomination. Beginning with Baylor University and then expanding his battle to include the entire SBC, Norris viciously attacked the denomination.

While compromise, modernism, complacency, and infidelity were the denominational sins condemned by Norris, attacks focused primarily on the issue of evolution.

Even feisty Texas Baptists had difficulty with Norris's extreme sensationalism and censoriousness. As a result of his antics, Norris's church was expelled from its local association in 1922 and from the Texas Baptist Convention in 1924.[16] After exclusion from the ranks of Southern Baptists, Norris continued his combative campaigns, aligning himself with a variety of fundamentalist organizations throughout North America.[17]

While the Southwestern tradition may not be as easily identifiable as earlier traditions, it permeates contemporary Southern Baptist identity. The Southwestern tradition's influence can be summarized this way: intensely conservative, fervently evangelistic, and spiritedly combative.

The Southwestern tradition's conservatism can be traced most directly to an inerrantist view of Scripture. For Southwesterners, both the message and the words of Scripture were infallible and should therefore be interpreted as literally as possible. Not only was the Bible the authoritative text for religion; it was the academic sourcebook for all areas of study. Whether the subject was history or ethics, agriculture or religion, the infallible Bible contained the perfect answer for every inquiry. This fundamentalist approach to Scripture also promoted a spirit of intense anti-ecumenism. In the opinion of Carroll and his followers, infallible Scripture did not provide a model for relating to those with contrary beliefs.[18] Open dialogue with those who possessed doctrinal error might contaminate the imagined purity of Southwestern Baptist orthodoxy.

Southwesterners also influenced Southern Baptist zealous emphasis on missions and evangelism. Politically and geographically, Texans lived by the code of conquest, fiercely battling any opposition until all foes were defeated. Texas Baptists "contended for lost souls" with the same unceasing evangelistic fervor. This zeal for winning souls dominated the doctrine and preaching themes of Southwestern Baptists. Not surprisingly, most worship had a revivalist, evangelistic flare.[19]

In religion as well as in politics, Southwesterners of the 19th and early 20th centuries would rather fight than switch. Like J. Frank Norris, Southwestern Baptists were apt to shoot first and ask questions later. That kind of fighting spirit does not die easily. That longstanding spirit of conflict and conquest continues to haunt the SBC, according to native Texan Leon McBeth, who stated,

> One is hard pressed to name a major Southern Baptist uproar of the twentieth century that has not centered in the newer territories west of the Mississippi.... Those in the Southwest seem to take to a row like Br'er Rabbit takes to the briar patch.[20]

While the Southwestern tradition was last in chronological sequence, it certainly was not least in denominational impact.

### Notes

[1]Leon McBeth, "A Study in Baptist Regionalism," lecture at The Southern Baptist Theological Seminary, Louisville, KY, recorded April 19–20, 1988.

[2]Ibid.

[3]Ibid.

[4]John Franklin Loftis, "Factors in Southern Baptist Identity as Reflected by Ministerial Role Models, 1750–1925" (PhD diss., The Southern Baptist Theological Seminary, 1987), 253.

[5]McBeth, "Baptist Regionalism."

[6]Ibid.

[7]Ibid.

[8]Ibid.

[9]Walter B. Shurden, *Not a Silent People—Controversies That Have Shaped Southern Baptists* (Nashville: Broadman Press, 1972), 26.

[10]McBeth, "Baptist Regionalism."

[11]Shurden, *Not a Silent People,* 28–29.

[12]Robert A. Baker, *The Southern Baptist Convention and Its People, 1607–1972* (Nashville: Broadman Press, 1974), 303.

[13]Loftis, "Factors," 253.

[14]Shurden, *Not a Silent People,* 90.

[15]Ibid., 91.

[16]Ibid., 90–92.

[17]Ibid., 93.

[18]Loftis, "Factors," 254.

[19]McBeth, "Baptist Regionalism."

[20]Ibid.

# Conclusion

In learning about, comprehending, and analyzing the SBC controversy, a review of key events in Baptist life is essential. We cannot understand who we are until we understand our heritage, that is, the streams from which we flow.

Baptists are a highly diverse people. Our diversity results from a variety of influences and experiences. We are a mixture. Some of us are three parts Regular Baptist and two parts Southern Orthodox. Others are one part Landmark and four parts Southwestern. Most of us are an unequal mixture of all five traditions surfacing at different times and places on our faith journey.

Prior to the mid-20th century, Southern Baptists functioned cooperatively despite their wide diversity. Indeed, numerous disputes erupted because of diverse patterns, but in every instance the desire to accomplish our central mission enabled us to see past our differences. While other denominations splintered into doctrinaire factions, Southern Baptists took pride in their ability to maintain unity in the midst of doctrinal and cultural diversity.

Southern Baptist pride eroded when unity faded. Diverse traditions that formerly collaborated soon collided. Instead of rallying around a common mission cause, Baptists drew denominational battle lines. The denominational giant experienced a great fall.

Part 2

# Factors Influencing the Formation of the Cooperative Baptist Fellowship

### Chapter 6

# Early Indicators of Denominational Conflict

I was a child of the sixties. Some called us hippies, some called us freaks, and many adults simply refused to call us at all. Our hair was long, and our skirts were short. We liked the Beatles and the Rolling Stones and wore bell-bottomed jeans. Peter, Paul, and Mary were not biblical names to us. Instead, they were prophets of protest decrying a war we did not understand.

We "Baby Boomers" were intent on changing our world. My generation tried to tear loose everything that was nailed down. We burned flags as we marched down streets. We extolled free love as we fought to end war. We ushered in a psychedelic revolution on the wings of mind-altering drugs. We concluded the past was all wrong and we were all right, and as we tore down the establishment, we established new expectations.

Today, my generation *is* the establishment. No longer do we seek to tear down tradition; rather, we are vigilant defenders of the status quo. Only now, after raising children, do I know how frightening my generation was for my parents' generation. In less than a decade our fathers and mothers watched their conservative world of traditional values become a seething cauldron of moral, ethical, and political change.

People in society tend to react to radical change in one of two ways. Some simply "go with the flow," making the personal adjustments required to embrace societal shifts. Others rebel against change, seeing it as a threat to their security and all they hold dear.

Southern Baptists were not immune to the radical changes of the 1960s. Rooted in theological and ethical conservatism, many Southern Baptists were frightened by the new social order. In an attempt to insulate the denomination from the threat of this new "liberalism," the convention began restricting expressions of theological diversity. Formal and informal systems were established to exercise more control over the convention's agencies and personnel. For these defenders of the status quo, expressions of diversity became a threat. In their minds the only safeguard against sliding down the slippery slope of theological liberalism was to erect intractable boundaries of theological uniformity.

The term *fundamentalist* is often used to distinguish extremist groups that aggressively resist religious or social change. These groups do whatever is needed to keep their society attached to a set of perceived "fundamentals." Any diversity that calls into question their chosen set of fundamentals is seen as a threat to survival.

Leon McBeth uses the term *fundamentalist* to identify Southern Baptist extremists who organized themselves in the 1960s and 1970s. McBeth stated,

> I intend nothing pejorative in applying the term to contemporary Southern Baptists who espouse ultraconservative theological and social views…[but] fundamentalism, in whatever religious group, tends to be unable to tolerate diversity and often seems determined to "rule or ruin" its group.[1]

I also use *fundamentalist* to describe those who represent the militant ultraconservative faction in the SBC. *Moderate* is the term I use for the denominational circle that advocates acceptance of theological diversity. These terms are descriptive, not divisive, for both sides are represented by people of integrity and value. As with any label, these two are woefully inadequate because they tend to suggest all people within a given group are the same. Nothing could be further from the truth. Not all fundamentalists are militant, ultraconservative, and exclusive. Not all who wear the name moderate are open to diversity. There is great variety within the ranks of both groups. Unfortunately, for lack of better terms, I use these.

Historically, fundamentalist groups had little success in controlling the affairs of the SBC. Because Baptists thrive on diversity, they tended to resist attempts to squelch the exercise of free thought and conscience. As stated previously, the term *theological uniformity* and the word *Baptist* are inappropriate bedfellows. William Screven moved to Charleston and established the Regular Baptist tradition because the religious leadership of Kittery, Maine, refused him the right to express his personal theological views. Even though Separate Baptists significantly differed from Regular Baptists in their theology and worship, the two diverse groups found denominational fellowship around a central mission purpose. In 1845 Baptists of the South formed their own convention because the American Baptist Missionary Society tried to squeeze them into a doctrinal mold. Despite the persuasive expertise of people like J. R. Graves and B. H. Carroll, Southern Baptists resisted efforts to coerce denominational theological uniformity. Baptists have not always agreed, but they never expected to agree. Common purpose, not theological uniformity, was the cement that held Southern Baptists together.

Dr. E. Y. Mullins, a past president of the SBC, was one of the denomination's greatest statesmen. On one occasion when Dr. Mullins disagreed with a colleague on a doctrinal point, he rejoined, "If we do not agree on this subject, let us be brothers and agree to disagree. Let us not be like some Baptists who will not be a brother to any other Baptist unless he is a twin brother." Indeed, the history of Baptists is one of denominational brotherhood where no one was expected to be exactly alike.

According to Southern Baptist historian Claude Howe, 1961 marked the beginning of an effort to develop a more uniform orthodoxy within the SBC. This fundamentalist effort began to overshadow the convention's original purpose of cooperative missions.[2] Several events illustrate this movement toward theological uniformity.

In 1961 the Sunday School Board of the SBC published *The Message of Genesis* by Ralph Elliott. Elliott was a professor at Midwestern Baptist Theological Seminary. In his book, Elliott suggested Genesis might have been written by authors other than Moses. He further conjectured that the first eleven chapters of Genesis were not literal accounts of history but parabolic stories depicting the beginning of humankind.[3]

Because Elliott's book created such uproar among Southern Baptists, the Sunday School Board decided against publishing a second edition. Ultimately, Elliott was fired by Midwestern's board of trustees because he refused to be censured.

As a result of the Elliott controversy, the SBC appointed a special committee to craft a new confession of faith, one that would more clearly define acceptable boundaries of Southern Baptist theological orthodoxy. In 1963 the convention adopted the revised "Baptist Faith and Message" statement at its annual meeting in Kansas City, Missouri.[4]

The parameters of theological expression continued to narrow as the Sunday School Board published volume one of *The Broadman Bible Commentary* in 1969. The Genesis section was written by G. Henton Davies, an English scholar. In his commentary on Genesis 22:1–19, Davies suggested God may not actually have commanded Abraham to sacrifice Isaac. Instead, suggested Davies, Abraham only understood that to be God's will.

In June 1970 when the convention met in Denver, the new Broadman Commentary became the focus of controversy. After lengthy periods of contentious debate, the convention voted to discontinue selling the current edition and to replace it with a revised edition.[5]

In the early 1970s several "watchdog" groups sprang up within the convention, intent on curbing a perceived drift toward theological liberalism. Most notable was the Baptist Faith and Message Fellowship. This group of right-wing fundamentalists advocated strict adherence to the "Baptist Faith and Message" as a test of orthodoxy for all employees of Baptist institutions.[6]

During the late 1960s and early 1970s several new educational institutions were independently established by fundamentalists skeptical of existing Southern Baptist schools. These institutions championed the causes of biblical inerrancy and theological fundamentalism. Among these institutions were Mid-America Seminary, Luther Rice Seminary, and the Criswell Center for Biblical Studies.[7]

These developments and others not cited demonstrated Southern Baptist reaction to the fear of denominational liberalism. While the events significantly impacted the denomination, they were random, reactionary, and uncalculated. For the most part, these theological skirmishes did not represent an organized effort to impose new theological restrictions upon Southern Baptist theological diversity.

In 1979 Southern Baptists entered a new era, the era of intentional political control. This new era was ushered in by two Texans, Judge Paul Pressler and Dr. Paige Patterson. Judge Paul Pressler, a state appeals judge in Houston, was the political mastermind of the takeover effort. His 35 years of secular political experience provided the fundamentalist coalition a wealth of expertise.[8]

While Pressler brought political expertise to the fundamentalist effort, Dr. Paige Patterson, president of the Criswell Center for Biblical Studies, contributed theological proficiency. Because the school was sponsored by First Baptist Church of Dallas, Patterson's position made him highly recognizable to more conservative members of the SBC.

Early in 1979 Pressler and Patterson announced a ten-year plan for gaining control of the SBC. By orchestrating the election of politically active, fundamentalist presidents, these two Texans hoped to establish a less diverse orthodoxy within the SBC.[9]

Their plan was as simple as it was effective. Here's how it worked: All Southern Baptist agencies and institutions are controlled by trustees who are elected by the convention to four- or five-year terms. These trustees are nominated by the Committee on Nominations. The Committee on Nominations is nominated by the Committee on Committees, but the Committee on Committees is appointed by the SBC president. Pressler and Patterson surmised that if the "right politically active" presidents could be elected, then the "right" Committee on Committees members would be appointed, and the rest of the process would simply follow suit.

Note the phrase *politically active*. For Pressler and Patterson's plan to work, they needed leaders who were more than theologically *acceptable*. They needed people who would take an active role in excluding those who were theologically *unacceptable*. Robert Tenery, editor of the *Southern Baptist Advocate*, a fundamentalist tabloid, said this about the takeover plan:

> If we fill vacancies with people who feel they have to be conciliatory to
> the liberals [that is, to moderates]…all our effort has been in vain.…
> They don't seem to have any use for a Jesus who plaited a whip and
> drove a bunch of phonies out of the temple.[10]

When Pressler and Patterson announced their plan, few Southern Baptists took their design seriously. The idea of a politically manipulated theological orthodoxy was so outrageous it was deemed incredible.

About one month prior to the 1979 annual convention in Houston, Patterson and Pressler conducted an intensive fifteen-state tour to enlist messengers to come to Houston and "fight liberalism in the convention." To the complete surprise of many, Adrian Rogers, the fundamentalist pastor of Bellevue Baptist Church in Memphis, Tennessee, was elected on the first ballot.[11]

Strange and unusual changes were taking place in the convention's normal process. Not only was the convention politicized prior to the meeting, but the voting process appeared to be manipulated during the meeting itself. Pressler, Patterson, and others occupied a command post in skyboxes above the convention meeting space and maintained contact with the floor below through an elaborate communications network.[12] After the election, accusations of parliamentary irregularities were voiced. Pressler, for example, was registered to vote at the convention as a messenger from a church to which he did not belong.[13]

When the 1979 convention was over, most rank-and-file Southern Baptists refused to believe their convention had significantly changed, but they were wrong. The political strategy devised and enacted by Pressler and Patterson proved to be effective, not only in 1979, but throughout the contentious decades that followed.

## Notes

[1]Leon McBeth, "Fundamentalism in the Southern Baptist Convention in Recent Years," *Review & Expositor* (Winter 1982): 86, 87.

[2]Claude L. Howe Jr., *Glimpses of Baptist Heritage* (Nashville: Broadman Press, 1981), 146–158.

[3]Rob James, ed., *The Takeover in the Southern Baptist Convention, A Brief History* (Decatur, GA: SBC Today, 1989), 15–16.

[4]Ibid., 16.

[5]Ibid.

[6]Howe, *Glimpses*, 146–158.

[7]Ibid.

[8]"Struggle for the Baptist Soul" (Dallas: Baptists Committed to the Southern Baptist Convention, 1988), 2.

[9]Claude L. Howe Jr., "From Houston to Dallas: Recent Controversy in the Southern Baptist Convention," *The Theological Educator*, Special Issue (Spring 1985): 31–37.

[10]Robert Tenery, "Remember the Little Red Hen," *Southern Baptist Advocate*, January 1989, 3.

[11]Howe, "From Houston to Dallas," 31–37.

[12]James, *Takeover*, 9.

[13]Ibid.

Chapter 7

# An Overview of the
# Southern Baptist Convention Controversy,
# 1980–1992

In 1979 the SBC embarked on a course that thrust her into waters of denominational turmoil for more than a decade. The emergence of purposeful political activism was something for which Southern Baptists were unprepared. Never before in the history of the denomination had an individual or group of individuals intentionally set out to control the denomination and its agencies. This, however, was clearly the goal of the Pressler-Patterson coalition.

In the decade that followed Adrian Rogers' election, both fundamentalist and moderate coalitions developed intricate political networks focused on registering the largest number of convention messengers—messengers who would support their candidates and their agenda.

Of the two political factions, fundamentalists proved to be the most effective in getting out the vote. Year after year, fundamentalists were able to secure the election of politically active presidents. Additionally, they approved motions and resolutions that narrowed the SBC's parameters of acceptable theological orthodoxy. The denomination that had once been a repository for diverse Baptist traditions quickly became one that excluded anyone who did not embrace fundamentalist views.

As the schism deepened and became increasingly hostile, groups of denominational centrists surfaced, looking for ways to bring reconciliation within the fractured denomination. To that end, in 1985 the convention elected a "Peace Committee," given the task to study the causes of controversy and recommend solutions for resolving differences. An attempt was made to fill the Peace Committee with an equal number of fundamentalist and moderate leaders.

Despite the convention's overt gestures toward reconciliation, peace proved to be an elusive dream. Before the committee met for its first session, some of its members expressed pessimism about the committee's success. Bill Sherman, a moderate member of the committee, recalls,

I met with Adrian Rogers and told him, "I don't see eye to eye with you theologically, but I can work with you, and you interpret Scripture as you wish." Quick as a flash Rogers snapped his fingers and said, "Bill, that's good enough for you, but I will not work with liberals."[1]

In 1986 the Peace Committee made its first convention report and stated, "The limits of legitimate diversity are at the very heart of our ongoing process to bring about reconciliation."[2] While moderates wanted to include denominational leaders from diverse Baptist perspectives, fundamentalists wanted to exclude all who did not adhere to their strictly defined parameters of theological orthodoxy.

Prior to the 1989 annual meeting, a centrist group called "Baptists Committed to the SBC" announced its intention to offer a "middle of the road" presidential nominee. Daniel Vestal, a well-known, conservative pastor from Atlanta (with Texas roots), was the choice of Baptists Committed. Commenting about the politicized convention, Vestal stated he wanted to help Southern Baptists become

a holy people, a loving people, and a great commission people.... We need to neutralize the spirit of militant partisanship (embodied by) this kind of control-oriented, militant people who have dominated our convention for a decade.[3]

Apparently, the "middle of the road" nominee offered by Baptists Committed was still too far left for the majority of convention messengers. Vestal was defeated in his bid for the SBC presidency by a 57 to 43 percent vote.

In addition to the election of fundamentalist presidents, the convention regularly adopted resolutions that moderates found unacceptable. Though these convention-adopted resolutions initially had no binding control, they eventually became the operating guidelines for convention agencies and institutions. For moderates, these resolutions flew in the face of long-cherished Baptist doctrines. Some of the resolutions excluded women from church leadership. One even suggested women were responsible for original sin.[4]

Instead of endorsing the separation of church and state, convention messengers began giving nod to organizations that fostered national political agendas. The fundamentalist position on separation of church and state was elaborated by Dr. W. A. Criswell on the CBS Evening News, September 6,

1984. In an interview Criswell stated, "I believe this notion of the separation of church and state was the figment of some infidel's imagination."[5]

The priesthood of the believer, once a cherished doctrine held by the majority of Baptists, began to be viewed with suspicion. When television journalist Bill Moyers asked W. A. Criswell about his belief in the priesthood of the believer, Criswell responded that the doctrine was "a ruse [a trick].... If the Holy Spirit is allowed to teach you the truth of God as you read the Bible, you'll come out saying the same thing I do."[6] Moyers then asked Criswell if there was room in the Baptist fellowship for those who disagreed with him. Criswell answered, "No. Not to me. Not to me. Let them go to some other school. Let them pastor some other churches. But to me, they don't belong with us."[7]

The crux of this new understanding of the doctrine was embodied in the resolution adopted at the 1988 SBC:

> Be it further RESOLVED, that the doctrine of the Priesthood of the Believer in no way contradicts the biblical understanding of the role, responsibility, and authority of the pastor which is seen in the command of the local church.[8]

The theological landscape moderates once found so inviting had disappeared, and in its place was a new denomination intent on excluding anyone who disagreed with its fundamentalist leaders.

By the end of the decade, moderates realized the Pressler-Patterson coalition had successfully accomplished its goals. The convention, its seminaries, its boards, and its agencies were now governed by trustees with a strict fundamentalist view, and anyone who did not agree with this view was excluded from denominational leadership.

Despite their political defeat, moderates were unwilling to give up. From August 23–25, 1990, moderate leaders met in Atlanta to discuss alternative ways of relating to a denomination that had disenfranchised almost half of its constituents. The meeting was convened by Daniel Vestal. At that meeting, moderate leaders proposed a new funding mechanism for denominational giving, an alternative giving program that bypassed SBC Executive Committee oversight.

As fundamentalists continued to exert control over the agencies of the SBC, moderates investigated new avenues of denominational support and fellowship. From May 9–11, 1991, more than 6,000 disenfranchised moderates gathered at the Omni Coliseum in Atlanta. By the end of the meeting, moderates had given themselves a name, a constitution, a budget, and a plan for advancing world missions.[9] The "Cooperative Baptist Fellowship" elected John Hewett of North Carolina as its first moderator and Patricia Ayers of Texas as moderator-elect. These words from Hewett's acceptance speech articulated the sentiments of many moderates who gathered in Atlanta:

> Though many of us still grieve over ongoing effects of the fundamentalist capture of the SBC, I see a people who are no longer incapacitated by that grief. Our period of denominational mourning is drawing to a close. We did not gather here this weekend to send a signal to the rulers of the new SBC. We gathered here to check signals with each other and to get a signal from God. That signal came through loudly and clearly: "Behold, I am doing a new thing; now it springs forth for those who have eyes to see" (Isaiah 43:19a).[10]

As 1992 dawned, moderate Baptists began searching for full-time directors to coordinate the work of their expanding mission ventures. On March 1, 1992, Cecil Sherman began serving as the first full-time coordinator of the CBF.[11]

On April 30 the fledgling CBF met in Fort Worth, Texas, to conduct its second annual assembly. During that meeting, messengers welcomed the Fellowship's first four missionaries and endorsed a plan to spend $2.5 million on global missions in 1993. Fellowship leaders reported that approximately 950 churches were contributing to the Fellowship. Additionally, messengers heard predictions that 1992 receipts would likely exceed six million dollars with five million dollars designated for traditional SBC causes.[12]

For more than twelve years, Southern Baptists experienced one of the most contentious denominational conflicts in the history of American Christianity. One cannot begin to estimate the time, money, and energy spent to sway denominational opinion and to influence partisan voters. Careers were crushed and reputations ruined as partisan zealots relentlessly sought to gain control. At the end of the conflict, fundamentalists celebrated victory, claiming the convention had returned to its historic roots. Moderates, on the other side, believed Baptist history had been rewritten, and they grieved the loss of a denomination that no longer embraced Baptist diversity.

And yet, rising from the ashes of smoldering hope, God gave birth to something new. From those wounded in a not-so-holy war, God brought healing and redemption. To those whose dreams had been crushed, God gave a new vision, and those of us who suffered the sting of rejection found new acceptance. Yes, we discovered fellowship, a Cooperative Baptist Fellowship, where Baptists with diverse views could come together in a place that finally felt like home.

## Notes

[1]James C. Hefley, *The Truth in Crisis: The Controversy in the Southern Baptist Convention* (Dallas: Criterion Publications, 1986), 131.

[2] Eugene Roehlkepartain, "SBC Moderates Prepare for Exile," *The Christian Century* 103, July 2–9, 1986, 604.

[3]"Centrists Gather Campaign Forces," *SBC Today* 8, July 1989, 3.

[4]"Resolution on Ordination and the Role of Women in Ministry," The Southern Baptist Convention Annual Meeting, Kansas City, MO 1984.

[5]"Struggle for the Baptist Soul" (Dallas: Baptists Committed to the Southern Baptist Convention, 1988), 4.

[6]Ibid., 3.

[7]Ibid.

[8]"Resolution No. 5: On the Priesthood of the Believer," *SBC Today* 6, July 1988, 3.

[9]Amy Greene, "Cooperative Fellowship Formed in Atlanta," *SBC Today* 9, May 31, 1991, 1.

[10]John J. Hewett, "New Moderator of Baptist Fellowship Articulates His Vision in Acceptance Speech," *SBC Today* 9, May 31, 1991, 2.

[11]"Sherman Accepts CBF Post as Coordinator," *Baptists Today* 10, February 6, 1992, 1.

[12]Greg Warner, "Fellowship Undergirds Missions While Grappling with Identity," *Baptists Today* 10, May 4, 1992, 1.

# Afterword

### *Gene Wilder*

At its best, history is rarely an objective recollection of people, places, and events; and for those of us who live through the history we record, objectivity is impossible.

I admit I did not record the SBC controversy objectively, nor are my conclusions without bias. I recorded these events as one who was injured. For over a decade, I saw people I loved and respected maligned with wounding words. Institutions that fed my mind and warmed my heart were suddenly ripped apart at the seams. Friends with whom I freely shared my life and ministry suddenly treated me like an enemy. Sadly, I was not just a victim. Because I was hurting, I'm sure I hurt others. May God forgive my trespasses as I forgive those who've trespassed against me.

I was the child of a denominational divorce. The pain I experienced, as well as the pain I inflicted, will forever be a part of me. Thankfully, our redeeming God does not want divorce to be the final word. Lovingly, God gathers the scattered bones of our broken relationships and creates in us something new.

For me, the CBF has been, and still is, God's new work of redemption. For 25 years I've found healing and health in this blessed fellowship. I've seen the birth of God's new work and found God's love in new faces. And for every door that closed, God has opened a hundred new doors, showing me new vistas both wonderful and divine.

Twenty-five years is but one millisecond on God's continuum of time, but in that one millisecond God has given me new life, new love, and new hope for the future. Granted, I cannot erase all the pain of the past, but surprisingly, I no longer feel the need to grieve. The same God who began a good work in me over 25 years ago is still perfecting it today. Praise be to God!

Reclaiming and Re-Forming Baptist Identity

Part 3

# Forming and Shaping the Cooperative Baptist Fellowship

Chapter 8

# Birthing the Cooperative Baptist Fellowship

Sensing a higher calling than the conflict, politics, and impatience of the previous twelve years, 6,000 moderates gathered in Atlanta, Georgia, on May 9, 1991, for the first General Assembly. There, the group officially adopted the name Cooperative Baptist Fellowship. John Hewitt, pastor of First Baptist Church in Asheville, North Carolina, was elected the first moderator.

A document called "Address to the Public—the founding document of the Cooperative Baptist Fellowship" from the Interim Steering Committee was adopted. This document outlined reasons for separating from the SBC. The text of the address, written by Cecil Sherman and Walter Shurden, is included here to preserve the original intent:[1]

Introduction
Forming something as fragile as the Cooperative Baptist Fellowship is not a move we make lightly. We are obligated to give some explanation for why we are doing what we are doing. Our children will know what we have done; they may not know why we have done what we have done. We have reasons for our actions. They are:

I. Our Reasons Are Larger Than Losing.
For twelve years the Southern Baptist Convention in annual session has voted to sustain the people who lead the fundamentalist wing of the SBC. For twelve years the SBC annual session has endorsed the arguments and the rationale of the fundamentalists. What has happened is not a quirk or a flash or an accident. It has been done again and again.

If inclined, one could conclude that the losers have tired of losing. But the formation of the Cooperative Baptist Fellowship does not spring from petty rivalry. If the old moderate wing of the SBC were represented in making policy and were treated as welcomed representatives of competing ideas in the Baptist mission task, then we would co-exist, as we did for years, alongside fundamentalism and continue to argue our ideas before Southern Baptists.

But this is not the way things are. When fundamentalists won in 1979, they immediately began a policy of exclusion. Non-fundamentalists are not appointed to any denominational positions. Rarely are gentle fundamentalists appointed. Usually only doctrinaire fundamentalists, hostile to the purposes of the very institutions they control, are rewarded for service by appointment. Thus, the boards of SBC agencies are filled by only one kind of Baptists. And this is true whether the vote to elect is 60-40 or 52-48. It has been since 1979 a "winner take all." We have no voice.

In another day Pilgrims and Quakers and Baptists came to America for the same reason. As a minority, they had no way to get a hearing. They found a place where they would not be second-class citizens. All who attended the annual meeting of the SBC in New Orleans in June of 1990 will have an enlarged understanding of why our ancestors left their homes and dear ones and all that was familiar. So forming the Cooperative Baptist Fellowship is not something we do lightly. Being Baptist should ensure that no one is ever excluded who confesses, "Jesus is Lord (Philippians 2:11)."

II. Our Understandings Are Different.
Occasionally, someone accuses Baptists of being merely a contentious, controversial people. That may be. But the ideas that divide Baptists in the present "controversy" are the same ideas that have divided Presbyterians, Lutherans, and Episcopalians. These ideas are strong and central; these ideas will not be papered over. Here are some of the basic ideas:

1. Bible.
Many of our differences come from a different understanding and interpretation of Holy Scripture. But the difference is not at the point of the inspiration or authority of the Bible. We interpret the Bible differently, as will be seen below in our treatment of the biblical understanding of women and pastors. We also, however, have a different understanding of the nature of the Bible. We want to be biblical—especially in our view of the Bible. That

means that we dare not claim less for the Bible than the Bible claims for itself. The Bible neither claims nor reveals inerrancy as a Christian teaching. Bible claims must be based on the Bible, not on human interpretations of the Bible.

## 2. Education.

What should happen in colleges and seminaries is a major bone of contention between fundamentalists and moderates. Fundamentalists educate by indoctrination. They have the truth and all the truth. As they see it, their job is to pass along the truth they have. They must not change it. They are certain that their understandings of the truth are correct, complete and to be adopted by others.

Moderates, too, are concerned with truth, but we do not claim a monopoly. We seek to enlarge and build upon such truth as we have. The task of education is to take the past and review it, even criticize it. We work to give our children a larger understanding of spiritual and physical reality. We know we will always live in faith; our understanding will not be complete until we get to heaven and are loosed from the limitations of our mortality and sin.

## 3. Mission.

What ought to be the task of the missionary is another difference between us. We think the mission task is to reach people for faith in Jesus Christ by preaching, teaching, healing and other ministries of mercy and justice. We believe this to be the model of Jesus in Galilee. That is the way he went about doing his mission task. Fundamentalists make the mission assignment narrower than Jesus did. They allow their emphasis on direct evangelism to undercut other biblical ministries of mercy and justice. This narrowed definition of what a missionary ought to be and do is a contention between us.

## 4. Pastor.

What is the task of the pastor? They argue the pastor should be the ruler of a congregation. This smacks of the bishops' task in the

Middle Ages. It also sounds much like the kind of church leadership Baptists revolted against in the seventeenth century.

Our understanding of the role of the pastor is to be a servant/shepherd. Respecting lay leadership is our assignment. Allowing the congregation to make real decisions is of the very nature of Baptist congregationalism. And using corporate business models to "get results" is building the Church by the rules of a secular world rather than witnessing to the secular world by way of a servant Church.

5. Women.

The New Testament gives two signals about the role of women. A literal interpretation of Paul can build a case for making women submissive to men in the Church. But another body of scripture points toward another place for women. In Galatians 3:27-28 Paul wrote, "As many of you as are baptized into Christ have clothed yourselves with Christ. There is no longer male and female, for all of you are one in Christ Jesus (NRSV)."

We take Galatians as a clue to the way the Church should be ordered. We interpret the reference to women in the same way we interpret the reference to slaves. If we have submissive roles for women, we must also have a place for slaves in the Church.

In Galatians Paul follows the spirit of Jesus who courageously challenged the conventional wisdom of his day. It was a wisdom with rigid boundaries between men and women in religion and public life. Jesus deliberately broke those barriers. He called women to follow him; he treated women as equally capable of dealing with sacred issues. Our model for the role of women in matters of faith is the Lord Jesus.

6. Church.

An ecumenical and inclusive attitude is basic to our fellowship. The great ideas of theology are the common property of all the church. Baptists are only a part of that great and inclusive Church. So, we are eager to have fellowship with our brothers and sisters in the faith and to recognize their work for our Savior. We do not try to make them conform to us; we try to include them in our design for mission. Mending the torn fabric of both Baptist and Christian fellowship is important to us. God willing, we will bind together the broken parts into a new company in preview of the great fellowship we shall have with each other in heaven.

It should be apparent that the points of difference are critical. They are the stuff around which a fellowship such as the SBC is made. We are different. It is regrettable, but we are different. And perhaps we are most different at the point of spirit. At no place have we been able to negotiate about these differences. Were our fundamentalist brethren to negotiate, they would compromise. And that would be a sin by their understandings. So we can either come to their position, or we can form a new fellowship.

In addition to adopting the "Address," participants at the first General Assembly constituted the new organization and adopted the name "Cooperative Baptist Fellowship." A leadership structure was put into place, including a coordinator, a moderator, and a representative governing body called the coordinating council.

You don't birth a new "movement" without convictions. Clearly, those who pulled away from the SBC to "form" the CBF did so out of deeply held convictions about very important theological issues. No longer could moderate Baptists be content to invest in political battles or striving to win elections. The SBC had become a "new convention" by virtue of turning over leadership to a different brand of Baptists, and the time had come for moderates to be true to their understanding of the gospel and once again live into historic and cherished Baptist principles.

### Preserving What Was Lost

When a new organization is birthed out of conflict over deeply held convictions, there is a natural tendency to preserve or recapture what was lost and to reestablish homeostasis (balance). This happened in the birthing process for CBF.

Because missions is the heartbeat of Baptists, the fledgling organization sought from day one to become a mission sending and supporting entity. Initially, mission dollars flowing into CBF coffers were directed to SBC missionaries. The first CBF missioners were appointed in 1992; Keith Parks was called to coordinate global missions in 1993. In 1994 the SBC voted to discontinue accepting funds channeled through CBF. That self-defining step on the part of the SBC was pivotal in birthing the global missions enterprise of CBF. In the early days of the movement, CBF committed to preserving SBC missionaries who could no longer work under the restrictive SBC system that required them to sign doctrinal statements.

Before long, state and regional branches of CBF began to form—typically along state lines—as was done in the SBC. Many of these formed as independent entities in response to disdain for the top-down approach they experienced during the SBC conflict.

### Denomination or Not? Creating Something New

From the beginning there was debate about whether CBF was forming a new "denomination." While possessing denomination-like qualities, CBF is a *fellowship* and a network of individuals and congregations. This issue was discussed at length at the 1996 General Assembly, and the assembly voted "no" to becoming a new denomination. Rick McClatchy, coordinator of the CBF in Oklahoma at that time, describes what the vote really meant:

> I think it meant at least three things. First, it meant CBF does not want its existence as a convention to be a divisive issue in many local churches which would be the case if it formally broke with the SBC. Second, it meant CBF wants to take the moral high ground of defining itself by its mission rather than by the people or groups it repudiates. Third, it meant CBF does not want its organizational structure to be viewed as a "mini SBC."... Our structure must gravitate around those things that commonly inspire us—missions, theological education, religious liberty, etc.—while respecting the differences we may have on some theological and ethical issues.... CBF must continue to reject a structure in which a centrally organized leadership tries to place its agenda upon the churches. CBF's goal should not be to produce uniformity but provide specialized services to empower diverse congregations.[2]

While seeking to preserve what had been lost, CBF was very intentional about shaping this new spiritual movement in significantly different ways from those practiced within the SBC. Some of the distinctions include:

Owning no property
Refusing to consider resolutions at General Assemblies

Welcoming diversity as a strength, not a threat to unity

Focusing on what binds us together, not what pulls us apart

Embodying an ecumenical spirit and practice

Organizing from the bottom up, not top down

Consisting of individuals and congregations

Honoring the autonomy of local congregations

Refusing to speak *for* local churches

Broadening the definition of global missions roles (to include more than church planting and evangelism)

## Notes

[1] Walter B. Shurden, "An Address to the Public from the Interim Steering Committee," presented to the CBF, Atlanta, GA, May 9–11, 1991.

[2] Rick McClatchy, "What Did Richmond's 'No' Vote Really Mean?" *Fellowship News* 6/8 (October 1996): 13.

### Chapter 9

# Shaping CBF Identity—The Early Years

Any time a new organization is birthed, efforts are made to craft and clarify identity. The following statements shaped CBF's early identity:

"We are a fellowship of Baptists, Christians, and churches who share a passion for the Great Commission of Jesus Christ and a commitment to Baptist principles of faith and practice."

**Our Vision:** "Being the presence of Christ in the world."

**Our Mission:** "Serving Christians and churches as they discover and fulfill their God-given mission."

**Our Core Values:**

*Baptist Principles*
Walter Shurden conveniently outlined the distinctives of Baptists in his book *The Baptist Identity—Four Fragile Freedoms.*[1] These common convictions are expressed in four freedoms Baptists embrace. Other Christian groups also embrace these freedoms, but Baptists cannot be understood apart from some reference to these four freedoms. The CBF claimed these four fragile freedoms as key core values, believing that when we embrace these freedoms, we become free and faithful Baptists.

1. Bible Freedom (Heb 1:1–2; 4:12): Baptists believe in an open Bible and an open mind: "Bible Freedom is the historic Baptist affirmation that the Bible, under the lordship of Christ, must be central in the life of the individual and church and that Christians, with the best and most scholarly tools of inquiry, are both free and obligated to study and obey the Scripture." The Bible is the sole authority for faith and practice for Baptists and "the criterion by which the Bible is to be interpreted is Jesus Christ." Baptists have historically insisted on freedom of access to the Bible and freedom of interpretation of the Bible to arrive at the mind of Christ. Baptists insist on this freedom for

the purpose of continuing obedience to God. Baptists have rejected creeds and insisted on *sola scriptura* (scripture alone).

2. Soul Freedom (Matt 16:13–16; 1 Pet 2:5, 9): Baptists believe in personal accountability to God: "Soul Freedom is the historic affirmation of the inalienable right and responsibility of every person to deal with God without the imposition of creed, the interference of clergy, or the intervention of civil government." Soul freedom affirms the sacredness of individual choice. This focus on individual choice is based on the biblical affirmation that every human being is created in the image of God and is, therefore, competent under God to make moral, spiritual, and religious decisions. More importantly, each individual is responsible to make those decisions. Baptists insist that saving faith is personal and relational. This does not mean that Baptists do not value community, but the Baptist theme is "individual in community." So Baptists insist on each person making a free and voluntary choice to follow Christ.

3. Church Freedom (Matt 16:18; Eph 1:22–23): Baptists affirm personal choice to assemble as the "body of Christ" in community: "Church Freedom is the historic Baptist affirmation that local churches are free, under the lordship of Christ, to determine their membership and leadership, to order their worship and work, to ordain whom they perceive as gifted for ministry, male or female, and to participate in the larger Body of Christ, of whose unity and mission Baptists are proudly a part." Baptists are part of the free church tradition, which affirms "the freedom and responsibility of the individual as being central in all matters of faith." The church is comprised of people who follow Jesus as Lord of their lives and who help each other struggle to follow Jesus as Lord. Church freedom has led Baptist churches to argue for the freedom of self-government, the freedom of worship style, and the freedom to carry out its ministry to Jesus Christ. Baptists follow a democratic form of government where the authority is placed in the hands of the members of the church. Baptists have never equated the voice of the majority for the voice of God but practice democratic church polity because it accents the role of the individual within the community. In other words, this allows the greatest number of people to have a say in the life of the church.

4. Religious Freedom (Matt 22:15–22): Baptists believe practicing the faith must be free from government intervention, involvement, or control: "Religious Freedom is the historic Baptist affirmation of freedom OF religion, freedom FOR religion, and freedom FROM religion, insisting that Caesar is not Christ and Christ is not Caesar." Jesus recognized the legitimacy of both

the church and the state. Baptists have tenaciously called for religious freedom and the separation of church and state, and they have anchored their passion for religious liberty to the nature of God, the nature of humanity, and the nature of faith. God is the source of our liberty. To deny freedom of conscience to any person is to debase God's creation. To be authentic, faith must be free. Genuine faith cannot be forced or denied by the state. So the historic cry of Baptists has been "a free church in a free state."

### Biblically Based Global Missions

All of us are called to be co-laborers in the task of fulfilling our Lord's Great Commission. We believe the Bible teaches that

- God is the one triune God, the creator of all people in God's own image.
- All people are separated from God by sin.
- Christ (universally understood) is the savior and redeemer for all peoples.
- The Holy Spirit convicts and converts all who believe in Christ, teaches the church in the voice of the living Christ, and empowers the church and all believers for the mission of Christ in the world.
- Christ calls us to minister redemptively to the spiritual, physical, and social needs of individuals and communities.
- Every believer and every church is responsible for sharing the gospel with all people.
- We want to enable believers and churches to work cooperatively with other Great Commission Christians to activate this global missions calling in their communities and throughout the world.

### Resource Model

We are committed to discovering and providing resources that will empower churches to fulfill their mission in their particular contexts and will equip individuals to fulfill their calling under the lordship of Christ. We prefer to cooperate in mutually beneficial ways with other organizations rather than to establish, own, or control our own institutions.

### Justice and Reconciliation

We are committed to a biblical vision of justice and mercy. We believe the call of Christ extends to every area and relationship of life.

### Lifelong Learning and Ministry

We believe in lifelong learning for laity and clergy for the ministry of the church. We are committed to Baptist theological education that affords

intellectual and spiritual freedom to both students and professors in an atmo-
sphere of reverence for biblical authority and respect for open inquiry and
responsible scholarship.

*Trustworthiness*
We will organize, make decisions, and carry out our mission in ways that earn
trust. United in our mission and our shared commitments, we will celebrate
God's gift of diversity among the individuals and churches of the Fellowship.

*Effectiveness*
We will organize in ways that encourage flexibility, responsiveness, and
accountability. We will monitor our progress and organizational structures in
light of our stated mission.

## CBF Strategic Initiatives
The following strategic initiatives guided CBF early in her history:
   1. Faith Formation: Encouraging all persons in their journeys toward
Christ-likeness by identifying and responding to the critical needs of congre-
gations in the following areas:
- Evangelism and outreach: Biblically wholesome and effective evangelism
  and outreach
- Spiritual growth: In areas such as corporate worship, spiritual disciplines,
  Bible study, Christian ethics, spiritual gifts, and discipleship

   2. Building Community: Nurturing authentic community within and
beyond congregations by identifying and responding to critical needs in the
following areas:
- Congregational health: Developing and sustaining healthy congregations
- Baptist identity and relationships: Understanding and embracing Baptist
  values that have shaped our identity and engaging in meaningful Baptist
  partnerships and dialogue
- Reconciliation and justice: Bringing wholeness to relationships within and
  beyond congregations through acts of reconciliation and justice
- Marriage and family ministry: Developing healthy individuals, marriages,
  and families
- Ecumenical and interfaith dialogue: Establishing meaningful ecumenical
  partnerships and encouraging interfaith dialogue

3. Leadership Development: Developing effective Christian leaders by identifying and responding to critical needs of congregations in the following areas:

- Congregational leadership development: Developing effective leaders among both laity and clergy
- Theological education: Building a strong foundation of theological education for church leaders
- Collegiate ministry: Developing effective collegiate ministry, including nurture and development of future leaders for churches and the larger CBF community
- Chaplains and pastoral counselors: Recognizing ministry in specialized settings and endorsing chaplains and pastoral counselors

4. Global Missions and Ministries: Engaging in holistic missions and ministries in a world without borders by identifying and responding to the critical needs of congregations in the following areas:

- Partnership missions with local churches: Engaging in effective missions and ministries in their communities and around the world
- Most neglected peoples: Establishing an effective Christian witness among the world's unevangelized and marginalized peoples
- Church planting: Assisting at the start of churches via research, recruitment, fundraising, training, and counsel

### Note

[1]Walter B. Shurden, *The Baptist Identity: Four Fragile Freedoms* (Macon, GA: Smyth & Helwys Publishing, 1993).

### Chapter 10

# Reshaping the Cooperative Baptist Fellowship— 2012 Task Force

As the CBF approached its twentieth anniversary, an intentional process was undertaken to consider next steps in its spiritual journey. To that end, the 2012 Task Force was established at the CBF General Assembly in Charlotte, North Carolina, in 2010. Moderator Hal Bass appointed this group, the Coordinating Council affirmed the election of the task force, and Executive Coordinator Daniel Vestal encouraged the Fellowship to wrestle with the following three questions:

- What is the best model of community that fosters missional collaboration rather than competition for resources?
- How can we refocus and streamline organizational structures in order to provide leadership and resources for churches and other ministries to respond more effectively to global challenges?
- How do we help Baptist churches and organizations embrace their identity as partners with this community?

Members of the Task Force held listening sessions across the Fellowship, and the following topics emerged as holding the best potential for positive change:

**Clarify Our Identity:** What is the clearest way to articulate the identity of CBF as we look to the future?

**Reform Governance:** How can the Coordinating Council be restructured so it can be a more effective governing body for CBF?

**Missions:** How can Cooperative Baptists be most faithful in following the Great Commission to share the message of Jesus Christ to the ends of the earth?

**Ministries:** What is the best model for resourcing congregations to be ministers of the gospel of Jesus Christ?

**State/Regional and National Relationships:** How can free and autonomous organizations relate to each other for a common purpose?

**Partners:** What should the relationship be between CBF and its ministry partners?

**Renewal in Funding:** Can something be done to our system of funding that might cause an increase in giving?

### Identity Statement

The 2012 Task Force crafted a new identity statement for CBF:

"For we are laborers together with God " (1 Corinthians 3:9).

The Cooperative Baptist Fellowship is a community of Baptist Christians and churches walking together and drawn toward the center of our common life in Jesus Christ. We share this fellowship with God, whom we have come to know through Christ. We serve as co- laborers with the Holy Spirit in God's mission. Within these relationships we freely offer this expression of our identity, not to bind the conscience of any believer or the freedom of any congregation but as an expression of the nature of our fellowship.

Our vision is to be a national and global community bearing witness to the Gospel in partnership with Christians across the nation and around the world. Our understanding of Baptist faith and practice is expressed by our emphasis on freedom in biblical interpretation and congregational governance, the participation of women and men in all aspects of church leadership and Christian ministry, and religious liberty for all people.

Our life together is also shaped by a common ministry focus. Because of our passion to obey the Great Commandment (Matthew 22:34-40) and the Great Commission (Matthew 28:19-20) of our Lord, we are committed to global missions with the least evangelized and most neglected persons of the world through sending vocational and volunteer missionaries. Because of our passion for called, gifted, and qualified ministry leaders, we are committed to effective leadership development in partnership with theological education institutions. Because of our passion for local churches as the locus of Christian formation and discipleship development, we are committed to a collaborative model of resourcing congregations through the development of a robust resource network.

Because of our passion for participation in God's mission beyond the capacity of most congregations, we are committed to supporting ministry partners who share our identity, values, and goals.

Our community consists of congregations, individuals, regional fellowships, and ministry partners. While we respect the freedom and individuality of each member of our community, we are committed to practices of cooperation, collaboration, and leadership that will enable us to be faithful and wise stewards of our common life and mission.

In summary, Cooperative Baptist Fellowship is a community of Baptist Christians who cooperate together to engage people in missions and equip people for ministry.[1]

## New Governance Structure

The 2012 Task Force also reshaped the governance of CBF. Here is the new structure approved by the General Assembly:

### Governing Board

The Governing Board took the place of the Coordinating Council. While it retained the Board of Directors function, including the legal and fiduciary responsibility for CBF, the Governing Body became smaller and more focused on governing national CBF than providing representation of the state/regional CBF organizations to the national CBF. The Governing Board has oversight of the Missions and Ministries Councils and develops policies that guide the practice of these two councils. Ultimately, the Missions and Ministries Councils report to the Governing Board. The Governing Board also has oversight of the Executive Coordinator, who (1) reports to the Governing Board, (2) supervises CBF staff, and (3) works with both staff and the two councils to ensure integration of the missions and ministries areas. Finally, the Governing Board has the responsibility of recommending CBF's Annual Budget to the General Assembly for its approval.

### Nominating Committee

The Nominating Committee is responsible for nominating to the General Assembly members of the three bodies—Governing Board, Missions Council, and Ministries Council. The goal is to develop a pool of committed, focused talent for these three bodies. The Nominating Committee replaced the representative state/regional feeder system that formerly populated the Coordinating Council.

## Missions Council

The purpose of the Missions Council is to bring together missions leaders and practitioners from across the CBF community and CBF Global Missions staff to provide vision, strategy, education, and sustainability to CBF's mission enterprise in accordance with policies established by the Governing Board.

The guiding philosophy of the Missions Council selection process is for CBF to identify, invite, and involve the best missions thinkers, leaders, strategists, and practitioners in the CBF community to provide vision and planning for CBF Global Missions. Although membership on the Missions Council includes people who are representative of the various mission partners in CBF life, the primary criterion for membership is expertise and gifts in missions leadership in the CBF community. A vital component of the body's effectiveness will involve enlisting passionate, gifted laypersons to serve on the council.

## Ministries Council

The purpose of the Ministries Council is to gather leaders from across the CBF community in a forum of collaboration, communication, and sharing of ideas. Having the broadest representation of the three bodies, the Ministries Council brings together people from throughout the Fellowship to identify, develop, and deploy assets of the CBF community. Along with identifying resources and sharing ideas, the council will empower shared ministry networks related but not limited to chaplaincy, church resourcing, community building, evangelism, faith formation, leadership development, and mercy and justice in accordance with policies set by the Governing Board.

## Partnerships

From its beginning CBF has operated with a "partnering paradigm," working with other missions and ministries organizations to accomplish much of its work of equipping individuals and churches. Through the years, the number and types of partnerships have grown and resulted in a rich community of relationships that allow CBF to do far more than it could do alone. Partnerships have expanded our community and our witness in the world.

Because we observed much discussion relative to partners centered on financial relationships between CBF (both national and state/regional entities) and those to which it sends money, we identified three categories of partnerships that represent CBF's shared funding priorities:

Theological Education Partners: CBF partners with schools and houses of Baptist studies that are members of the Consortium of Theological Schools Partnering with the CBF.

Resource Partners: CBF entities choose to partner with other organizations that provide resources for the spiritual growth of individuals and congregations.

Membership Partners: CBF entities choose to be a member body in Baptist and ecumenical organizations that help us live out our mission and clarify our identity.

To strengthen our work, enhance cooperation, and encourage giving, the funding of such partnerships should be encouraged and evaluated based upon how the partnerships serve the needs of the CBF community. The Task Force affirmed the "Guiding Principles" recommended by the 2005 Partnership Study Committee:

- Partnerships must be voluntary.
- Partnerships are born out of desire to achieve a goal that cannot be achieved alone.
- Partnerships are based on mutual trust and respect.
- Partnerships require persistence, patience, and planning.
- Partnerships function most effectively when accountability is built into the relationship.

### Funding Strategy

We believe a shared funding strategy can move us in the direction of increasing cooperation while reducing competition for financial resources. This practice will represent an unprecedented level of cooperation between CBF and state/regional CBF organizations, and it will be an extremely significant stride in "fostering missional collaboration rather than competition for resources." While contributions from individuals are a vital component of financial support, this strategy focuses primarily on contributions from congregations. Our shared values suggest a funding strategy is best based on the following guiding principles:

- Foster unity of mission within diversity of giftedness of each CBF entity
- Bring value to the entire CBF community
- Clarify giving and empower decision-making for congregations
- Ensure freedom for congregations in implementing funding plan
- Recognize the uniqueness of each state/regional organization

- Respect the autonomy of CBF entities (congregations, state/regional CBF organizations, national CBF, partners)

### CBF Rebranding Journey

The 2012 Task Force report was foundational for understanding CBF's identity and ways folks within the Fellowship work together to accomplish CBF's mission. The adoption of the Task Force Report served as the launch pad for the future of the Fellowship. In January 2013 CBF engaged in a year-long process to assess our brand. The branding journey yielded new words and images to describe CBF, improve our identifiability, and increase our visibility:

**New Tagline:** "Forming Together"
**Our Core Purpose:** We exist to partner in renewing God's world.
**Attributes to which we aspire:**
- Christ-like: First and foremost, we witness God's work in the world, both as a witness to others for Christ and an observer of God's grace.
- Innovative: CBF is ever exploring ways to renew the church and the world—from how we start churches to our partnerships that bring clean water to impoverished areas.
- Authentic: CBF values and nurtures genuine relationships built on respect where we create opportunities for dialogue about issues facing the modern church and the modern Christian.
- Global: Fellowship impact reaches every corner of the globe, with a CBF presence spanning from rural villages in Thailand to the United Nations office at Geneva, Switzerland.
- Excellence: The Fellowship is raising the bar with inspiring partnerships, ministries, and missions and insisting on integrity in our work and in our being.
- Diverse: Cooperative Baptists are strongly committed to hearing and respecting different perspectives and to creating sacred space to hear God in multiple ways.

Below is an executive summary written by Jeff Huett, Associate Coordinator of Communications and Advancement, describing the branding journey:

*What is a brand, and why did CBF need a new brand strategy?*
Our brand is our reputation. It's what people perceive about CBF and what they say about us when we're not in the room. We sought profes-

sional guidance to find innovative ways to tell the CBF story that precisely articulate who we are without resorting to who we are not. We started with a guiding question posed by the 2012 Task Force, which was a group brought together in 2010 to help CBF live into its future. "How do we help Baptist churches and organizations embrace their identity as partners within this community?"

*What did we learn?*

Key insights told us Cooperative Baptists see ourselves as a "both/ and" organization—opposite sides of the same coin.

We appreciate, even celebrate, the fact we are comprised of individuals and congregations, while autonomous, invite collaboration.

Clergy and laity from across the Fellowship interviewed during this process used words for CBF such as "family" and "freedom," "connected" and "forming." CBF was described as "local" and "global." When asked what CBF does best, many responded "missions" and "local church support."

*How does this work hearken back to CBF's founding?*

We're living into the same values that CBF's founders instilled nearly 25 years ago. We strive to be the presence of Christ—to be Christ-like— to be innovative, authentic, global, and to raise the bar on excellence with inspiring partnerships, ministries, and missions.

We are this way because the approximately 1,800 congregations that comprise our Fellowship are this way. CBF partner congregations are innovative in their ministries and seek global impact through their mission work. They strive for excellence in the ways they carry out ministry and missions. Like CBF partner congregations, CBF aspires to be diverse—in race, in gender, in geography, and in age. These words describe our past and will describe our future.

*What is the new way to tell the CBF story?*

We developed a visual identity system and messaging that would reflect the fruitful and global nature of the ministry and missions efforts of CBF. The new look and feel is fresh, thoughtful, and flexible. For a tagline, we decided on "Forming Together." As CBF partners to renew God's world, we do so by collaboration and spiritual growth. Abstract enough to be left up to interpretation, "Forming Together" is as much an invitation and challenge as it is a method of operation.

*How does the branding work clarify our core purpose?*

CBF Exists to Partner in Renewing God's World.

God calls us and equips us to spread the hope of Jesus Christ to the least evangelized, most marginalized people on earth. Whether we're feeding the hungry, lifting up the voiceless, digging for water, or helping families get back on their feet after a disaster, we and those we are serving are remade a little more nearly into God's image.

Renewing is spiritual. It's a movement that takes faithful believers and active participants. Participants don't just talk the talk but are Christ's presence in the world.

*What is the real value of this work?*

Ultimately, the real value of this work will depend on how helpful it is to the people, churches, and partners that comprise the Fellowship as, together, we partner to renew God's world.

Part 4 of this book is an intentional effort to help unpack the potential value of CBF's branding journey. We seek not to take away from a church's journey to understand or live into "forming together" and "partner in renewing God's world." Our goal is to broaden the conversation.

## CBF's Visual Identity

### 1997 Logo

In early 1997 CBF's newsletter, *Fellowship News*, became *fellowship!* Along with the new look and format for the newsletter, CBF launched a new logo design reflecting the promising future of the Fellowship, CBF's commitment to reach out to a new generation of Baptist Christians, and CBF's priority on using cutting-edge communication and information technologies.

Cooperative Baptist
**FELLOWSHIP**

The globe form communicated the worldwide scope of the Great Commission and CBF's emphasis on "doing missions in a world without borders." The spiraling ribbon form symbolized the energy and vitality of the

Fellowship's mission to "network, empower, and mobilize" Baptist Christians and churches. It also signified the free and faithful commitment to Baptist principles. The subtle arrow at the top of the spiral communicated forward movement and progress toward shared goals. The typography emphasized the word *Fellowship* to underscore the spiritual nature of CBF. The cross formed between the "l" and "P" represented Christ, in whose name we minister. The italicized letter-forms emphasized growth, progress, and openness to the future.

This logo served CBF well for 18 years. The logo also pointed to openness to the future. Subsequently, the 2015 branding campaign yielded a new logo.

## 2015 Logo

Visually, CBF's new logo is part of a system that represents the individuals, congregations, and partners that comprise the Fellowship, first and foremost, to witness God's work in the world. In this logo "parts make up the whole" because that is our strength.

The CBF monogram is a visual representation of "forming together." It is a combination of squares, circles, and the cross, each having a visual purpose and a deeper meaning with the context of our mission, vision, and work (this architecture cannot be seen in this single-color monogram above).

Squares: In the CBF monogram, squares represent individuality and foundation. Affiliation with CBF is measured by contribution. Any church or individual who sends a contribution of any amount is considered a member of the Fellowship. This kind of connectivity at a personal and individual level is foundational to the Fellowship.

Circles: In the new logo, circles and curvature represent community and the formation of unified partnerships that renew God's world. Circles allow for fluidity in the design. One of the strengths of CBF is our ability to be nimble, meeting needs of our local and global communities as they arise.

Cross: The cross in the "f" signals that, first and foremost, we are here to witness God's work in the world. By design, our monogram is easily recognizable as Christian.

## New CBF Mission Distinctives

Under the direction of Missions Coordinator Steven Porter, the following Mission Distinctives were crafted to offer Fellowship Baptists shared language for our common witness to the triune God. The *commitments* reflect the values inherent to the Fellowship's mission engagement, while the *contexts* focus more intentionally on the work of our Global Missions field personnel. CBF field personnel live out the following commitments alongside CBF congregations within the contexts of global poverty, global migration, and the global church.

### Our Mission Commitments

- Cultivating Beloved Community: We cultivate communities of reconciliation and hospitality that serve as instruments, signs, and foretastes of the kingdom of God.
- Bearing Witness to Jesus Christ: We bear witness to the gospel through words that invite faith in Jesus and actions that embody the way of Jesus.
- Seeking Transformational Development: We seek to transform systems that suppress the capacity of individuals and communities in order to recognize, claim, and celebrate the God-given gifts of all people and places.

### CBF Mission Contexts

- Global Poverty: In a world where 1 in 8 persons suffers hunger, 2.8 billion live on less than $2 per day, 1 billion lack access to clean water, and 35.8 million are enslaved, Cooperative Baptists seek sustainable responses to systems of poverty that devalue life and diminish the image of God.
- Global Migration: With over 232 million migrants in the world, including 16.7 million refugees, we live in an age of unprecedented human mobility. Such movement affords Cooperative Baptists the opportunity to extend hope and hospitality to those who are driven by circumstance or drawn by opportunity away from their homes.
- Global Church: We live in the era of a global church in which no single tradition or culture can lay claim to the center of Christianity. Cooperative Baptists befriend Christians from around the world to share and receive gifts and to engage in God's mission together through worship, fellowship, education, and service.

### Note

[1] Identity Statement included in the 2012 Task Force Report.

### Chapter 11

# Impact of CBF Executive Coordinators

O ne cannot discuss the CBF without giving proper credit to the three Executive Coordinators who guided and shaped the Fellowship through their gifts, passions, and influence. In this chapter, we seek to outline major contributions of each. We tell the story of our leaders using the CBF acronym. We acknowledge up front each coordinator cared deeply about and invested in all three: cooperation and collaboration, Baptist identity, and building the Fellowship.

### *Cecil Sherman (1992–1996): "B" is for Baptist*

Cecil Sherman, pastor of Broadway Baptist Church in Fort Worth, Texas, was tapped as the first coordinator of the CBF and began his service on April 1, 1992. Highly invested in groups that opposed the fundamental-conservative takeover of the SBC, Sherman was a key leader in bringing together the moderate movement. He was a founding member of CBF, Baptists Committed, the Southern Baptist Alliance, and the SBC Forum.

CBF needed someone like Sherman, with his deep love and commitment to Baptist distinctives. Sherman arrived in Atlanta with a briefcase, one change of clothing, and much enthusiasm for championing Baptist principles.

In reviewing early CBF documents and *Fellowship News* magazines, we see clearly what was important to Sherman. Resounding themes were Baptists and freedom. Sherman often wrote about what a Baptist is, what a Baptist is not, and how to tell the difference. Sherman strove to clarify and help readers understand our Baptist identity—apart from a written creed. Hear our first coordinator in his own words:

> The big idea for all Baptists was freedom. A lot of people who worship in churches that have "Baptist" on the sign haven't the faintest idea what it means to be a Baptist. But sad people and entrapped people are the people who for the sake of a job or the prospect of a job or for

the hope of peace are willing to give up on the first principle of being Baptist. They are not free.[1]

Baptists were people who believed in freedom.... The freedom was given in two places: 1) The individual was given great freedom in the exercise of his or her religion. 2) The congregation was given great freedom.... Freedom and conformity are enemies.... People who don't understand Baptist polity are pushing toward a denomination that is more interested in standardizing orthodoxy than in cooperating in missions.[2]

The controversy will come into your church no matter how detached you try to be.... Why not do the Baptist thing? Why not tell the people and let them sort this out as they will?[3]

Baptist headquarters belongs in the local church. Baptists are a "bottom up" outfit rather than a "top down" people.... Should a Baptist church have women deacons? Who gets to decide? The convention meeting in annual session? Or will it be (ordinary) Baptist laypeople with the New Testament in hand, sorting out the mind of Christ and the leadership of the Spirit, and then deciding where women will stand in that congregation?[4]

[Sherman's response when asked what kept him at CBF]: This is the right thing to do. We are caretakers of Baptist ideas, we are teachers of Baptist ideas, and we are promoters of doing missions in Baptist ways.[5]

I vision a day when the larger Christian community can draw near to Baptists.... Jesus prayed that we might all be one: must we wait until heaven for everything? I dream of a day when Baptists will not be afraid. You can't know how many people are enslaved and intimidated today. Young ministers are afraid to speak their minds, tell who they are, say what they think. And to think, Baptists began as a freedom movement.[6]

Fighting for Baptist principles was a defining issue for Sherman. He was also deeply committed to the Great Commission. Sherman made certain CBF channeled resources to take the gospel to a world without borders. On his watch, the Fellowship moved from a dream to a vibrant entity supporting 120 missionaries around the world.

The Fellowship owes a huge debt of gratitude to Cecil Sherman for heavily investing in and guiding the early days of CBF. He traveled tirelessly from state to state and church to church telling the CBF story, inviting congregations to journey with CBF and support CBF missions, and answering questions about this new Baptist entity. In fact, Sherman logged 180,000 miles on Delta in 1994. Under Sherman's leadership, the budget grew from $600,000 to $14,000,000. Contributing churches increased from 481 to 1,500. That is huge growth in only four years. The Fellowship's true strength is found in the Baptist ideal of freedom that our first Executive Coordinator Cecil Sherman strongly advocated.

### Daniel Vestal (1996–2013): "F" is for Fellowship

Daniel Vestal was tapped as the second coordinator for CBF. He came from the pastorate of Tallowood Baptist Church in Houston, Texas. Vestal needed no introduction to the CBF family. He was a key figure in CBF's founding after serving on the SBC Peace Committee and running twice as the moderate candidate for SBC presidency (1989, 1990). Vestal chaired the interim steering committee for CBF and served on the search group that called Cecil Sherman as CBF's first coordinator.

Vestal came to CBF with a compelling sense of inward calling from God, a desire to energize young Baptists, to unite moderate Baptists around common convictions and mission objectives, and to build on the strength of diversity. Moments after his election, Vestal outlined five commitments that would inform and guide his vision for the Fellowship:[7]

1. The Fellowship is "a way for us to do cooperative missions with integrity, with vision, and with freedom."
2. The Fellowship will be "a voice for Baptist principles and ideas."
3. CBF will be "a resource center" for spiritual renewal, moral decision-making, and "faith formation," stressing that, "deep in the heart of Baptists, there is a hunger and a thirst for authentic spirituality."
4. CBF will be a place of "genuine fellowship," bridging the diversity of "gender, geography, and generation…I don't see our diversities as weaknesses; I see them as strengths."

5.  The Fellowship will be "a laboratory for learning." "This fellowship is still learning what it is and what it will become. We're still in process. We are still being shaped by the Spirit of God."

When asked in 1997 about his vision for CBF, Vestal indicated his reticence to project what he believes into the CBF movement. What he really desired "is to call forth the dreams of Baptist Christians—young and not so young—and then to challenge us to turn those dreams into a vision that guides us into the 21st century.... The collaborative journey—with others and with God—represents much of what the Fellowship is all about."[8]

In his first General Assembly address, Vestal outlined a vision for CBF characterized by three broad priorities:[9]

1.  Authentic spirituality: "I believe within the heart of Baptists is a yearning for spirituality.... We must abandon a performance-based religion, a corporate mentality that diminishes and even depletes spiritual formation.... I am on a spiritual journey, a journey of discovering the life of prayer. And I very much want others to join me in that journey. And I very much want CBF to help others in that journey."
2.  Community: "Spiritual health must translate into community in family relationships and in churches. I believe with all my heart that to grow a church and to love church requires the building of community."
3.  Global missions: "Baptists believe in cooperative missions. They know they can do more together that they can alone.... I dream of churches taking the initiative in global missions, undergirding Fellowship missionaries with prayer and financial support, starting new churches and involving lay people in missions.... World missions is a passion more than it is a program. It is a compelling conviction, a motivating, unifying urge."

Let's hear directly from former CBF Executive Coordinator Daniel Vestal for additional historical insight. Dr. Vestal graciously responded to several questions I sent to him.

**Terry:** As you began your term of service as Executive Coordinator, did you have specific values or convictions in mind you hoped to inculcate in the Fellowship? What end did you have in mind, i.e., "When I come to the final days of my service, I will consider my ministry effective or faithful if we accomplished ____ together?"

**Dr. Vestal:** I certainly brought the values and convictions of my own Christian faith and experience as a pastor to bear on the CBF role. I had served as a pastor for 27 years, so I believed deeply in the local church and loved the local church. I felt from the beginning CBF should support and extend the ministry of the local church. As a Baptist I believed in the autonomy and freedom of each congregation, but equally I believed in the principle of voluntary cooperation among congregations, which had been a bedrock conviction of my pastoral ministry.

The idea of local churches cooperating with one another in ministry and mission is woven deeply into the fabric of my identity, so I wanted to communicate that idea and encourage it within this newly formed community named CBF. Cooperation involves mutual respect, shared decision-making, prayer, and financial support. Being cooperative is more than a shibboleth to me. It is part of the gospel.

I have also been committed to the missionary enterprise since childhood and felt from the beginning of my tenure I wanted to grow and expand the mission vision of CBF. We were already appointing missionaries, and I wanted to see that effort expand. For me missions is not so much a program as it is a passion. It's a romance that's deepened and strengthened through fervent prayer and active participation. I came to CBF hopeful that the global reach of the gospel could be extended by what we did in CBF.

Most of the new seminaries were already begun when I came into leadership, and the birth of each was amazing. CBF didn't begin any of the new schools, but the schools wanted relationship with CBF. And, of course, they each wanted more money. That was a struggle, because there just wasn't enough money to go around. Cecil Sherman felt we should fund only two, or perhaps three, schools. But the pressure for me was too great to defund any of them. I felt a strong conviction at the beginning of my tenure that our future and the future of these schools were tied together. Leadership development, especially partnering with seminaries, was a priority.

One last priority for me from those earliest years was resourcing congregations in ways that would strengthen them and make them more effective. We had already written a mission statement in which we had declared CBF would not try to be a convention of churches that everyone looked to for all their resources. But we knew that churches needed support and suggestions in fulfilling their mission, so there were strong feelings we needed to equip, network, and mobilize laity. In all candor, we didn't have much money to do this, but it was still important.

To the second question the short answer is "no." I didn't come with an end in mind. You must remember that in 1996 CBF was only five years old and still very fragile. The SBC was spending considerable money and time undermining us. There were concerted efforts to spread false information and question our legitimacy. There was considerable conversation in Texas and Virginia about another organization being formed that was more conservative. There was also conversation in various circles about CBF merging with the Alliance of Baptists or becoming a regional body within American Baptist Churches, USA. Our very existence was being challenged, not to mention our identity or mission.

In the eyes of many, CBF was suspect, and all kinds of predictions were being made that we wouldn't last very long. At the congregational level it wasn't always easy to identify with CBF. For many pastors it took courage to lead their congregations toward CBF and a genuine risk to their future opportunities in ministry. Also, the wounds from battling fundamentalism were very real for a majority of CBF folk. We were still healing, and as many would say, "We're building the plane while we're trying to fly it." There was no model or blueprint for what we were trying to do. It was both a challenging and an exciting time.

**Terry**: You came to CBF quite early in our history. Cecil Sherman kept the focus on being true and free Baptists. How did the foundation Dr. Sherman laid affect how you went about your work?

**Dr. Vestal**: First, let me say Cecil was one of the most remarkable Baptist leaders I have ever known. I have spoken and written on this before. He was a person of impeccable integrity, practical wisdom, and unflinching courage. I was on the search committee that asked him to be our founding coordinator and am convinced he was the right person at the right time for that position.

One of the greatest gifts Cecil brought to the early years of CBF was a "life wish" for it and a deep conviction that CBF was not only needed but had a future. He was a true believer in the principles Baptists hold dear and was convinced those principles were not only vital and viable but were still relevant. They were not only relevant for local churches but also for a denomination-like organization such as CBF. His belief and conviction gave encouragement to a lot of people, including me.

Sherman's unwavering commitment to Baptist tradition helped not only to preserve it, but also to shape it for the future. Cecil was an apologist and spokesman for Baptist identity. His was a clear voice; it is impossible to over-state how important that voice was in the early years of CBF. For those of us who love Baptist tradition and its witness to the gospel, Cecil was an exam-ple and an important reminder that we must not take Baptist principles for granted. We cannot assume everyone (not even every pastor) knows Baptist heritage or what it means to be Baptist.

One practical way this expressed itself in Cecil's leadership was his unwavering commitment to theological education. Cecil was a champion for supporting newly formed schools of theology because he believed these schools formed future ministers who would know and love Baptist tradition. In addi-tion, because he believed in the Baptist witness, Cecil strongly supported the Baptist Joint Committee and a free Baptist press.

I was aware of Cecil's convictions, and because I shared many of them, I felt a deep kinship with him. He was very helpful to me, always encourag-ing and counseling but never interfering. Because I love the Baptist tradition, community, and witness, I have always felt a strong sense of indebtedness to Cecil Sherman.

Given all the negative connotations of the word "Baptist," some have wanted to diminish or even eliminate our Baptist identity. I hope we do not do that but instead celebrate a noble tradition and do what we can to strengthen a distinct witness to the gospel.

**Terry**: In what ways did you and those working with you seek to bring folks together for common purposes, build up and strengthen the Fellowship, and enhance the sense of community?

**Dr. Vestal**: I think it's safe to say that when CBF began, it was a support group for wounded Southern Baptist moderates. We had come through a terrible conflict, and we had lost a great deal. In the beginning our commu-nity was created out of a shared experience of grief and loss. We also felt our Baptist heritage had been forfeited and Baptist principles we cherished had been violated. Our shared commitment to these Baptist principles created a genuine community. They brought us together.

Once one got beyond these facts, the reality in the early years was that this Fellowship was fragmented and fragile. We were wounded Southern Baptists who shared a passion for Baptist principles and found community with one another around those principles. Before long, however, we realized there were many differences among us: theological, sociological, and geographical. Before I became coordinator, the Fellowship adopted an identity statement: "We are a Fellowship of Baptist Christians who share a passion for the Great Commission and a commitment to Baptist principles." We had a mission statement: "To network, empower, and mobilize Baptist Christians for effective service in Jesus' name." But these didn't do much to unify us.

Not too long into my tenure, I appointed a "task force/team" to draft a new vision statement, mission statement with core values, and a strategic plan. It took two years of many conversations, surveys, and gatherings to craft these statements. They were adopted, almost unanimously, in 2000, and I believe they helped us unify into community. The vision statement was "Being the Presence of Christ," and the mission statement was "To serve Christians and churches as they discover and fulfill their God-given mission." Leadership at all levels worked hard to keep these two statements before us at all times and order/organize in ways that implemented them. This gave us focus.

In many ways CBF is a community of multiple communities, and that's not a bad thing. People have passion and energy around their calling and gifting. Chaplains and pastoral counselors are different than missionaries and church planters, and they create their own communities. Those who have a lifelong love for theological education and leadership development share community with each other as do those who have a passion for community development and social justice. Of course there is overlap, but the fact is, within CBF, there are many streams flowing into the river.

The challenge of leadership is to nurture a broader community between these "communities of practice." There were two places we worked hard at doing this: in the budget and at our General Assemblies. The budget is a reflection of shared commitments. Each year we worked hard to create a budget that fostered and nurtured community. Anyone who has worked on budgets knows how difficult this is, but we did our part to encourage a sense of community.

Also, we tried to make our annual gathering "a Baptist meeting" that cultivated community and strengthened fellowship. I honestly believe the General

Assembly of CBF is the premier gathering in Baptist life. It is unlike any other "Baptist meeting" I know. It is a combination family reunion-convention-revival-retreat-continuing education-party. The General Assembly was intentionally the single largest "line item" in the budget during my tenure. Nothing can take the place of Baptist people worshiping, deliberating, discussing, and having fun together in order to create community. Many people work very hard all year to make the General Assembly meaningful.

**Terry**: In what ways did the ideas of "shaping" or "forming" inform how you thought about or went about your work of guiding the Fellowship?

**Dr. Vestal**: I believed from the very beginning of CBF that we are a work of God's grace. God brought good out of bad, beauty out of ashes, joy out of mourning in creating CBF. Whenever God's grace is at work, new life, new relationships, and new ministries as well as new hope and new joy will result. So the ideas both of creation and redemption have been very prominent in my own mind, which perhaps is very similar to the metaphor of forming or shaping.

One of the convictions that sustained me through the years was that this organization and its various ministries were God's creative and redemptive work among us. I never believed God caused the controversy in the SBC, but I continue to believe that out of that controversy, God created something beautiful. As time unfolded, I witnessed the creative work of the Spirit again and again.

Think about it for a minute and consider all that God created in the past 25 years: a worldwide mission enterprise, a chaplaincy-endorsing body, a center for congregational resources, a denominational-like structure with state and regional organizations, 14 new seminaries and divinity schools, institutions and ministries of all kinds. In addition to this are the profound personal relationships and the thousands of friendships that would not have happened without CBF. This is the work of the Lord, and it is marvelous in our eyes.

**Terry**: What resources were developed during your tenure that you believe helped shape the future direction of CBF?

**Dr. Vestal**:
*Resources for Spiritual Formation and Missional Church:*
"A Vision of Hope," by Daniel Vestal. This booklet was my inaugural address delivered at the 1997 General Assembly in Louisville, Kentucky.

"It's Time: An Urgent Call to Christian Mission," by Daniel Vestal. This book became the basis of an eight-week congregational study in discovery and discerning how a congregation might participate in God's mission. It was published in both English and Spanish.

"It's Time: A Journey toward Missional Faithfulness," edited by Bo Prosser. This workbook was produced to accompany an eight-week congregational study in discovery and discerning how a congregation might participate in God's mission. It was published in both English and Spanish.

"It's Time: Fulfilling God's Mission in the World: A Catalogue of Resources for the Church's Ministry," by Terry Hamrick. This catalogue was produced to provide information about available resources to help congregations discover and fulfill their God-given mission.

"It's Time: Missions Education Curriculum." This was a full line of missions education curriculum designed for various age groups.

"The Missional Journey: Being the Presence of Christ," by Terry Hamrick, Bo Prosser, Greg Hunt (principal writer), Doris Nelms, Dennis Foust, Michael Tutterow. This booklet introduced the meaning of "missional church."

"Missional Journey Guide," by Greg Hunt, Doris Nelms, Dennis Foust, Michael Tutterow. This workbook/notebook provided practical guidance for congregations in becoming a missional church.

"Glimpses of Missional Faithfulness," edited by Rick Bennett. This booklet/workbook offered stories of inspiration and examples of spiritual transformation and missional engagement.

"Klesis: God's Call and the Journey of Faith," by Kathy Dobbins, Colin Harris, Doris Nelms. This workbook was developed to equip laity in discipleship and discovery in the missional journey.

"Destinations: Mapping Your Congregation's Missional Journey," by Rick Bennett. This booklet provided more resources for congregational planning.

"Blueprints," by an eight-member design team. This booklet provided a resource for annual church planning.

"Missional Church Bookmarks and Links," by Bo Prosser. This booklet provided additional information for churches seeking to become missional.

"Light for the Path: A Guide to Spiritual Formation Resources," by Rick Bennett. This resource book provided extensive information to help churches in caring for the spiritual life of their members.

"Resources in Spirituality," by Bill Clemmons. This resource book provided additional information for churches in caring for the spiritual life of their members.

"You've Got the Time: A Journey of Biblical Faithfulness." In partnership with "Faith Comes by Hearing" we offered a free 40-day Bible listening program for congregations to listen to the New Testament as a part of their spiritual formation or outreach ministry.

*Being the Presence of Christ: A Vision for Transformation*, by Daniel Vestal. This book was published by Upper Room, but CBF provided study guides for congregations that wanted to participate in a 40-day study.

*A Quest for Renewal: Reflections from My Journey with Cooperative Baptist Fellowship*, by Daniel Vestal. This book was a collection of selected sermons, addresses, and articles during the 15 years I was coordinator.

*Missions Education Resources:*

The resources listed below have been significant in shaping the Fellowship at various times in its history to continue in its commitment to global missions. They have been educational and inspirational in forming CBF as a missional movement.

"The Missionary Card Collection" (1997). These 2 x 3-inch cards featured personal information about CBF missionaries and were very popular in encouraging prayer and financial support.

"Partners in Prayer: CBF Missionary Prayer Calendar." This calendar listed the birthdays of missionaries and their children and provided practical prayer for congregations.

"Unreached People Group Video Series." These videos were effective tools for missions learning when CBF focused on unreached people groups. They were used extensively in homes, congregations, and CBF gatherings.

"Unreached People Group Flyers." These brochures provided mission study material that educated CBF on the 25 unreached people groups on which CBF focused.

"Global Missions Offering Promotional Material." Each year CBF prepares and offers these materials to local churches to raise mission consciousness in the local church. This resource has been valuable in helping churches support global missions.

"It's Time: Missions Education Curriculum." CBF offered a full line of missions education curriculum designed for preschoolers, children, youth, and adults.

"Affect/Spark: Missions Education Resource." For several years CBF offered missions education curriculum in the monthly news magazine. This included printed stories, worship guides, practical suggestions, and suggested readings to educate congregations in our global missions enterprise. It was both age-graded and formational.

"Prayers of the People." Several years ago we began to publish a yearlong guide to prayer, including the names and birthdays of missionaries, chaplains, and church starters accompanied by devotional and formational thoughts.

**Terry**: How did your own bent toward spirituality inform or drive CBF's focus on spiritual formation?

**Dr. Vestal**: One of the first things I did as coordinator was appoint a "task force" or "team" to offer suggestions on how we as a fellowship might broaden and deepen our understanding of prayer and spiritual formation. It was a diverse group of folks that included both academics and practitioners. This group took its work very seriously and set a direction for CBF that I believe continues to this day.

Partly because of my own journey, I was convinced then and remain convinced now that Baptists have much to learn about prayer and spirituality from other Christian traditions. I felt for many years both pastors and laity are hungry and thirsty for spiritual renewal and reality that is simply not being offered by our Baptist tradition alone.

The task force recommended we call Rick Bennett as a specialist in congregational life. Rick devoted much of his time and energy to developing resources to assist churches in learning about prayer and spiritual formation. The first publication was "Resources in Spirituality," which remains to this day one of the finest listings of resource persons in spirituality as well as available workshops, training programs, networks, professional organizations, publications, links, and personal retreat centers.

In addition to resources, Bo Prosser, Rick Bennett, and I led a number of pastor/minister prayer retreats across the Fellowship. These were well received and showed a deep desire among clergy to learn more about prayer life and practice. We created formal partnerships with Upper Room and Renovare, two premier organizations in Christian discipleship. Marjorie Thompson of

Upper Room introduced us to "Companions in Christ," an excellent adult curriculum designed to help Christians grow in their faith. We introduced the Academy for Spiritual Formation and the regional conferences sponsored by Renovare.

Richard Foster, Trevor Hudson, Marjorie Thompson, Roberta Bondi, Tilden Edwards, Glenn Hinson, Bill Clemmons, Jeannie Miley, Ruth Haley Barton, and many other "thought leaders" in Christian spirituality were invited to preach and teach at our gatherings. The focus on spiritual formation was given priority in state/regional events as well as national events, on our website, and in all of our publications.

**Terry**: Much has been written about what was accomplished during your tenure as Executive Coordinator. What do *you* think the major accomplishments of CBF were during your term as leader?

**Dr. Vestal**: I am not comfortable talking about accomplishments or achievements because it focuses too much on what we do as human beings. I like to talk about what gifts were given to us and how God used our human efforts in ways beyond what we could have imagined. In retrospect regarding my 15 years as Executive Coordinator, it is impossible to name all of God's blessings. They were so many, and they came in unexpected ways.

Perhaps I am most grateful for the ways we as a Fellowship of individuals and churches have responded in times of great challenge. From the earliest years, when being identified with CBF took real courage, to the later years, when earthquakes, hurricanes, and natural disasters required great energy, we as a Fellowship have "stepped up" to challenges. We have seen opportunities where many only saw problems. God has used us in ways far beyond what our size or numbers would suggest.

I think it is difficult for those of us who lived through the past 25 years to grasp how much of a deconstruction and reconstruction we experienced. Spirit let us be part of that transformation. We probably don't have eyes to see how dramatic the differences actually are. Without sounding proud or boastful I really believe we have been part of a renewal movement within the Baptist family and the broader Christian community.

Our Baptist understanding of missions has been significantly broadened from simply the church's efforts to evangelize the world to the church's participation in the mission of God, a mission of reconciliation and justice. Baptist "connectionalism" has been revisioned from a convention model to a networking model. Women serve at all levels of leadership in CBF life. The Baptist World Alliance is a different body than it was 25 years ago. Baptists are learning about prayer and spirituality from Christians in other traditions. Baptists are engaged in significant ecumenical initiatives and serious dialogues about human sexuality, interfaith and interreligious relationships, world hunger, and so much more.

All this is not to say the kingdom is here in its fullness. We still face many problems and challenges, but it has been that way from our beginning. We surely are not perfect. We are still forming and becoming a Fellowship that pleases God, but I remain convinced we are a part of something much bigger than we are. I felt that during my tenure of leadership and feel it still.

**Terry**: Anything else you would like to say about your journey as leader of CBF?

**Dr. Vestal**: My journey with CBF has been a gift from God. I am deeply grateful for the divine providence and presence I experienced as well as the many friendships I have been given through CBF. Words can't express my amazement and awe as I reflect over the past years. I have experienced a rich diversity as well as deep unity in CBF that made me a better person, a better Christian, and a better minister.

My leadership role was not something I sought. I will always be thankful for the search committee that was patient with me until I could discern a divine call to it. When I did sense that call, I came to realize I had been preparing all my life for this role of ministry. Both my journey with CBF and my leadership of it were not easy, but they have been richly rewarding and deeply satisfying.

Finally, I must say none of this would have been possible without the loving support and encouragement of my wife, Earlene. In many ways Earlene sacrificed the most when we left the pastorate and when I assumed a ministry that required a great deal of travel, public scrutiny, and the loss of a way of life in a local congregation that we loved dearly.

Our journey together has been rich and sweet. In the struggle for the soul of the SBC, in the formation of CBF, in the discovery of a much broader Baptist family, in the relationships with the global church, and in the many, many opportunities for shared ministry, we have experienced abundant and amazing grace. Thanks be to God!

### *Suzii Paynter (2013–present): "C" is for Cooperative*

On March 1, 2013, Suzii Paynter began her work as CBF's Executive Coordinator. She came to CBF from Texas, where she served as director of the Texas Baptist Christian Life Commission and director of the Advocacy Care Center of the Baptist General Convention of Texas. In addition, Suzii oversaw church outreach; the Texas Baptist Hunger Offering; community care ministries of restorative justice, anti-human trafficking, hunger and poverty; healthcare ministries; the Texas Baptist chaplaincy program; and Texas Baptist counseling services. These leadership roles uniquely prepared Suzii to guide the work of CBF.

Daniel Vestal described Suzii Paynter this way: "Suzii Paynter is a person of Christian character with impeccable integrity, and she is my friend. She has a strong commitment to the local church, as well as to Baptist organizational life. She will inspire and lead all of us in caring and creative ways. I believe the Cooperative Baptist Fellowship has a bright future."[8]

As she prepared to begin her work with CBF, Suzii established "cooperative" as an imperative for the Fellowship: "I think the idea of cooperating, collaborating, empowering—co-empowering—means passing energy back and forth in order to empower multiple facets of our life together. That is the future. To me that is so exciting. It's about a partnership future. It's about a collaborative future. And the whole idea of cooperating is a word we've become familiar with.... We've got to move forward with energy. And where are we going to get that energy? It's going to come from maximizing our energies together toward some central themes that are important to everyone.... So cooperative means this energetic collaboration toward the kingdom vision that we're going to embrace together for the future."[10]

Suzii described the launch of her ministry as a "liminal moment" for the Fellowship. She described ways in which CBF was standing at the threshold of a new day marked by "renewing community, embracing a large mission endeavor, and expanding partnerships."[11] Paynter went on to say this liminal moment demands building three critical structures—governance, missions, and ministry—in response to the work of the 2012 Task Force. Her goal was "to restructure staff and operations functions to align with new priorities and to explore, renew, and hopefully, expand partnerships and affiliations."

Much has happened in the life of the Fellowship during Suzii's brief tenure as Executive Coordinator. Suzii responded to questions about her role:

**Terry**: As you began your term of service as Executive Coordinator for CBF, did you have specific values or convictions in mind you wanted to inculcate in the Fellowship? For example, did you begin with the end in mind, i.e., "When I come to the end of my service, I will consider my ministry effective or faithful if we accomplish this together?"

**Suzii**: My dream for CBF is to become the most vital, vibrant religious community in the United States and to have a voice here and around the world, a voice that we're proud of, that is reflective of our churches, that is reflective of the freedom in Christ we experience as individual Christians.

Specifically, I would like to effectively implement the new structure flowing out of the 2012 Task Force, to bring an ethics and justice effort to the CBF (expand our public witness), engage the larger Christian community on behalf of CBF, strengthen relationships with existing partners and friends in Baptist life, start new churches and strengthen existing congregations, and elevate the gifts of leaders across the Fellowship.

**Terry**: I would like to write about your tenure as it relates to building capacity for *cooperation and collaboration*. In what ways do/did you and those working with you seek to bring folks together for common purposes or to fortify partnerships, i.e., the call to be more together than alone?

**Suzii**: Each congregation within the Fellowship is a living congregation. Each one of us is a unique expression of the gifts and callings of committed Christians—the lives within each church provide energy and growth as we form together toward God's kingdom vision. Whether reading the Bible, singing God's love, caring for children, feeding the hungry, digging for fresh water, or tending the sick and bereaved, each person is remade just a little more nearly into God's image. There are no experts in the kingdom of God, but brothers and sisters who are at once both caretakers and caregivers who share together and are forming together toward a new heaven and earth. Through this process of forming together, God is yet transforming each heart and mind.

But we are not congregations alone, *For we are laborers together with God (1 Corinthians 3:9)*. Our statement of identity from the 2012 Task Force Report says of our Fellowship: We are a community of Baptist Christians and churches walking together and drawn toward the center of our common life in Jesus Christ. We share this fellowship with God, whom we have come to know through Christ. We serve as co-laborers with the Holy Spirit in God's mission.

Within these relationships we freely offer this expression of our identity, not to bind the conscience of any believer or the freedom of any congregation but as an expression of the nature of our fellowship.

Consider, for example, how flocks of birds are able to demonstrate such amazing coordination and alignment, with thousands of independent bodies that move as one, reacting together in nanoseconds to changes in geography, topography, wind currents, and potential predators. Scientists have discovered that just three simple rules govern their interaction: maintain a minimum distance from your neighbor, fly at the same speed as your neighbor, and always turn toward the center. All three rules are essential for flocking. When they are in place, it is as if all birds collectively "see" what each bird sees and "respond" as each bird responds.

Taken from the field of complexity science, *emergence* is a term to describe events in human endeavors which, like flocking, are unpredictable and which seem to result from the interactions between elements, and which no one organization or individual can control. The Fellowship is an emergence endeavor. Although autonomous congregations, we are constantly forming together in responsive mission and ministry. Is it any wonder that Celtic Christians chose the image of a flying wild goose as the picture of the Holy Spirit that forms and guides us? Like soaring birds, as a Fellowship, we are flocking toward our center of the Christ way, living and loving in varieties of congregations and missional expressions. As we travel together on this holy emergence endeavor, we can be responsive to the leading of the Holy Spirit; we can fulfill God's imaginative vision for our community.

Our vision is to be a national and global community, bearing witness to the gospel in partnership with Christians across the nation and around the world.

Individuals, churches, and field personnel of CBF join together in ministry and missions to advance the work of God's love. Where does forming together as a soaring flock happen? In 1,800 congregations and in more than 70 places around the world through collective ministries, we are forming together. Be on the lookout, just a little to your left and just a little to your right, fly together, and turn toward Christ, our center. We will be forming together.

While we are passionate about forming together, we must stay aware that the Four Fragile Freedoms we enjoy yield diversity in the forms and practice of faith. While that diversity is threatening to some, it flows naturally from Baptist preoccupation with the right of choice.

Don't think God is in a predictable box or that church is a cookie-cutter endeavor—not in the Fellowship. We find our beauty in our diversity, but it takes practice to appreciate diversity, and it takes an intentional effort to reach out and celebrate the beauty of it. Humility and kindness are our companions to experiencing the lessons God has been patiently waiting for us to receive. There is much to learn from exploring the diversity of our Fellowship.

**Terry**: In what ways does your understanding of *shaping* or *forming* inform how you think about or go about your work of guiding the Fellowship (I'm referring to the time before and after this became CBF's Big Idea)?

**Suzii**: Throughout the Fellowship we see sustaining vitality uniquely expressed in the variety of our congregations. There is genuine care in our communities—shepherds who love the flock, friends who have supported each other over many seasons of life, families cherishing each others' kids into adulthood, student friends encouraging each other into their dreams. We must continue shaping and forming these qualities in Fellowship congregations.

Our congregations are loving, joyful, enlightened, and educated. So raising this picture of identity, and expanding the visibility and vitality of our churches through branding and outreach, is one of our Fellowship priorities.

Part of my goal has been to take a mirror into different congregations and to remind them who they are. I think the most powerful things in our world—the spiritual things—are invisible, and we live in a very material world. What concerns me is we've not become experts at making the invisible visible. We need to reclaim that and make visible the things we seek to form: love, joy, peace, kindness, faithfulness, perseverance, expressing fruit of the Spirit.

I do love systems, and I love this system, this denomi-network system of our Fellowship that allows for decision-making and friendships and collaboration and flexibility. I love the dynamic nature of it, and I look forward to what it will mean in the future, how it will be further shaped and formed. Religious life today in a denomi-network like the CBF is more like coalition work. You have to respect the interests and the focus of everyone at the table, and you have to understand their focus and their interests are not your interests, but you can still accomplish a lot of things together.

The challenge of global Christianity is calling us to more active global engagement. I think that's a challenge we've been prepared for in some ways, but we've not been focused on it. We know how to go and do a global missions trip, but do we really know how to be globally engaged as brothers and sisters in Christ in supportive ways that honor the churches around the world? We have to put our minds to it and really make some intentional preparation.

The culture of call over a lifetime is a journey that's going to have many expressions. First of all, we need to covenant to be in partnership with people from the time of their exploration, and whether that exploration ends up in an ordained clergy position or expresses itself in secular employment, our commitment is to the personal development of the young explorers in our network. This is a pipeline for everyone to engage, with an opportunity for expression and engagement for public witness all along that pipeline. You don't have to wait until a certain point and then be allowed to lead or be in service, but all along the pipeline opportunities present themselves.

One thing we're doing in order for that to happen is putting all of our young Baptist programs in what we're calling an ecosystem and staffing it with people who are under 40. We see this step as key to forming and shaping leaders for the future.

**Terry**: How did your experience with collaborative partnerships while at BGCT inform, inspire, and/or drive your leadership of CBF?

**Suzii**: I feel my time with the Baptist General Convention of Texas prepared me for leadership within the Fellowship in so many ways:

1.  I learned how to understand the concentric circles of an organization (especially staff and stakeholder relationships), identifying funding streams, shaping an organizational structure in line with its vision, and crafting new position descriptions for needed leadership.
2.  I learned how to meet and connect with major stakeholders, identify funding streams, and build collaborative partnerships.
3.  I learned the importance of "having the right people on the bus," i.e., having the right people in the right roles for the success of the organization.
4.  We built relationships with Baptist and non-Baptist entities across the country. I learned to work across denominational lines to accomplish kingdom work and how to craft shared resources agreements.
5.  I gained experience advocating for important causes in the Texas legislature, enhancing the public witness work of the BGCT.

6. I nurtured my passion for addressing poverty and food insecurity. This fueled my commitment to tell powerful stories in order to raise funds for the Texas Baptist Hunger Offering.

7. I learned to write grant requests to help fund major initiatives.

**Terry**: Anything else you would like to say about your journey as leader of CBF?

**Suzii**: Christ's love has compelled us—each one—on a journey of faithful and adventurous obedience. We constantly hear stories that tell of the incomplete but elegant connection that is the work of God's creative hand in our very lives and the churches gathered in CBF. Stories challenge us to attend to and visualize ourselves as a constellation of witnesses. We are many voices, many hearts being called and drawn toward the center of our common life in Jesus Christ.

Our CBF story is relevant and full of surprising gifts because it is grounded in the greater gospel story. We are not the creators of spiritual gifts nor the blessing of Christ-like living, but we acknowledge the bounty given to us and seek stewardship into our future. The strength of a fellowship is in its aspirations and the authenticity of mentors, pastoral inspiration, friendship, common purpose in mission across miles and times. The blessing of community is also a signpost of hope in the valley of our shadows. During both the light and dark, CBF has been a community of imperfect but strong spiritual connection.

Outwardly, CBF connections have been characterized by sincere ecumenical friendship across the larger Christian community and positive collegiality in interfaith endeavors as well. In a context of U.S. religious pluralism and the expanding outreach of the global church and world religions, CBF will invest toward diversity in our leadership and deeper, productive ecumenical and interfaith connections. The near future calls for a public witness of common purpose for biblical justice, racial healing, and an amplified voice for religious liberty, "a gift from God, not nations."

CBF pioneered the structure for a global organization of churches and individuals to provide identity and collective missions based upon a network that serves Baptist Christians and churches. I served on the first interim steering committee for CBF (it later became the Coordinating Council). Our discussions were deliberately exhaustive because everyone was keenly aware we were building the enabling structures from the ground up and that, for better or worse, structure begets potential. This is true of our past, and it will be true of our future. Now, in the Executive Coordinator chair to navigate the 21st-century religious landscape, it is clear that the flexible expressions of connectional life expressed in CBF are firm enough to provide organizational structure yet nimble enough to allow for adaptation and restructuring. Rather than aspiring to be something else, CBF is a denomi-network and is defining its identity as such. Central to this identity are the practices of friendship among individuals and partnership with other, mostly autonomous, organizations.

This is a genuine web of diverse organizations that are autonomous and interdependent that will chart a course into a changing future. Loose affiliations and independent funding of the partners allow for partnerships to come and go. The evolving nature of the collection of CBF partners is not accidental, but intended to change and to add vitality to CBF as new and varied partners are explored for scale, strength, common Christian aspiration and impact. There are always tensions for funding when so many organizations coexist, but the priority of *freedom* referenced so often is reflected in this partnership paradigm. CBF will extend this sustainable model by exercising the art and practice of faithful friendship and collaborative partnership.

CBF has reaffirmed a primary commitment to cooperative global engagement, thus continuing the tradition to make disciples of all nations that Baptists have been forming together for more than two centuries. The CBF endeavor of cooperative missions is complex, substantial and long term (compared to a general missions landscape of drive-by projects and missions tourism). This is co-missioning—it is not cheap, nor is it the kind of venture that can be supported with the change left in your car cup holder. This type of 21st-century Christian engagement is worth the lives of our partners and field personnel, and it is worth our serious investment. Be clear—the gospel task, bringing the word that GOD is with us, *Imago Dei*, and *Missio Dei* is not "just another charity"—it is a way of being, a way of living, and a way of sharing God's love and the witness of Christ. This is eternal.

CBF is embodying Mission Distinctives to offer Cooperative Baptists common framework missions engagement and is committed to local and global missions focused on Beloved Community (to love and empower people), Bearing Witness to Jesus Christ (to speak of and show Christ), and Seeing Transformational Development (to use assets to make meaningful change).

(NOTE: These are outlined in the previous chapter. CBF field personnel serve in many places around the globe and in the United States. CBF's Global Mission Enterprise focuses on three broad contexts: Global Poverty, Global Migration, and Global Church.)

At the core of our Fellowship is a journey of forming together. We each move within our time—we are on a pilgrimage that includes both decline and hospice and renewal and movement toward our spiritual home. How do we find tomorrow's church? The answer, of course, is to BE tomorrow's church.

One reason to join in fellowship of CBF is for the present journey. It has been my practice to visit CBF churches widely and often. Every week I meet people who have made great journeys to find God.

The friendship, witness, wisdom, scriptural insight, and care from the people and practice of their CBF church is repeated in stories of genuine inspiration, joy, and healing. The sacred pours forth. The depth of an authentic faith narrative repeated by simple witness of church members is stunning and so hopeful. They are true followers of Christ. The congregation may be limping in another way, but undoubtedly the miraculous and beautiful manifestation of tomorrow's faithful church resides in us. It is our mission to tune our ear to the work of the Holy Spirit and amplify the beautiful strength in the church right where we are but with new and diverse fellow pilgrims. Nurturing this journey is not an institutional given but a process of honest sharing and a practice of blessing the important transformational moments of God at work even if they are not the headline events.

There is no doubt that the need to manifest God's kind of love is urgent in our context of objectification, hate, and despair. "For God so loved the world that he gave his son" is a radical message and a simple call to bring love, compassion, and humaneness to bear everywhere. CBF churches are responding to their communities with life-changing—if not always headline-making—ministries. We need the help that comes from those also committed to Christ-like living to navigate our course. I am very sure that tomorrow's church will grow from the seeds and good soil that are already here, but likewise, not many new pilgrims will be drawn to Christ because a church is focused on celebrating its past. In comparing the American church to the Chinese church, a lay pastor in Chengdu said, "Perhaps the U.S. church has been more comfortable being the loaf, not the yeast." We are in for a yeasty future. God has called us into this time and is asking something creative, fragrant, and dynamic of us. CBF is committed anew to supporting and equipping churches, pastoral leaders, and young Baptists for tomorrow's church.

As CBF we have shared aspirations for lives of spiritual vitality and peace, for renewal of the church in our time, for discarding the encumbrances that would hinder us from God's great realm that is both at hand and yet to come. We all need a journey, and we all need a home.

## Notes

[1]Cecil Sherman, "Baptist and Freedom," *Fellowship News* 3/3, September/October 1993, 8.

[2]Cecil Sherman, "Thinking About Freedom," *Fellowship News* 4/2, March/April 1994, 2.

[3]Cecil Sherman, "The Highest Good," *Fellowship News* 4/3, May/June 1994, 2.

[4]Cecil Sherman, "Bottom Up," *Fellowship News* 5/2, March/April 1995, 2.

[5]"Sherman Marks Third Anniversary as Fellowship's First Coordinator," *Fellowship News* 5/2, March/April 1995, 21.

[6]"Sherman Sound Bites," *Fellowship News* 5/2, March/April 1995, 22.

[7]Adapted from ABP report by Greg Warner, "Newly-Elected Coordinator Sounds Leadership Themes for Fellowship, *Fellowship News* 6/8, October 1996, 3.

[7]Daniel Vestal, "A 'Fellowship of Hope,'" *fellowship!* 7/6, July/August 1997, 2.

[8]Daniel Vestal, "Dreaming and Visioning," *fellowship!* 7/5, June 1997, 16.

[9]Daniel Vestal, "Meet Suzii Paynter–CBF Executive Coordinator," *fellowship!* 23/2, April/May 2013, 25.

[10]Suzii Paynter, "Q&A with Suzii Paynter," *fellowship!* 23/2, April/May 2013, 26–27.

[11]Suzii Paynter, "At the Front Door of Our Future," *fellowship!* 23/2, April/May 2013, 2.

Chapter 12

# CBF—Shaped by the Stories We Tell

Every person committed to the mission and ministry of CBF shares responsibility to tell the story of what God has done and is doing in and through the movement. According to the Apaches, stories are like arrows. They are told to us—or aimed at us—to awaken us to the experiences of others. Often they bounce away; sometimes they penetrate us and work on us.

The person on the CBF staff assigned direct responsibility for telling CBF's story and CBF stories is the Communications Director. Three persons have served in this role during the past 25 years: David Wilkinson, Ben McDade, and Aaron Weaver. Each of these gifted journalists helped shape and form the Fellowship by the stories they told and the images they used in telling them. Specifically, they and those who worked with them crafted inspirational stories from the life of the Fellowship and from field personnel to awaken our consciousness about important kingdom work we do together.

Carrie McGuffin, Communications Specialist for the CBF since October 2014, describes "the work of words":

> For me, being part of the Cooperative Baptist Fellowship is being part of a movement that I believe in. As a Communications Specialist for CBF Global, I have been privileged to share the stories of our missions and ministries as we celebrate the freedom of being Baptist. That privilege extends to creating resources, providing news, curating views, and keeping Cooperative Baptists informed on a daily basis.
>
> I grew up as a Cooperative Baptist, and from the time I was six years old, I knew the language of partnership; I understood the equality of women in leadership; I embraced liturgy; I celebrated Global Missions. I learned the language of CBF through attending a CBF church, going to PASSPORT Camps, serving as a Student.Go intern at a Together for Hope site, and joining the communications staff of CBF—first as an intern and then as a full-time member of the team.

Shortly after I began my time on the staff of CBF, we adopted the language of "Forming Together," and "Partnering to Renew God's World." The six attributes of CBF were also introduced: Christ-like, diverse, innovative, global, authentic, and excellence. Through all of the work that we do as an organization, especially in communications, I believe these attributes are the threads that bind us to our commitments to form together and partner to renew God's world, as well as express our core values of soul freedom, biblical freedom, church freedom, and religious freedom.

The ways in which we express the views of the Fellowship should at all times reflect some aspect of these values, attributes, and commitments and, in practice, deeply involve partnership.

In every piece that we write, curate, or create, partnership is the key to taking an idea from concept to reality—from an idea on a white board or stated in a meeting to seeing the concept through the writer's eyes to layout in a magazine or formatting on a blog, creating a social media campaign, reviewing videos, editing curriculum, posting photos on Instagram, or sharing articles on Twitter. Each team member on the communications staff is key in keeping the Fellowship informed at whatever level they connect with us—from email to social media, from blog readers to readers of hard-copy magazines.

The message of CBF is intended to be managed by this core group alongside the leadership of the organization—shaping the way that we connect with our constituents through the annual campaigns like the Offering for Global Missions and one-time responses to global disasters.

Through this dedication to shaping the language and images that we share with the broader Fellowship, our hope is that all of our materials speak to our attributes, connect to our commitments, and influence individuals and churches to partner with us as we seek to share Christ's love. Christ's love compels us to engage on personal, intellectual, theological, and social levels with those who partner with us. We strive to create conversation and prompt our constituents in sharing about their lives in the pews of a Cooperative Baptist church, to encourage their prayers and hopes for our missional endeavors, to impart their wisdom of experience as chaplains and pastoral counselors or graduates of our partner seminaries.

As the public voice of the Fellowship, we as a team aim to share from every perspective. We seek to show the faces of the Fellowship around the world. We strive to show impact and increase impact of our field personnel and partners.

The work of words is beautiful and engaging; it is difficult and sometimes requires a thesaurus; it reaches people through emotion and through calls to action. The work of words is the work of breathing life into the stories that the people of the Fellowship need to hear.

### Chapter 13

# What We Learned in the First 25 Years!

Attempts to thoroughly and comprehensively articulate what we learned during the first 25 years of CBF are almost overwhelming. Acknowledging that no exploration is exhaustive and lessons continue to be learned, I have done my best to fairly represent what I have seen, heard, and experienced in CBF life. God's Spirit moved in the past and continues to move among us. For that we are grateful.

## CBF Is Tethered to Jesus

CBF exists to be a community bearing witness to the gospel in partnership with Christians across the nation and around the world. This good news inspires us to become like Jesus in word and deed, invest in kingdom ministries, and advocate for the poor and needy (more about this in Part 4).

## Baptist Ideals Are Worth Preserving

Baptist convictions and values that birthed the CBF are worth preserving. Cherished beliefs like separation of church and state, autonomy of the local church, and religious liberty for all continue to be threatened. CBF commits to countering the threat.

## Commitment to Missions

From its inception CBF has shown remarkable commitment to engaging in global missions. We have called out and commissioned gifted missioners to serve the most marginalized and least evangelized around the globe. We birthed Together for Hope to provide missionary presence in the 20 poorest counties in the United States. We secured important leaders with sound missiology to guide CBF's global mission enterprise: Keith Parks, Gary and Barbara Baldridge, Rob Nash, and Steven Porter. Finally, in response to changing times, we designed a new and sustainable model for global missions.

## The Joy of Being Together

I cannot say I looked forward to attending contentious SBC meetings. There was little joy because believers felt divided. Growing intolerance for diversity within the system created suspicion and separation. Fellowship gatherings are different. Annual General Assemblies are like a family reunion. Friendship networks and supportive encounters are rich. The Gathering Place draws me into a world of deepening friendships old and new. I walk away from the experience feeling refreshed and uplifted and can't wait until next year's General Assembly.

## The Value of Cooperation

*Cooperative* is not only part of our name; cooperation is woven into the DNA of the *Cooperative Baptist Fellowship.* We collaborate with other believers. We forge sustainable partnerships. We believe in the divine value of working alongside others to accomplish kingdom goals.

## Congregational Renewal Is Continually Sought

Congregations desire spiritual vitality, so they constantly seek resources to aid the journey. Dawnings has proven to be an excellent congregational process to help churches find new life and vitality through visioning, forming, and engaging.

## Church-Shaped Mission vs. Mission-Shaped Church

While institutional think still controls many Baptist congregations, others find life by engaging in God's mission in the world. Efforts at becoming more missional have blessed congregations and the kingdom. Some of our congregations are growing incarnational ministries in which deeper relationships develop with those we serve. Churches are relationship systems that prioritize relationship and love over rules and principle. Christ's mission of loving people into the kingdom is our mission too.

## Peer Learning Groups Are of Great Value

Peer learning groups that educate and provide support are extremely important gatherings for clergy. Vocational ministers who invest heavily in caring for others need places to connect with colleagues who motivate them and understand the work. Peer learning groups provide a network of encouragement/accountability and foster continuing education. Given the demands of ministry, having a place where others help carry the load is essential.

## Necessity of Enlarging the Christian Education Conversation

Many CBF congregations have discovered the necessity of focusing on spiritual formation that leads to transformation, not just "growing the Sunday school." This will be discussed in detail in Part 4.

## Moderate Baptists Could Not Abide Fundamentalism

When the reins of the SBC were turned over to fundamentalists, moderates chose to build a new fellowship. Fundamentalism as a mindset is not compatible with the gospel of love and grace. So when Baptist-style fundamentalism attacked the church of Jesus Christ, we could not ignore the impact. We were compelled to follow the Spirit's leadership in birthing a new faith-based movement.

Pat Anderson said it well, "The Baptist landscape is littered with craters left by Fundamentalist bombs: innumerable characters attacked, seminaries dismantled, missions recruits narrowly chosen, creedal beliefs imposed, connections with right-wing secular politics embraced, relationships with indigenous Baptists around the world destroyed, Baptist history rewritten, dissent stifled, intimidation and mind control ruled the day.... So distasteful are the machinations of the Fundamentalists that we turn our faces and gladly cling to this new thing God is doing in and through the CBF."[1]

## Institutional Tug of SBC

We learned early in CBF's history that many individuals and congregations were excited to journey with and support new mission and ministry initiatives of CBF. I think some were surprised by how many congregations could *not* make the shift away from the SBC even though congregational and leadership values and convictions aligned with those of CBF. SBC indoctrination worked well and led to statements like this: "The SBC was good enough for my grandparents, and it's good enough for me" or "We can't take away support from missionaries we sent to the field." The tug of institutional connection, reactions to propaganda efforts by SBC leaders seeking to discredit CBF, and fear about minister placement and ministerial retirement funds often superseded values and convictions. The power of "institutional think" led many congregations to choose dual alignment.

## Courage Needed to Affiliate with the Fellowship

CBF Executive Coordinator Daniel Vestal acknowledged much courage was required to lead a congregation to leave the SBC in order to embrace CBF or even to claim dual alignment. Though excitement was palpable as moderate Baptists responded to the movement of God's Spirit, early adopters experienced huge personal and professional uncertainty in the early days of CBF life. Many ministers paid a huge price for encouraging their congregations to stay true to their Baptist convictions. Even today tensions exist in many congregations that are dually aligned because of how difficult remaining true to two different versions of Baptist Christianity is.

## The Value of Staying Nimble

Unlike older, established denominations, CBF has remained flexible and malleable. Many denominational leaders marveled at CBF's ability to totally restructure in a brief period of time. Staying nimble has allowed us to be responsive to the needs of our constituents and the changing world in which we live.

## Folks Don't Want to Live in the Past

CBF is a youthful movement. Many who engage with the Fellowship today never experienced being a part of the SBC. They have heard and respect the "war stories," but these women and men are ready to move boldly into the future together. We know the value of celebrating our rich heritage but not dwelling on the conflict that birthed us. We are compelled by the love of Jesus Christ to follow a new vision into brighter days ahead.

## The Value of Diversity

Being Baptist means freedom, and embracing freedom as a value connotes we welcome diversity. The Fellowship is not threatened by diversity. In fact, we see diversity as a beautiful part of God's creation. Naturally, diversity can lead to disagreement—even conflict. CBF values the ability and willingness to have difficult conversations—especially when we know there is disagreement. We believe ability to have hard conversations in which all perspectives are respected as a gift to the kingdom.

## CBF College Student Ministries Are Life-giving

I am very pleased with the many resources CBF offers college students. CBF's Young Baptist Ecosystem may be one of our best-kept secrets. Lives are being changed because of Student.Go, Student.Church, and SelahVie. Many students in CBF congregations also appreciate opportunities to serve through Passport. Experiences for students tether them to CBF in powerful ways. Spread the word!

## The Value of Women in Leadership

How blessed the Fellowship is to have a female Executive Coordinator—an impossibility in many Baptist circles. CBF places high value on elevating leadership roles of women in our organization and in our congregations. We've made great progress over the past 25 years, but we have a ways to go. Many of our congregations still balk at calling women as senior pastors. This must change. So even as we celebrate the leadership of women in CBF life, we acknowledge we still have work to do in moving the conversation along.

### Sound Theological Education Is Vital

CBF's connection to many divinity schools and seminaries is a gift. Trained clergy are key to our future. We need connection to a network that provides sound theological education for those responding to the call to vocational ministry. CBF congregations depend upon these schools to prepare vocational ministers who assist in the foundational work of local congregations.

### The CBF "Seal of Approval" Means Something

More and more folks depend on CBF to vet resources, speakers, and consultants. Having the CBF "seal of approval" is increasingly important to our constituents.

### CBF Is a Movement of God's Spirit

We embrace the word *movement* to describe the CBF. While I served as convener (2013–2014, 2014–2015) of the Movement Leadership Team (state and regional coordinators plus global representatives) for CBF, we engaged in honest conversations about whether or not we needed a new name. Some felt the word *movement* connotes something short-lived. Ray Higgins, coordinator for CBF Arkansas, led a discussion on the subject. He shared this quote from the introduction of Brian McLaren's book *We Make the Road by Walking*:

> So our world truly needs a global spiritual movement dedicated to aliveness. This movement must be global, because the threats we face cannot be contained by national borders. It must be spiritual, because the threats we face go deeper than brain-level politics and economics to the heart level of value and meaning. It must be social, because it can't be imposed from above; it can only spread from person to person, friend to friend, family to family, network to network. And it must be a movement, because by definition, movements stir and focus grassroots human desire to bring change to institutions and the societies those institutions are intended to serve.[2]

Ray concluded his comments by reminding us of a powerful passage of scripture. When Paul and Silas came to Thessalonica, some Jews attacked

Jason's house looking for them. They dragged Jason and others before the authorities, shouting, "These people who have been turning the world upside down have come here also" (Acts 17:6 NRSV). Ray responded:

> That's what movements can do.
> They can set the world on fire.
> They can turn the world upside down.
> They can do it through hatred and violence.
> Or they can do it through love, peace, justice, grace, and hope.
> They can do it to conquer and destroy.
> Or they can do it to love and redeem.

CBF is a movement of God's Spirit, inspired by love, peace, justice, grace, and hope. We celebrate what God has accomplished in and through the CBF movement over the past 25 years, and we are excited about the future. A historical timeline prepared by Aaron Weaver is provided in Appendix E to prompt our thanksgiving and gratitude to God.

### CBF's Story Continues

This section of the book is designed to give insights in the formation and re-formation of the CBF. Leaders of the Fellowship care deeply about this movement of God and carefully crafted language to help folks understand our identity. Some have struggled to say who CBF is in a reasonably short, clear, and understandable way. A summary of who we are and what is important to us is helpful at this point. I turn to the words of my friend Marion Aldridge, former coordinator for CBF of South Carolina, who offered the top twelve distinctives of CBF in his "elevator speech":

1) We think God's grace trumps everything else. We believe in the Law, but the grace of Jesus Christ needs to be the last word. Refer to the 1963 Baptist Faith & Message statement: "The criterion by which we interpret scriptures is Jesus Christ."

2) We believe the great commandments (to love God, neighbor, and self) are the most important directives in Holy Scripture.

3) We affirm the role of women in the church in every capacity, as lay leaders and as pastors.

4) We empower the laity. We don't believe there are any second-class citizens in the kingdom of God, neither women nor laity.

5) We foster ecumenical and interfaith relationships. We are committed to civility rather than demonizing those who are different from us. (If I am feeling feisty, I say, "We are the Baptists other people can get along with.")

6) We emphasize four particular freedoms:
   a) Bible freedom, meaning each person interprets through guidance of Holy Spirit.
   b) Soul freedom, meaning the individual stands before God alone without mediation by any other human—parent, pastor, or pope;
   c) Church freedom, each local church acts independently;
   d) Separation of church and state.

7) Our mission efforts pay attention to and attempt to promote justice for the most marginalized members of society.

8) We are often a sanctuary for marginalized churches that have not fit into the prevailing denominational culture. (This is where I begin my elevator speech with some pastors or laity or churches who have been ostracized in some way.)

9) We value conversation and formation (for adults) more than indoctrination. We value biblical scholarship as distinct from a literal or legalistic or narrow worldview.

10) The focus of our ministry is on congregations. We resource local congregations so that they can thrive.

11) We believe in partnerships and networking (we feel no need to do it all on our own).

12) We like to develop young leaders.

A long elevator ride would be necessary to talk about all of these important distinctives that uniquely describe CBF. Use this list to engage others in conversation about CBF.

CBF has preserved important Baptist tenants while staying alert to where the Spirit blows. That's why "forming together" and "partnering to renew God's world" inspire our ministry into the future. The CBF story continues as we learn to more faithfully embrace and embody the convictions flowing out of the 2015 branding campaign.

## *Notes*

[1]"Facing Fundamentalism," *Fellowship News*, 6/4, May 1996, 16.

[2] Brian D. McLaren, *We Make the Road by Walking* (New York, NY: Jericho Books, 2014), xvi.

**Reclaiming and Re-Forming Baptist Identity**

**Part 4**

# What Inspires CBF's Future?

After exploring values and convictions that influenced the birthing of CBF and sharing a brief history of the Fellowship, we now focus on the future. While moderate Baptists are wary of a prescriptive approach to following Jesus, the next chapters make a case for building our future by "forming together" and "partnering to renew God's world."

### Chapter 14

# Forming

No scripture passage provides a visual image for "forming" better than the parable of the potter and the clay found in Jeremiah 18:1–11. Recall the story. God invites Jeremiah to a potter's house to hear a message from God. At his wheel the potter crafts a vessel. As sometimes happens, the vessel became misshapen, causing the potter to rework it into a different vessel, "as seemed good to him." Then comes God's probing question to the nation of Israel: "Can I not do with you, O house of Israel, just as this potter has done?"

The potter's house was a workshop in which the potter crafted much-needed, practical containers. God frequently describes something familiar to teach life lessons. In this tale we understand God is the potter, the maker, the creator of what is useful. God shapes and forms people and nations. When they become rebellious and resist the shaping process, God's powerful hand re-forms people and/or nations into something purposeful. If, however, the clay becomes too hard and immovable, it is thrown onto the discard pile.

The parable teaches us clay must retain pliable qualities in order for the potter to reshape it into different vessels when necessary. Only flexible, malleable, responsive clay may be shaped and formed.

What human truths may we draw from this parable? We must recognize our innate tendencies to resist God's shaping forces upon our lives. Most of us have authority issues, don't we? We prefer to be in control or at the very least believe we are in control of our lives. We want to be "in charge" and choose our own way instead of yield our lives into the Master Potter's hands. God knows who we are and continues to woo and encourage us onto the potter's wheel for shaping and changing, though we are predictably often stiff-necked and resistant regarding the Master's conversion efforts. Choosing our own (false) sense of control over consent to the efforts of God the creator leads to rigidity and resistance to change, transformation, and something new.

Because the Christian life is a journey of faith (believing in something unseen; trust), we absolutely must remain open, responsive, and pliable under God. If we react favorably to God's intentional forming and shaping at each stage of our lives, we are always "new." Trusting our lives into God's capable hands allows us to discover the joy of becoming God's "perfect" and useful vessel.

God's methods are keen. Sending Jesus to learn about us, live like us, love us, and leave us the plan is masterful. When we refuse to learn about God's presence (Jesus) and how he showed us to live and love, we resist God's efforts to shape and form us. We hurt ourselves when we try to take over and commandeer our faith development. God the Spirit stayed to show how to be moldable in God the Father's hands. Jesus showed us how to remain responsive to our Master Potter.

### What Is Faith, and How Is It Formed?

What is faith? How is it taught or transmitted? These questions beg thoughtful and reflective responses.

First, an attempt to define *faith* is illuminating and helpful. Richard Osmer says, "Faith is a relationship of trust in God whose loving-kindness and faithfulness have been shown in Jesus Christ. This is the heart and soul of Christianity. The core of the Bible is a story of God's faithfulness to creation and to humanity, a story that culminates in the life, death, and resurrection of Jesus Christ. It is God's faithfulness that brings Christian faith to life. God is trustworthy, and in faith, we recognize and accept this trust."[1]

Osmer also describes four sides of faith that guide the teaching/learning process in a church[2]:

1. *beliefs* about God that serve as the basis of our trust
2. an ongoing, personal *relationship* with God that brings us into a relationship with other persons of faith
3. a *commitment* to God as trustworthy that shapes the way we invest our time and energy
4. an awareness of the *mystery* that surrounds God and places limits on our understanding and control of God

These four sides of faith, rightly understood, could revolutionize our understanding of faith and how we "teach for faith" in the church. Without holistic awareness we can easily focus our energy on "getting our beliefs right" to the neglect of other dimensions of faith. This is damaging to the believer, the church, and the kingdom. Expanding consciousness about the nature of faith is required if we seek to nurture trust in God, to help people understand all aspects of their lives in light of their faith, and to rightly recognize there are limits to what we can comprehend about an infinite God.

We must acknowledge faith cannot be taught in the same way we teach math or science in school. Why? Because we seek to educate for faith in the person of Jesus Christ—not simply facts about Jesus. We cannot cause another to have faith. Faith is a free gift from God that is awakened and enlivened as we respond to God's grace. We know God also uses the witness of faith communities to bring faith to life. I love Osmer's understanding of the purpose of teaching in the church:

> The purpose of our teaching in the church is to create a context in which faith can be awakened, supported, and challenged.[3]

Osmer is on target! The teaching ministry of a church is vitally important because it creates a context for faith to live and grow. Teachers don't give faith to their students, but they do use tools and methods to awaken, support, and challenge the faith of fellow pilgrims on the spiritual journey.

Finally, we recognize that our understanding of what faith is and how it is transmitted is influenced by many cultural factors. Challenging the culture can be threatening for many. Christians have a difficult time examining the human systems that formed them. Ralph Linton said, "For a person to discover culture is like a fish discovering he is living in water."[4] Critical reflection is required of each generation because culture is man-made. Each congregation is responsible to wrestle with the meaning of faith in light of its history, relationships, and societal events. Ellis Nelson says culture has to be "opened up for critical examination if faith in God is ever to lead us to a different style of life."[5] This is why the congregation is the educator, developing a contemporary understanding of faith before passing it on to the next generation.

### Spiritual Formation Defined

Formation captures the essence of CBF. In fact, the first section of our birthing document, "Address to the Public—the Founding Document of Cooperative Baptist Fellowship," begins with the word *forming*: "Forming something as fragile as the Cooperative Baptist Fellowship is not a move we make lightly." Whether intentional or coincidental, the big idea coming out of the 2015 CBF rebranding process was *forming together*. From our inception, leaders in the Fellowship movement were confident a new way of being Baptist Christians was being shaped and formed by God.

*Forming* is key for CBF and drives our understanding of spiritual formation:

> Spiritual formation is the process of being formed in the image of Christ by the gracious working of God's Spirit in community for the transformation of the world.

This profound definition is a contextual rewording of Robert Mulholland's seminal work *Invitation to a Journey*. This understanding of spiritual formation reminds us faith is formed in and by God, is shaped in the context of Christian community, cannot be programmed, and is "caught" more than taught. We also voice the conviction that our formation is not complete until we invest our lives in others—that is, Jesus' command to love God AND love neighbor.

Formation is a process much like shaping pottery vessels is a process. As clay cannot become a useful vessel without the careful craftsmanship of the potter, Christ-followers do not arrive at spiritual maturity apart from life-shaping personal and corporate spiritual practices. Though we don't do the shaping—God does—we are prompted by the Spirit's forming forces in the midst of our life experiences. Engaging in spiritual practices or disciplines makes us more aware, pliable, and responsive to God's work in our lives. How do we know which practices will mold and shape us? The disciplines exercised by Jesus are foundational, and we benefit greatly from studying and practicing them. The formation of our faith is purposeful and enables us to become more like Jesus—to *want to* emulate his life and ministry. The goal of the ongoing process of spiritual formation is to nurture believers to become like Jesus in attitude, conviction, intent, and action. We discover how to be like Jesus from the New Testament.

The apostle Paul was fond of using the phrase *in Christ* when encouraging the churches he planted. He changed his language slightly when writing to the church at Galatia: "My little children, with whom I am again in travail until Christ be formed in you" (Gal 4:19). Paul's life and ministry were all about telling the story of what Christ did in his life and helping others embark on a similar journey toward God. Paul sees potential for Christ to be birthed in the lives of believers at Galatia. For that to happen, Christ must first be "formed" in them. It seems the Galatian converts responded favorably and showed signs of growth as long as Paul was physically present. In Paul's absence the Galatians appeared to lose their way—an observation that caused Paul great anxiety.

Clearly, Paul expected Christ to be formed in the lives of the Galatian Christ-followers, but this formation did not happen immediately or automatically. A variety of interpretations for Paul's use of *formed in you* have been suggested: (1) Paul is referring to Christ being born again in people's lives (incarnation); (2) Paul expects a quality of life that leads to Christ-like behaviors; (3) Paul sees a well-balanced life resulting from moving in a Christ-centered direction; and (4) Paul sees Christ as the core that provides hope, joy, and grounding for daily living.

All who welcome Christ accept the invitation to be formed. Formation begins with Christ and continues because of the Spirit's initiative and our willingness and our efforts to grow (form) into the image of Christ. As Paul "parented" the Galatians in their progress, we, too, seek wisdom and guidance in the process of our own faith formation.

### Awakening Consciousness

Joan and I have a pet parakeet we call Sky because of the beautiful blue and white colors of his feathers. Sky has an extensive vocabulary. One of his favorite things to say is, "Wake up, Sleepyhead!" Of course, he has no idea what it means, but Sky knows he gets a good reaction when he says it. I wonder if that is what God wants to cry out to Christ-followers and congregations today, "Wake up, Sleepyheads!" In God's case, God knows the meaning of the call to wake from our slumber.

How can God get our attention in the midst of our own and the world's busyness? How does God awaken us to gaps between our current reality and what God desires? We "wake up" because the Spirit invites us and calls us to respond to realities beyond our present perspective on life. The Spirit then calls us to redefine and realign our lives in relationship to God in ways beyond our present circumstances and understanding. Some call this realignment *transformation.*

David Benner says transformation is an enduring expansion of consciousness that expresses itself in four ways:[6]

1.  Increased awareness
2.  A broader, more inclusive identity
3.  A larger framework for meaning-making (how we understand and make sense of our self, others, God, and the world)

4.   A reorganization of personality that results in a changed way of being in
     the world

Difficult or new life experiences have potential to awaken consciousness.
Transformation is, however, not the same as self-improvement. We certainly
play a role in the transformative process, but true transformation is more gift
of God than achievement.

Benner says it this way,

> Shifts in our consciousness involve a spiritual response. The spiritual
> nature of these responses is seen in (the fact that they are) acts of
> openness to something larger than and beyond our self as it presently
> exists. In every case this involves a posture of willingness (rather than
> willfulness), faith and trust (as opposed to fear and caution), surrender
> (rather than an attempt to control), and consent to awakening (rather
> than a return to sleep). It means offering a full-hearted *yes!* to life, to
> love, to others, to the world.... By responding in these ways, we open
> ourselves to the possibility of becoming more than we presently are.[7]

When the Spirit wakes us up, we can choose to hold on to the life we now
live, the status quo. There may be spiritual significance in that choice. Being
"stuck" (or going back to sleep) where we are on the journey of faith, however,
is not contentment. In fact, Benner says, "It is saying 'no' to 'the unceasing
invitation of God's Spirit to become more than we are.'"[8]

Too often we speak of the spiritual journey solely in terms of what *we do*,
and we become convinced that is how God defines faithfulness. What God
really desires is our *consent* to be awakened. If we reduce faith to our own
efforts, we run the risk of strengthening the false self and turning the spiritual
journey into a self-improvement project. This is disastrous because doing so
wrongly convinces the ego it is even more in control than before the spiritual
journey began. Ignoring or running from the Spirit's invitation can have devastating consequences for our development.

Again I turn to Benner: "Awareness is the fruit of such an unobstructed
opening of self.... The risk of awareness is that we might have to change....
More fundamental than what we do or think is our openness to the Spirit."[9]
It is this openness that enables the Spirit to shape and form us on the journey
of faith. How do we discover ways in which the Spirit desires to form us? We
turn to the life and ministry of Jesus—the author and sustainer of our faith.

## The Centrality of Jesus

The only true center of Christian discipleship is Jesus—not the Bible, not the Law, not tradition, not personal interpretation. This truth should go without saying. Faith and trust are essential for a Christ-follower, but if we focus on *our* faith—disregarding the person of Jesus and his teachings—we turn our attention away from our obligation to be obedient to Christ. Salvation is much more than personal redemption (assurance of an eternal relationship with God); it is about participating in God's redemption of the world.

Jesus showed us by how he lived that God cares about what happens in the material world. He wasn't simply focused on the eternal destination of souls. That's why Jesus spent so much time showing us how to care for earthly things. Jesus embodied grace and love as he reached out to people. He healed the sick and fed the hungry. He spoke in parables listeners could understand. He celebrated at weddings and played with children. Jesus' life was marked by compassion for what happened in the world around him. To call ourselves disciples of Jesus, we can do no less.

If we are honest, we admit our tendency to urge others to see things *our* way and in so doing believe we are engaging in genuine discipleship. Again, in our limited understanding and experience, we "have usurped the role of Jesus Christ in these matters. We have determined what is appropriate discipleship, and we have presumed to judge who meets our criteria of personal faith."[10] What happens as a result? The norms *we* establish for Christian discipleship fall far short of Jesus' teachings, actions, and expectations. Theologian David Watson says it well: "Instead of serving as salt and light and leaven and seed as Jesus commissioned us, we have created congregational 'safe houses,' offering the benefits of salvation, but doing little to further God's salvation of planet earth."[11] We cannot make Christian discipleship *primarily* about comforting and supporting people. We must take the next steps toward deeper understanding of our faith.

Are our congregations failing to produce disciplined followers of Jesus? Yes, I believe there is strong evidence to support such a claim. Is this because our discipleship efforts are too focused on our *human* understanding of discipleship, our *human* concept of faith, and our *human* assumptions of what it means to live for Christ? As long as the only objective of discipleship is to strengthen our faith, to deepen our spirituality, to utilize our gifts, or to fulfill our potential, the resulting homogeneity (everyone believes the same) leaves little room to follow Jesus through radical acts of compassion, justice, worship, and devotion.

Do not hear me saying personal growth and spiritual development are wrong. They aren't wrong. God calls each of us to greater understanding and higher, holier functioning. Here, however, we are considering the life of the community, individuals who band together in faith families for purposes beyond their ability to perform in isolation. God loves each one of us, but he sent his son Jesus to empower our unity for godly influence in the world God the Father created. We are the "bride of Christ" and must neither diminish nor underestimate the importance of what we are called to do—together.

What happens when we disempower Jesus' expectations? We become preoccupied with ourselves. This leads to congregational maintenance and self-indulgence. Instead of places where people come together to be formed into Christian disciples, congregations become places where people seek the enrichment of God's love and grace. Instead of places where the blessed come together to bless others, churches focus on personal growth and development—while neglecting being Christ's compassionate hands and feet in ministry. Jesus' presence brings grace, peace, and justice to the world. The church does not exist for itself; it exists for the world (John 3:16).

How does a congregation avoid the pitfall of focusing all its energy and passion on itself alone? I believe it begins with acknowledging the reality that we have removed Jesus from center stage and replaced him with *our* beliefs, *our* perceptions, *our* intentions, and *our* activities. When Jesus and God's mission are at the center of congregational life, the reason we are together is obvious. We don't have to sit around trying to figure out what God's will is for the church. The reason the church exists is to see the world God loves with Jesus' eyes of compassion. God's will is for the church to act on what it sees by going with Jesus into the world (near and far) to minister (love) and serve (action). We need congregational leaders who center the life and work of the church on the person and teachings of Jesus. Faith communities can do better in helping believers understand God's will as our compass (direction) rather than a map (turn-by-turn directions). God welcomes variation under the umbrella of the Christ ethic (see above) and encourages examination and expression of our giftedness, recognition of our personal call to ministry, and response to Spirit nudges both personally and corporately. Allowing Christ to assume center stage in our personal and corporate lives fosters greater clarity in discerning God's will in all matters.

### Jesus' Mission Statement

After his temptation in the desert, Jesus' ministry exploded in Galilee. He preached and healed. News about Jesus spread far and wide. You can imagine how excited people in Nazareth were when they heard Jesus was coming to town. On Sabbath, people flocked to the synagogue to listen to this person who had done great things in other places. Jesus stood to read passages from Isaiah that later became his mission statement. Jesus went on record about what would give shape and form to his earthly ministry:

> *The Spirit of the Lord is on me, because he has anointed me to preach good news to the poor. He has sent me to proclaim freedom for the prisoners and recovery of sight for the blind, to release the oppressed, to proclaim the year of the Lord's favor.* (Luke 4:18–19 NIV)

Jesus let the home-folks know he was the fulfillment of this passage from the Old Testament. All was well until Jesus said something highly offensive— he lifted up specific examples of God's favor shown to non-Jews (widow in Zarepath and Naaman the Syrian). Immediately, the crowd turned on Jesus and wanted to kill him. What made the people so mad? Jesus dared articulate a vision of the kingdom for *those* people—the labeled and rejected ones, the unclean and unworthy. Jesus' ministry leaned toward those who didn't have it all together—the poor, the hungry, the marginalized, folks unacceptable to the hometown crowd.

This kind of "good news" is highly offensive to us too, isn't it? Imagine Jesus walking into your worship space and announcing the kingdom is not about you—it's about _____ (fill in the blank with the people for whom you have the most disdain or hatred). Our hypocrisy is revealed.

If we desire to be (and I assume we do) authentic Christ-followers, we must wrestle with the implications of Jesus' mission statement. In what ways do Jesus' expectations for his own ministry shape and form our mission statement as Christ-followers today? To what degree is there alignment between Jesus' values and convictions and how we engage the world?

### Jesus' Instruction Manual

An excellent way to study Jesus is to examine the new order he describes in the Beatitudes and the Sermon on the Mount. Matthew sees these teachings as central to understanding Jesus and the kingdom he proclaimed. Jesus' words illustrate the kingdom of God (God's reign on earth) and give us the "instruction manual" for living the Jesus way. These rich statements from Jesus must, however, be seen through different lenses in order to understand their intent. To awaken consciousness about what Jesus means by the "kingdom of God," I include a summary of Jim Wallis's comments in *The (Un)Common Good*. Wallis draws from Matthew's Gospel what Jesus wants us to invest in and value. His ideas are summarized here:[12]

*Blessed are the poor in spirit, for theirs is the kingdom of heaven.*
- Jesus cares about people who suffer from spiritual and physical poverty.
- Caring for those in physical poverty is a frequent subject in the kingdom.
- Caring for the affluent is necessary because they no longer depend on God.
- The kingdom will be a blessing to both.

*Blessed are those who mourn, for they will be comforted.*
- Those who have capacity to see the needs in the world and express compassion for them will be comforted.
- Empathy is seen as strength, not weakness.
- To feel the pain of the world is to participate in the heart of God.
- Compassionate people respond to human suffering.

*Blessed are the meek, for they will inherit the earth.*
- The humble are the favored ones (defies the world's logic).
- Humility is greatly needed in the highly competitive world in which we live.
- The greatest are the ones who serve.

*Blessed are those who hunger and thirst for righteousness, for they will be filled.*
- Jesus cares about justice.
- To love the kingdom is to pursue justice for all.
- Pursuing justice in all arenas of life demonstrates we understand God's justice and prove it by our engagement.

*Blessed are the merciful, for they will receive mercy.*
- Christ-followers show mercy and forgiveness.

- Showing mercy and forgiveness acknowledges our own need for God's grace and forgiveness.
- Christ-followers practice reconciliation.

*Blessed are the pure in heart, for they will see God.*
- To be pure of heart is to have integrity—truthfulness, honesty, and follow-through.
- Only leaders with integrity are trusted; trust is foundational.

*Blessed are the peacemakers, for they will be called children of God.*
- We need to do more than talk about peace; we must live peace.
- We need leaders who know how to resolve conflict.

*Blessed are those who are persecuted for righteousness's sake, for theirs is the kingdom of heaven.*
- A special place of honor is given to those who sacrifice their lives for just causes.
- Those who sacrifice for the kingdom inspire others to follow in their footsteps.

*Blessed are you when people revile you and persecute you and utter all kinds of evil against you falsely on my account. Rejoice and be exceedingly glad, for your reward is great in heaven, for in the same way they persecuted the prophets who were before you.*
- If you live according to Jesus' new order, you will be persecuted because you threaten the status quo (counter-cultural like Jesus).
- You are in good company with the prophets of old and Jesus himself.
- God rewards good and world-changing behavior.

Seeing the world with the eyes of Jesus and serving in his strength are daily choices and patterns. Short- and long-term mission engagement is purposeful and part of every good mission strategy, to be sure, but as Christ's representatives we must be faithful in the simple, repeated movements of our daily lives. Christian discipleship usually isn't flashy!

Glen Stassen offers keen insight for moving Jesus' teachings in the Sermon on the Mount from "ideals beyond our reach" to transforming initiatives that change us and the world. Stassen calls Jesus' statements *The Fourteen Triads of the Sermon on the Mount.*[13]

| Traditional Righteousness | Vicious Cycle | Transforming Initiative |
|---|---|---|
| 1. You shall not kill | Being angry or saying, "You fool!" | Go; be reconciled |
| 2. You shall not commit adultery | Looking with lust is adultery in the heart | Remove the cause of the temptation |
| 3. If divorcing, give a certificate | Divorcing involves you in adultery | Be reconciled (1 Cor 7:11) |
| 4. You shall not swear falsely | Swearing by anything involves you in a false claim | Let your yes be yes and your no be no |
| 5. Eye for eye, tooth for tooth | Retaliating violently or vengefully, by evil means | Turn the other cheek Give tunic and cloak Go the second mile Give to beggar and borrower |
| 6. Love neighbor and hate enemy | Hating enemies is the same vicious cycle that you see in what the Gentiles and tax collectors do | Love enemies, pray for your persecutors; be all-inclusive as your Father in heaven is |
| 7. When you give alms... | Practicing righteousness for show | But give in secret; your Father will reward you |
| 8. When you pray... | Practicing righteousness for show | But pray in secret; your Father will reward you |
| 9. When you pray... | Practicing righteousness for show | Therefore pray like this: Our Father... |
| 10. When you fast... | Practicing righteousness for show | But dress with joy; your Father will reward you |
| 11. Do not pile up treasures on earth | Moth and rust destroy, and thieves enter and steal | But pile up treasures in heaven |
| 12. No one can serve two masters | Serving God and wealth, worrying about food and clothes | But seek first God's reign and God's justice/righteousness |
| 13. Do not judge, lest you be judged | Judging others means you'll be judged by the same measure | First take the log out of your own eye |
| 14. Do not give holy things to dogs or pearls to pigs | They will trample them and tear you to pieces | Give your trust in prayer to your Father in heaven |

Jesus' teachings found in the Sermon on the Mount turn the world upside down. Allowing these words to form and shape our everyday lives impacts God's kingdom in powerful ways. Imagine what would happen if Christ-followers defined faithfulness in relationship to the Beatitudes and the Sermon on the Mount. Lives would certainly begin to reflect the Jesus Dash!

### The Jesus Dash

A significant challenge many Christians face is a tendency to reduce faith to beliefs. This approach causes us to put our trust in a set of statements *about* Jesus rather than nurturing a relationship *with* the living Jesus. Statements of belief alone will never capture the essence of God. Also, reducing faith to beliefs weakens the impact of faith on our lives, often causing us to isolate our relationship with Jesus from the rest of our being.

Pragmatically, what does "reducing faith to beliefs" look like? Worship may be understood as a singing and preaching event instead of "beggars searching for bread," bowing knees to acknowledge God is God, and offering praise and thanksgiving to the living God. Proclamation can become myopically focused on "getting people saved" while ignoring the demands of discipleship (help-ing people become like Jesus in thought and action). Christian education may be unintentionally limited to "teaching scripture" with no expectation of life transformation or putting hands and feet to our faith. How we think about the gospel's ethical demands may be diluted by our political persuasion. Capacity for meaningful conversation about the real stuff of life is replaced with pithy statements backed up with very little substance. An attitudinal shift is neces-sary—first.

I've heard a number of funeral sermons in which a pastor talks about the DASH of the person who died, that is, what happened between the birth and death dates—the deceased's meaningful relationships with family and friends, kingdom impact, service to God, community engagement, etc. The dates carved on tombstones are facts, but these "bookends" reveal nothing about the intervening years or the DASH.

I fear something similar happens in the church. Much attention is given to the birth, death, and resurrection of Jesus, and rightly so. Is it possible, though, that we focus too much of our attention on the bookends of Jesus' earthly life and not enough on how Jesus lived, what he did, his teachings, ways he modeled godliness, etc.? Ought not we who call ourselves Christians care as much about the narrative of Jesus' life as we do the beginning and the end?

Now is the time to focus on the Jesus Dash. We Christ-followers are called and compelled to study and pattern our lives after Jesus. Reflecting theologically on the Jesus Dash guides us in discerning how God desires to shape and form us.

### Jesus' Priorities (as revealed in the Jesus Dash)

How do we determine what was important to Jesus so we can discern what is important to his followers? We study Jesus' life and ministry to determine what he valued and in whom he invested. Christopher Maricle, Catholic layman, teacher, and educator, analyzed the teachings and actions of Jesus and summarized them in *The Jesus Priorities—8 Essential Habits*.[14]

Priority 1: Heal
- Stay deeply connected to compassion.
- Say "yes" to strangers.
- Do what is within your power to do.
- See with the heart.

Priority 2: Love
- Show mercy no matter what.
- Extend forgiveness without limit.
- Love others as your expression of love for God.

Priority 3: Pray
- Pray alone.
- Pray persistently.
- Pray with others.
- Pray simply.

Priority 4: Spread the Word
- Share the mission with others.
- Invite everyone to God's banquet.
- Challenge others and yourself to live the gospel.

Priority 5: Build Up Treasure in Heaven
- Detach yourself from possessions.
- Maintain an abundance mentality.
- Act justly in all things.

Priority 6: Seek God's Will

- Rely on the example of Jesus.
- Maintain a sense of urgency by seeking to be in a state of grace.
- Focus daily on God's will.
- See all tasks as acts of love.
- See sacrifice as gain.

Priority 7: Accept Children as Precious
- Protect children.
- Welcome children.
- Seek to be child-like.

Priority 8: Live with Humility
- Rely on God's mercy—not your own merit.
- Presume the lowest place.
- Sacrifice your ego.

Maricle backs up his convictions about Jesus' priorities with abundant scriptural support. I encourage you to study the life and ministry of Jesus. A list you compile may look slightly different, but if Maricle's list accurately describes what Jesus most consistently invested in and practiced, we have discovered an excellent pattern for forming and shaping faith in Jesus. At minimum, we have insight into the qualities Christ-followers must desire to emulate.

Make time to evaluate how well you embody Jesus' priorities. Where are the gaps between your current practice and the practices embodied by Jesus? We will visit these priorities again as we explore forming faith in community.

## Barriers to Effective Formation

During my years serving local congregations in the role of Christian educator, I frequently noticed barriers to effective Christ-like formation. The following list and explanations are by no means exhaustive, but they offer insight into how these barriers thwart faith formation in many Christian congregations.

### Failure to Prioritize the Fundamental Teachings of Jesus Blocks Formation

In the previous section we talked about the importance of studying the life and ministry of Jesus in order to know what he prioritized. We acknowledge that following Jesus' teachings is very challenging. Western culture tends to distort Jesus' words in order to make his teachings more compatible with our practice. This smacks of what some call "putting God in a box." We "force" our own

interpretations onto Jesus' words and actions. Some suggest we have domesti-
cated Jesus, cleaned him up, and made him respectable. In doing so, we fail to
take seriously Jesus' counter-cultural teachings. The result is that the church
forms cataracts that distort his words and intent and our vision of God's kingdom. We must not compartmentalize our faith by making Jesus Lord in some
arenas but not in others.

We need the teachings of Jesus to reveal our self-serving approach to
Christianity. We need Jesus' teachings to reveal our pride, ambition, lust,
greed, and egocentrism. We need the light of Jesus to illumine our hearts and
minds. We need Jesus to tell us how our practice is Christ-like and how it is
un-Christ-like. We need Jesus to show us the path of discipleship, not mean-
ingless ritual. "Christianity without discipleship is always Christianity without
Christ," declared Dietrich Bonhoeffer. Without commitment to Jesus' teachings (the Way), how can we learn to love our enemies, share our provisions,
work for peace, and forgive those who hurt us? We must allow Jesus' insight to
inform our attitudes and drive our actions—in all areas of our lives.

## Preference for "Popular Jesus" Blocks Formation

I love this blog article from Drew Smith, an ordained Baptist minister and director of international programs at Henderson State University in Arkadelphia,
Arkansas:

> We can point our pious fingers at people who reject Jesus, shaming
> them for not embracing the person and words of Jesus. But are we not
> just looking into the mirror at our own faces? Was not their problem
> with Jesus the same as our problem with Jesus?
>
> We embrace the Jesus we want, the popular Jesus who listens to our
> problems, offers us comfort and easily forgives our sins. But we quickly
> reject the unpopular Jesus, the Jesus who offends us.
>
> The Jesus we want is our friend. He is our ally in the face of our
> enemies. This Jesus is always on our side, answering our prayers and bless-
> ing us. This Jesus tells us what we want to hear, makes us comfortable,
> and looks pleasingly at our self-righteousness.
>
> The Jesus we want permits us to wage unjust violence against our
> enemies in the name of national security. He allows us to hoard money
> and possessions in the name of financial security. He allows us to be
> unconscious of the sufferings around us and to replace real discipleship

with a pseudo spirituality that manipulates us into thinking we are close to him.

He consents to our prejudices that we not only hold against people of other races and genders, but especially against those of other religions and sexual orientations. Yes, this is the Jesus we prefer. He is the Jesus we can accept. He is the popular Jesus.

But this is not the real Jesus. The real Jesus is the one who calls us to turn the other cheek, to love our enemies, to sell all we have and give to the poor, and to take up the cross and follow him. This is the Jesus who calls us to reach out to others and cross the boundaries of race, religion, culture, and gender. This is the Jesus who dined with tax collectors, beggars, diseased persons, and various others of questionable social standing.

This is the Jesus who compels us to repent of our insular lives and to commit ourselves to work for justice, peace, and hope in our world. This is the Jesus who desires for us to be inclusive and affirming of others. This is the Jesus who calls us to rethink our theological assertions and to open ourselves to being moved by his Spirit. And this is the Jesus who, by being so offensive and so scandalous to his contemporaries, was crucified on the most offensive and scandalous instrument of Roman power—the cross.

Yes, this is the offensive Jesus, the one who is not so popular. This is the Jesus, who, if I am honest, I do not like, for instead of comforting me and affirming what I want, he haunts me. But he is the real Jesus. He is the radical Jesus. He is the biblical Jesus. Indeed, this Jesus refused to be popular, for although he called folks to follow him, he called them to embrace his radical, and dare I say, unpopular way of living. Is this Jesus popular? As I look around, I would have to say, I don't think so.[15]

I think Smith hits the nail on the head. We prefer the version of Jesus that accommodates our cultural expectations. Clinging to "Popular Jesus" blocks us from seeing and living into Jesus' expectations of us.

## Busyness and Distractedness Block Formation

Baptists began with a strong (almost single-minded) emphasis on spirituality and listening to and for God. We have evolved over these four centuries into a more practical faith that, unfortunately, often leaves God out of the equation. Talk to many Baptists today and they are very content telling God what to do rather than listening to God.

I attended an Academy for Spiritual Formation in Atlanta, Georgia, a few years ago. One of our presenters, long-time professor and spirituality guide Glen Hinson, contended there are two facets to our inattentiveness to God: our busyness and our distractedness. Who can argue with this astute observation? Personal calendars, even church calendars, are crowded with activities. When people ask how we are doing, we tell them how busy we are. Don't get me wrong; meaningful activity is incredibly important, but excessive activity means we reserve too little concentrated time and attention for God.

Our Baptist forebears could not imagine all the distractions we face today. I think how different my life was before I owned a computer or cell phone (and I was a late adopter for both). Computers and cell phones are incredible inventions, and their potential is mind-blowing, but these tools also create huge distraction for us. How often do you see family members in a restaurant texting instead of talking with those present around the table? How often do you observe parents staring at their phones instead of interacting with their children on the playground? If our own children struggle to get our attention, can you imagine how difficult it is for God to garner some of our focus?

Yes, the Internet is an incredible tool, but the level of distraction it engenders is overwhelming. Hear how Hinson describes the impact of the Web:

> In *The Shallows: What the Internet Is Doing to Our Brains*, Nicholas Carr reports this disturbing news. "Dozens of studies by psychologists, neurobiologists, educators, and Web designers point to the same conclusion: *when we go online, we enter an environment that promotes cursory reading, hurried and distracted thinking, and superficial learning.*" He observed later, "With the exception of alphabets and numbers systems, the Net may well be the single most powerful mind-altering technology that has ever come into general use. At the very least, it's the most powerful that has come along since the book." What is particularly disturbing and has special relevance to attentiveness to God in the spiritual life is that "the Net seizes our attention only to scatter it...*presenting us with far more distractions than our ancestors ever had to contend with.*" Carr goes on to point out that the distractedness the Net encourages differs from intentional diversion of the mind to weigh a decision. "The Net's cacophony of stimuli short-circuits both conscious and unconscious thought, preventing our minds from thinking either deeply or creatively."[16]

Prayer is at the heart of spiritual living, and at its core prayer is attentiveness to God. We can see how busyness and distractedness are major impediments to formation. Unfortunately, churches are often complicit in contributing to people's over-busyness—leaving them even less time for contemplation. Church leaders are sometimes guilty of encouraging members to engage in ministry without the ongoing prayer and contemplation necessary to do the work. We seek to "impose" compassion, empathy, *koinonia*, and radical hospitality on congregants when these must be acquired, shaped, and formed by God through contemplative practices. Because faith is shaped and formed in community, we are wise to help followers address their busyness in order to foster their faith development.

Not only do busyness and distraction block spiritual formation; they keep people from listening to one another. Our faith practices include hearing and supporting each other along the journey. How many times have I heard people say, "People in the church just seem too busy to listen to me"? Churches are relationship systems in which people are prioritized, but distractedness communicates things are more important than people. Attention proves to others you care about them and love them. Listening is a lifeline in times of stress, sadness, and separation. Jesus was a champion listener. He learned about people and knew their hearts and minds. We, too, must practice Jesus' listening skills in order to be more like him and to love more like him.

## Unholy Alliances with Ideologies

An ideology is a system of ideas and ideals, especially ones that form the foundation of economic or political theory and policy. Glen Stassen says,

> By "ideological" I mean a belief system invented in order to defend special privilege for an in-group and provide justification for excluding other groups while covering up what the belief system is doing. It becomes a rival to God's truth, which is higher and more inclusive than our special privileges. The prophets called it idolatry, and Jesus called it hypocrisy. It distorts people's understanding and blinds them from seeing the truth.[17]

What happens if we unwittingly hitch ourselves or our churches to an ideology that is incongruent and incompatible with Jesus' kingdom vision? When attempts are made to manipulate us into believing competing claims, we trust and obey Jesus. That's what it means to submit to the lordship of Christ. Jesus is the standard to which we cling.

From 2015–2016 intractable political ideologies in the United States inflicted great damage on Christ-followers and faith communities. The incivility permeating our political process pushed people to their respective corners, discouraged cooperation and collaboration, and encouraged resistance to focusing on "the common good." That incivility spilled into our faith communities and affected our capacity to work together. Following are a few observations that lead me to believe political extremism blocks spiritual formation:

- Pastors fear preaching prophetic words of Jesus lest they be accused of pushing a political agenda.
- Christian leaders state willingly and overtly, "If you vote for the other party, you are not Christian."
- The strength of the political divide keeps congregants from engaging in open dialogue about important life issues (including social-political concerns, recognizing all of life is "spiritual") because they may be considered divisive.
- Church members stop going to a particular church because the pastor says something they believe supports the other political party's agenda.
- Lay leaders tell their clergy, "If I found out you were a Democrat, I would lose all respect for you and could no longer regard you as my minister!"
- Lack of respect for people on the "other side of the aisle" bleeds over into the church—including lack of respect for clergy.
- Political divisiveness causes some to flee from advocacy and justice issues.

Perhaps the saddest result of embracing a political ideology over Jesus' teachings is how it has the potential to disrupt relationship. How many well-meaning Christians have been unfriended on Facebook during this last election cycle? People who sit next to each other on the pew on Sunday morning no long speak to each other. This flies in the face of Jesus' prayer that we be united as one. We must not allow overly zealous political debate to fracture the body of Christ. The world is watching and judging our Christianity by what we say and how we say it, what we post, and the issues for which we advocate. The world will know we are Christians by our love.

Political parties by their very nature are partial and communicate "we are right…they are wrong." This *us vs. them* mentality shuts down important and meaningful conversation that might lead to an understanding of what is best for all ("common good"). One ugly aspect of partisanship is that people are encouraged to stay divided and use every resource available to denigrate the other side. Once we categorize people, we more easily demonize them, and we know what happens when we demonize people—we begin to believe they are all "bad" (evil, unredeemable) and should (must?) be destroyed.

Jim Wallis's perspective on working for the common good is insightful. In his book *(Un)Common Good* Wallis urges serious public discourse among conservatives and liberals. Both sides offer something of value to the conversation. Suggesting the best conservative idea is *personal responsibility*, Wallis says, "Individuals making good, moral, virtuous, noble, and courageous personal choices are absolutely essential to the well-being of society and the outcome of history."[18] The best liberal idea, according to Wallis, is *social responsibility*. Wallis contends being responsible for oneself or one's family is not enough: "Compassion is not weakness, and concern for the unfortunate is not socialism."[19] As Christ-followers, we must insist our leaders cease these ideological fights and work together to find common ground that gives attention to both personal responsibility and social responsibility.

To lop off folks on either side of the political spectrum halts conversation, hurts our country, and, most importantly, hurts God's kingdom. Certainly, Christians are diverse, but we are one under the lordship of Christ. How we choose to disagree is extremely important in determining the nature of the faith we shape and form.

Another illustration shows how commitment to an ideology can block formation. I love facilitating small-group discussions—especially when resources used to guide discussions are open-ended and encourage folks to speak out of their faith journeys instead of offering "church answers." I will never forget the small group I facilitated using the book *Red Letter Christian* by Tony Campolo. Believing Jesus is neither a Democrat nor a Republican, I hoped we would be able to discern Jesus' thoughts on hot-button social and economic issues plaguing our country.

I had no idea what I was getting myself into and must confess it was the most difficult group I ever facilitated. All of us in the group were conditioned by our culture (including church congregation culture) to take sides (partisanship), which blocked us from hearing anything different from what we already "knew" was "true." Beliefs and convictions of participants were pre-shaped by the ideology of political parties, resulting in strong resistance to applying

Jesus' teachings to the current context (at least in the way Campolo attempted to do so).

On no subject was resistance stronger than when addressing spirit-driven vs. market-driven wages. Campolo advocates raising the minimum wage— giving workers fair pay for hard work. Properly understanding passages that address injustice or abuse is nearly impossible when a political system blindly supports a free market that protects profits more than the working poor. Jesus had much to say about how we treat those with less; how we treat the poor is a reflection of our relationship to Jesus and our understanding of who Jesus is and what he values. Though Jesus speaks truth to power, participants had difficulty hearing it because their vision of how the system is designed to work was shaped more by political and economic perspectives than the words and intentions of Jesus.

Unholy alliances with ideologies can block our formation. We must be honest about self-interest and protecting (our) positions of influence, confess our willingness to put earthly powers above God's, and allow Jesus' teachings to form and transform our discipleship. Remember: Faith and patriotism (nationalism) are *not* the same things, contrary to popular assumptions! Decisions affecting community living and who and how to govern our common life must be informed by faith-based ethics. We practice our faith in all matters, not just those inside church walls.

Though one of my many experiences leading small groups was difficult, I continue to believe small-group conversations are an excellent way to increase understanding in ideologically divided times. Prophetic preaching that calls believers to a higher plane of behavior is always appropriate. Preaching through a book that clearly illustrates Jesus' ethic may help broaden understanding. Strong worship music can deepen the emotional connection between congregants. Singing together is bonding. Small acts of kindness toward those whose political and ideological leanings differ from your own go a long way toward bridging gaps. Focus on what we have in common and how we can work together in ministry and mission. Annual church-wide missions bring members together. Make the Great Commandment the big idea before, during, and after each church gathering and effort. Host speakers of different faith persuasions, and expose members to different thoughts and ideas under the faith umbrella. Remember, "variety is the spice of life." Different isn't bad; it's just…different. "Different strokes for different folks" is a positive concept. Try to leave the world better than you found it and make a difference where you are. We can only influence the sphere closest to ourselves, but the concentric circles move outward far beyond where we stand. Know and be known. Play together. Smile more. Speak softly. Hug often. Remember that all of us are products of our past, our life experiences, our innate desire to learn, our emotional make-up, and our willingness to respond to Spirit nudges. Shoot high, be noble, and God will bless.

### Dualistic Thinking Blocks Formation

From childhood we are taught about opposites: hot-cold, good-bad, happy-sad, etc. Comparing and observing opposites are ways children learn; they are an early way to understand and explain reality.

Unfortunately, many Christians spend much of the rest of their lives organizing beliefs around neat delineations between who is "in" and who is "out" of favor with God. This "tribal" approach to religion attempts to create clear boundaries in faith communities. Ego prefers to make one side better than the other. This dualism leads to all kinds of unhealthy comparisons and judgments. My wife likes to call this tendency toward one-upmanship "the sin of comparison."

How does this dualistic (either-or) thinking affect us? It leads to statements like the following: America is better than Russia (or any other country you might name); Democrats are better than Republicans (or vice versa); men are better than women—you get the idea. If we buy into dualistic thinking, we have a clear framework for making decisions—everything is understood in opposition to something else. This kind of decision-making limits capacity to be shaped and formed—not to mention causes us to ignore Jesus' teachings about loving enemies. When Jesus talks about love, he means inclusive action, not divisive emotion.

Once we understand how dualistic thinking works, we wake up to the reality that labels we use to describe folks who have opposite perspectives are false. The words used in both religious and political circles to describe opposite perspectives as "liberal" and "conservative" are good examples. No matter how we are instructed by the culture or how offensive rhetoric lulls us into thinking this way, the categories themselves are false. In reality, liberal and conservative are two parts of a whole. Truth is found on both sides of the divide. Adam Hamilton makes this point very well:

> If liberal is a synonym for "broad minded" or "open-minded" then, yes, I wish to be a liberal!... Yet, if conservative means holding on to

what is good from the past, and being cautious in embracing change for the sake of change, then mark me conservative![20]

In answering the question about whether one is liberal or conservative, it really depends on who is asking. Let me illustrate. I have friends who are theologically liberal AND politically conservative. They fight for equal rights for homosexuals at their church, AND they vote for very fiscally conservative values in political elections. Are they conservative or liberal? It depends on who wants to know.

I can speak more personally on this issue. I grew up in a world of black and white categories (very much driven by dualistic thinking). My spiritual journey has challenged me to recognize those false categories, so now I refuse to be defined by them. As are many people, I am *both* liberal and conservative. I value historic doctrines of the Christian faith and our rich heritage (conservative); I believe each generation must "work out its salvation" in the midst of the culture in which it finds itself; that is, Christ-followers must remain open to where the Spirit blows (liberal). Am I comfortable being categorized as both? Yes, because that is exactly how I see Jesus at work in the Gospels. He consistently lifted up tradition while challenging its flawed practices and inconsistencies.

Earlier I alluded to the vicious 2015–2016 U.S. presidential campaign. Dualistic thinking dominated the airwaves: Hillary Clinton is liberal; Donald Trump is conservative. We know these are false categories, but both campaigns spent millions of dollars trying to convince us that if the other candidate won, the end of America as we know it would be at hand. The fact that Clinton is conservative on many issues and Trump is liberal on many issues was lost in the midst of divisive accusations. Extremist rhetoric pushes us to the edges and blinds us to the truth, which is usually somewhere in the middle. In reality, our tendency is to latch on to one or two issues we are convinced capture our "values" and declare nothing else matters. Thus, we are left with incivility, name-calling, false statements, and immature behavior. Dualistic thinking blocked the candidates from engaging in substantive conversation on issues that matter.

To see the devastating impact of dualistic thinking, all we need to do is look at the political gridlock in Washington, DC. Parties often assume and stay in their respective corners, preventing healthy debate in order to arrive at solutions that benefit the country. In fact, we have devolved so far that some candidates run on platforms promising voters they will *never* compromise or work with leaders on the "other side of the aisle." This is the byproduct of extreme dualistic thinking.

How does dualistic thinking block formation? If we believe God desires to shape and form us, we know we need to be in Christian communities hearing and expressing diversity of thought. Our assumptions must be challenged. Non-dualistic thinking allows us to learn from one another and gives opportunity for the Spirit to nudge and transform us.

How might we nudge folks in our congregations toward non-dualistic thinking? I have found much value in personality and relationship tools like Myers-Briggs and Enneagram. These tools help people understand the beauty of diversity built into creation (which God called good!). The better we know people and understand what makes them tick, the easier it is to work toward understanding one another. Read broadly, and select authors who challenge your thinking. Exposure to new ideas need not shake your belief in God. Rather, hearing how other serious people of faith understand Jesus and what he modeled offers us new perspective and fresh insight that raises our awareness and opens our spiritual eyes. Do not be afraid of spending time with those "different" from yourself. Chances are you will discover more similarities than differences, and you may make a new friend. Teach your children about world cultures by reading books about them, visiting folk festivals, preparing cuisine from around the world, and watching educational programs about people from other places. "Love your neighbor as yourself" is a word we need to hear today and every day.

### Rituals Can Block Formation

Rituals are series of religious actions performed in prescribed orders that are important and grounding to faith development. We need rituals in worship—they shape and form us over time. If rituals become too routinized and congregants go mindlessly through the motions, rituals lose their effectiveness. Don't hear me say we need to do away with rituals. The challenge is to keep worship fresh. An occasional break from or shift in rituals gives opportunity for the Spirit to speak in new ways.

How often did I hear, "Don't mess with rituals, especially those related to Christmas or Easter"? An unspoken rule in some churches is if we engage in a meaningful routine for one or two years, we are stuck with it forever. Though the statement sounds a bit extreme, it is not far from reality. For example, think about the Christmas Eve service at your church. Typically, folks see this service as the most meaningful of the year. Try to change the time or the format, and people protest. The ritual has become patterned, and changing the pattern raises anxiety and resistance.

I love Advent. I didn't grow up in a tradition that appreciated this time of preparation and reflection leading up to Jesus' birth, but after I personally experienced the power of Advent, I was hooked. As a staff minister, several rituals became important to me: taking the congregation on a *unique* journey toward Christmas each year, crafting an Advent devotion guide in order to increase understanding of this season of the church year, and thinking about the significance of the candles lit each Sunday of Advent. For years we assigned traditional names like hope, peace, joy, and love to the Advent candles. Certainly those words embody who Jesus was, and writing devotions around these names for Jesus was easy. After several years, I felt the need to refresh our congregation's Advent journey by assigning different names to the candles. Using new names for the candles allowed people to think about our Christmas journey in unexpected ways. This attempt at creativity was not always welcome—primarily because many adults valued the traditional names and children's Sunday school teachers believed the name changes confused their pupils. I'm convinced there was great faith-forming potential in periodically taking the congregation on an alternative spiritual journey toward Christmas by assigning lesser-used terminology to the candles. I believed engaging in the same pattern (ritual) over and over was somewhat self-limiting.

Rituals are important for nurturing faith in individuals and congregations. Ruts or mindless repetitions offering little creativity, innovation, thoughtfulness, or intentionality can become an impediment to effective formation.

### Inherited Cultural Understandings

How do we know if practices of our congregation help shape and form faith in Jesus or are simply cultural expectations? To learn more, we must examine what we do and how we do it in light of Jesus' expectations regarding the kingdom of God. What if our understanding of "church" is in opposition to what Jesus meant by "kingdom"?

We are not surprised Jesus made his ministry about the kingdom of God. Jesus knew what people longed for: trustworthiness, closeness, and meaningful connections. Masks, assumptions, and flawed expectations had to be removed. We believe God's grace (i.e., the unmerited assistance of God given to humans) shows us the way to our heart's desires. Church done well can be a microcosm of heaven. Is today's church a place of love and encouragement that calls us to our best selves under God, or has church become a cultural cocoon where people hide from God's call to be salt and light to the world?

I'm reading the challenging book *Dirty Words—The Vulgar, Offensive Language of the Kingdom of God* by Presbyterian pastor Jim Walker. Throughout the book Walker shows great capacity to rethink church. Walker highlights three kingdom of God characteristics: authenticity, intimacy, and tightly knit relationships. Unfortunately, Walker admits that his own congregational experiences revealed the opposite—superficiality, isolation, and individualism—much like our culture does.

Walker maintains expectations of the church should align with expectations of the kingdom. To awaken consciousness about ways in which the kingdom of God and church are not the same, Walker provides an insightful chart:[21]

| Kingdom of God | "Church" |
| --- | --- |
| Authenticity | Superficiality |
| Assurance | Fear |
| Belonging | Rejection |
| Meaning/compassion | Luxury |
| Intimacy | Isolation |
| Tightly knit relationships | Individualism |
| We | Me |
| Communion with God | Religion |
| Sharing in community | Advancing politics |
| Heart for the suffering/poor | Idol of "big, bigger, biggest" |
| The Word of God | Cultural values of beauty, fame, and wealth |

Walker's lists prompt me to ask: Is the "church" list a fair representation of what is happening in congregational life today? Is the "kingdom of God" list accurate for God's expectations of Christ-followers?

Some are confused about the meaning of the kingdom of God or the spiritual reign and authority of God. According to the Gospel writers, the kingdom of God is the central theme of Jesus' ministry and teaching, so we must seek to understand the concept. Literally, the kingdom of God means God is king.

N. T. Wright, in *How God Became King*, provides additional insight. He says the story of Jesus is told in ways that underscore the tension between God's kingdom and Caesar's kingdom. Jesus knew this competition for loyalty would play out in the lives and witness of his followers. Wright writes, "Caesar's kingdom will do what Caesar's kingdom always does, but this time [in Jesus] God's kingdom will win the decisive victory.… Jesus explains his kingdom is not the sort that grows in this world. His kingdom is certainly *for* this world, but it isn't *from* it. It comes from God.… The difference between the kingdoms is striking. Caesar's kingdom and all other kingdoms that originate in this world make their way by fighting. But Jesus' kingdom—God's kingdom enacted through Jesus—makes its way with quite a different weapon: telling the truth (see John 18:37-38)."[22] Wright also notes, "All is to be done within the bounds of God's kingdom. It cannot be otherwise. That kingdom is universal, all-present, and all-powerful."[23] Earthly power will vie for our loyalty and attention, but the kingdom of God is the ideal toward which Christ-followers strive.

Cultural expectations are powerful. Look at how important specific programs, even styles of worship, have been for the church. Unexamined, these expectations reinforce religion rather than faith. Culturally driven practices must be confronted by characteristics of the kingdom as expressed by Jesus. If they aren't, we keep doing church in culturally driven ways, blind to kingdom expectations.

Is there room for established cultural patterns in our faith lives? Are cultural ways and methods good, neutral, or distracting? Cultural norms become entrenched because we practice them regularly. We are familiar with and practice cultural/familial habits and patterns and often label them godly. Repetition seems to be the best teacher. It behooves us to examine whether kingdom of God and culture can interact in healthy ways. Think of examples from your own life that prove God's reign and earthly norms can happily coexist.

### How We Read Scripture Can Block Formation

The biggest challenge to faith formation is our tendency to read and understand Scripture in preconditioned ways. Robert Mulholland, in *Shaped by the Word*, says,

> You are the victim of a lifelong, educationally enhanced learning mode that establishes you as the controlling power (reader) who seeks to master a body of information (text) that can be used by you (technique, method, model) to advance your own purposes (in this case, spiritual formation).[24]

Either consciously or unconsciously, we approach biblical texts with a personal agenda, our own understanding, and our worldview intact. The result is we seek to control what the text says and means instead of allowing the text to *read us*. Trying to control the meaning and impact of Scripture is the opposite of spiritual formation that allows God to speak to us through the Word.

Mulholland asserts, "We manipulate the scripture to authenticate our 'false self' and resist God's call to our true self, that self that is actualized through radical abandonment to God."[25] This tendency certainly impacts how we understand ourselves and others. In reality, the cultural lenses we bring to Scripture often become a prison that works against openness to God when, in terms of formation, a primary goal of reading Scripture is to liberate us and open us to hearing new truth, which nurtures us into wholeness.

Common practice in Baptist life has been to read the Bible for information. This is a necessary and important discipline. This type of reading relates to our *minds*—using cognitive skills. Certainly we desire to understand the context of scriptural passages, how the first readers heard and understood them. At some point, however, we must move from an informational approach to a formational one—which relates primarily to our *hearts*. The formational approach is powerful because it allows Scripture to tell us truth about ourselves—the truth our false self cannot hear on its own. Formational reading of Scripture makes us receptive to needed change. We are transformed by God's Word as it probes the depth of our being—but only if we are willing to surrender control of the text to the transformative power of the Spirit. Relinquishing control of anything, let alone our heads and hearts as we read Scripture, is extremely difficult for American Christians. In general, the American psyche relishes control and self-determination. Asking American believers to "let go and let God" speak and work in mysterious ways makes us very uncomfortable.

## Institutionalism Blocks Formation

In the movie *The Shawshank Redemption* a poignant scene depicts an elderly man preparing to be released from prison. Brooks Hatley filled an important position as prison librarian. As his release day approaches, Brooks intentionally causes a crisis in the prison so he is deemed unfit to leave the prison that has become safe and familiar to him. In the courtyard following the incident, other prisoners talk about what happened. Astutely, the character Red (portrayed by actor Morgan Freeman) points out that Brooks is not crazy; "he's just institutionalized." Brooks fears he will have no purpose or role outside the prison—on the outside he'll simply be a common ex-con. For a while longer Brooks chooses institutionalization, enjoying the comfort of the known over freedom and the unknowns associated with it.

The events from *The Shawshank Redemption* sound strangely similar to the story of the Israelites. When God delivered Israel from exile and slavery in Egypt and things got tough in the wilderness on the way to the promised land, the people grumbled and complained. They cried out, "If only we had died by the LORD's hand in Egypt! There we sat amongst pots of meat and ate all the food we wanted, but you have brought us into the desert to starve to death" (Exod 16:3). The Israelites, too, had become institutionalized—desiring the known (slavery in a foreign land) over the unknown (freedom in God's promised land).

In similar fashion, congregational ways of doing ministry can easily, even unknowingly, become set. Familiar patterns (traditions) are comforting and not inherently bad. When a church gets stuck, however, it can, without intending to, say "no" to new directions God might lead. Faithfulness to God demands congregations remain pliable in God's hands and always open to the Holy Spirit's leadership.

Some say Baptist ways of "doing" Christian education have become institutionalized. Well-crafted Christian education materials of the past several decades helped congregations reach people and engage them in Bible study through Sunday school. The incredible "success" of this approach encouraged Christian education to remain largely unchanged and unchallenged for generations. According to Eddie Hammett in *Reframing Spiritual Formation*, "Most churches continue to believe and practice Christian education that is done in classrooms, driven by printed literature, and tied to institutional loyalty and preservation."[26]

Ours is a living faith, so we dare not dwell in the shadow of old ideas or inherited dogma. Authentic faith demands boldness and courage from believers. Knowledge of past traditions is helpful and is the reason a brief journey of Baptist heritage is included in this volume. However, our task is to integrate the abiding teachings of the past into present-day thinking and practice in order to expand our understanding and foster creativity—not simply repeat what we inherited. Ours is a living faith in a living community, and each successive generation must wrestle with what living faith means in its current context.

The goals of Christian education through Sunday school (an institution in Baptist life) are worthy, but the approach has become institutionalized, which induces fear about moving outside the bounds of "teaching lessons" on Sunday mornings. We are stuck, and our patterned ways of doing Christian education can, and often do, block authentic faith formation.

### Certitude Blocks Formation

I grew up in a cultural setting that valued certitude in matters of faith. In fact, faith in God was equivalent to being absolutely certain about who God is and what God expects. I confess this assumption led me to become arrogant and judgmental ("I'm right; you're wrong"), resistant to engaging people who did not measure up to my limited understanding of God's standards, and in many ways blocked me from learning more about the nature of God's grace and God's unconditional love.

How did I miss the biblical message regarding the dynamic nature of faith and each believer's journey (priesthood of all believers) toward God? How did I, a deeply religious person, misunderstand the gospel's explanation of the devastating impact of certitude?

In an uncertain world, people, especially people of faith, seek a solid foundation on which to stand. When everything in the world seems out of control, we desperately want a faith with no gray area. If we know something without a shadow of a doubt, we feel secure—even smug—about our eternal destination. When we believe our understanding and methodology are the best, often the next step is judging others' behavior more severely than we judge our own.

Our Creator knew humans would struggle with the mystery of God and would strive to reduce faith to beliefs and something manageable. We read many Bible passages in the Old and New Testaments in which God seeks to break people free from the grip of certitude. Here are three key examples:

1.  The story of Job is a classic Old Testament example of certitude. Job is certain he knows everything about what it means to be in right relationship with God. He dares to challenge God's perspective on life and suffering. In fairly harsh tones, God asks Job tough questions to help him realize there is much Job does not understand. In addition, Job's friends believe they know all they need to know about God and how being in right relationship with God works. They are certain Job's suffering is directly tied to his sin. The friends' certitude is evident in their haughty advice and pious

platitudes that only make Job feel worse, and their overly simplistic faith assumptions reduce Job's suffering to clichés and Bible verses. Though well intentioned, Job's friends add to Job's suffering.

2.  The story of Saul's conversion on the road to Damascus is a good example of certitude in action (read Acts 9:1–10). Paul's certainty about God's desire to destroy Christ-followers blinded him to seeing God's Spirit at work. Saul's faith was formed in ways that made Saul absolutely certain he was on the right and only path to God. When confronted by Jesus Christ, Saul begins to see through new eyes of faith—even though he is struck blind by a light. When his spiritual eyes are opened to this new thing God is doing through the risen Christ, Saul, now Paul, is transformed and becomes an apostle to the Gentiles. Paul had to turn loose of the certitude that controlled him.

3.  Another key New Testament example of certitude is found in Acts 10:9–48. In this story, Peter has a vision from God. A sheet descends from heaven, and Peter is instructed to kill and eat "unclean" animals. Peter's tradition clearly taught him what is kosher (suitable for consumption) and what isn't (unsuitable for consumption). Without hesitation, Peter says "No!" to God. God breaks down Peter's certitude and changes his mind in order to use Peter in sharing the gospel with Cornelius, a Gentile. Peter's consciousness is awakened, and he proclaims, "God has shown me I should not call anyone profane or unclean…. I truly understand God shows no partiality" (vv. 28, 34).

Unfortunately, over time, faith has been reduced to beliefs about God. How many times have I heard well-intentioned church leaders say, "We've got to get our beliefs right if God is going to bless our church"? This understanding of what God wants from us diminishes the good news and turns it into statements of faith ignoring what God really desires from us—unconditional love, obedience, allegiance, and faithfulness revealed in our attitudes and behaviors.

Why describe certitude as a barrier to authentic faith? Patricia O'Connell Killen and John deBeer offer insight:

Certitude prevails when Christians accept the Bible or official teaching of the church literally as God's Word, providing an absolutely clear set of directions for life. We blindly accept these rules, truth, or general principles and apply them in every situation that might arise.

When we apply absolute rules to situations, we avoid having to look deeply at the situation and people involved; to take responsibility for interpreting and acting in the situation with the eyes and heart of faith; to be responsible carriers of the Christian heritage.[27]

Ironically, sometimes Christians who insist on a specific, prescribed path to God (certitude) can miss the presence of God in daily life. How? Killen and deBeer astutely identify the problem. Dogmatic certainty causes us to pretend we know what God desires in every situation (similar to the *What Would Jesus Do?* approach from a few years ago). This is particularly dangerous when we use our ingrained understanding to either deny God's action in the world today or blame God for everything that happens. Said more plainly, we can really make God look bad by projecting a rigid understanding onto every situation. The more insular the community in which we live, the greater the likelihood we expect all people in every unique situation anywhere to understand and practice faith the way we do.

Some of you may have seen the 1966 movie *Hawaii*, starring Julie Andrews and Max von Sydow. This older film depicts an American missionary couple intent on converting indigenous people in the kingdom of Hawaii. Absolutely convinced that all faith must look like Western-style Christianity, the well-meaning missionaries experience tragedy as the two cultures clash in more areas than religion. God's love for his creation is the "same yesterday, today, and tomorrow," but God is dynamic and welcomes, even encourages, variety. God surprises if we remain open to see with eyes of faith.

We must resist the temptation to fit life experiences into a predetermined framework. That is not theology but ideology designed to support the status quo. We play God when we assume we know how God thinks and acts; God's movement in the world is rife with mystery. We must resist the temptation to "put God in a box" of our own making. Our job is to remain open to Holy Spirit nudges and prompts, discern God's heart, sense God's movement, and follow to the best of our humble, finite ability.

If people of faith have been shaped by a context that demands certitude or self-assurance, they can become blind to the ways they distort God's intended design for humankind. The rich young man in Mark 10:17–22 is a good example of this principle. The man believed he was okay with God because he kept the rules. Only when confronted by Jesus' challenge to "sell your material possessions and give proceeds to the poor" did the confident one comprehend how distorted his faith understanding was.

Certitude that possesses all the answers about God is a barrier to forming deeper faith. We have no need to dig deeper and wrestle with difficult questions or challenging life experiences if conclusions are foregone. The Christian pilgrimage is by faith—not by sight. Certitude is the opposite of faith and leaves little room for the Holy Spirit to speak truth that can lead to deeper understanding of God and richer connection to God.

### Fear of Education Blocks Formation

In 1979, when I announced my sense of call to vocational ministry, a number of friends and family members encouraged me to attend an ultra-conservative seminary that practiced indoctrination. Oddly, these well-meaning Southern Baptists did not want me to attend one of the six Southern Baptist-supported seminaries. The words I heard often were, "Seminary will ruin you." That phrase was an expression of fear, informed by the belief that too much education is not a good thing. Education will "shake your faith" and "pull you away from what we taught you." Bottom line: Exposure to different ideas, understandings, and perspectives (especially regarding Scripture interpretation) is bad.

My observation is that many Baptists are open to education, but they are quick to let you know how far that "openness" goes. In this regard, Baptists are aware of the shaping and forming power of education, which is why incredible resistance arises when church leaders suggest changing curricular resources. I have led the charge in churches to move away from highly prescriptive resources—those that tell disciples exactly what to believe and how to interpret—toward ones that promote discovery learning and incorporate reflection.

People in some cultures are fearful of education. Sometimes communities open to higher education relative to the marketplace remain suspicious of theological education in the church, Baptist congregations included. Good folks in some churches even allow their fear of theological education to overshadow their faith. When fear takes the day, God's prophetic voice is silenced. Personal security becomes more important than serving people who we perceive are in a different place on the theological spectrum. Conversations about difficult subjects are avoided because we fear offending someone who may then choose to leave the church.

Yes, fearful Christians look very much like people who profess no faith at all. Genuine faith, though, produces trust, not fear. God gave us mental capacity to think, learn, wonder, and imagine. We must welcome our God-given drive to explore and learn more. Be assured that God's kingdom is not diminished when we encourage more, not less, theological education.

## Judgmental Attitudes Block Formation

Judgment is the ability to make considered decisions or come to sensible conclusions (a positive thing). The term *judgmental*, however, has negative connotations. In Christian circles, we call someone "judgmental" who unfairly or in exaggerated fashion makes a critical statement about another's behavior, implying the other's words or actions are un-Christian, sinful, or, at the very least, questionable. Be certain, judgment itself is *not* bad (see definitions above). Judgment meaning discernment or wisdom is a skill we all aspire to, but judgment meted out as a way to "lord it over" someone else indicates deviation from a Christ-like attitude.

I have watched judgmental attitudes determine how much people allow God to shape and form them. Growing up in the Deep South, I observed how snap judgments about people's appearance or race determined whether or not those people were "acceptable" and welcome in the church building. Even though we were taught at church that God loves all equally, that conviction did not play out in everyday life. Assumptions about others (also known as prejudice) convinced us we were better and were justified in excluding those who weren't like us.

What was really sad was how judgmental attitudes even separated Christians from one another. How many times did I hear pastors say, "God has called Southern Baptists (alone) to win the world for Christ"? Thinking back, I remember saying it too! Judgmental attitudes toward others cultivated and allowed arrogance to form. Arrogance led church leaders to say things like "Catholics are not Christians," "God doesn't hear the prayers of the Jews," or "Other denominations may do some good work, but they have flawed beliefs, so they are not really Christian; they might even be considered cults."

How does a judgmental attitude block formation? A few examples:

- Unwillingness to fellowship with believers of different stripes causes us to miss out on ways God wants to shape our thoughts, beliefs, and practices.
- Judgmental attitudes keep us from hanging out with people we perceive to be different than ourselves and diminish opportunities to be grace, extend grace, and receive grace.

- Pious assumptions keep vocational ministers from performing marriage ceremonies for divorced persons, losing opportunities to allow God to offer grace and wholeness to what was broken.
- Close-minded attitudes that say women cannot serve as deacons or ministers, deny "God is no respecter of persons" (Acts 10:34; Gal 3:28), and the kingdom is robbed of gifts God entrusted to the church.

Judgmental attitudes damage the body of Christ, invite people outside the church to call Christians hypocrites, cause the church to miss ministry opportunities, and shape a people in ways that are incompatible with the gospel of Jesus Christ.

### Role of Theological Reflection in Formation

Thus far we have examined the concept of being formed to become like Jesus—caring about what he cared about, investing in those outside the "in crowd," and striving to embody and live out his values and convictions. Then we looked at a few issues and perspectives that block effective formation. Next we explore an essential practice that can help bridge the gulf between what God seeks to form and shape in us and what hinders formation. Consider the practice of theological reflection.

Patricia O'Connell Killen and John deBeer define theological reflection this way: "allowing the thoughts, feelings, images, and insights that arise from the concrete events of our lives to be in genuine conversation with the wisdom of the entire Christian community throughout the ages."[28] Theological reflection is a group process in which participants attempt to suspend their own agendas so the wisdom gained doesn't bend Christian heritage to their preconceived expectations. The goal is to engage all of Christian heritage (Scripture, life of Jesus, history of the church, etc.) to allow life-giving insight to emerge. Theological reflection challenges certitude and blind self-assurance by including the wisdom and rich resources of the Christian faith in the conversation.

Because certitude and arrogance adamantly state what we already believe is unrivaled, reflection is discouraged and formation is hindered. We think we can ignore what our experiences teach us when we unreflectively keep supporting beliefs and values we assume benefit us. No matter what new insight is offered we cling to our assumptions. Instead of helping us become more like Jesus, these qualities keep us from mediating the care, agape, righteousness, wholeness, pardon, and unity of Jesus toward others. Patricia O'Connell Killen and John deBeer say it this way:

> Repetition [of what we already know] and dismissal [of anything else the Spirit desires to teach us] leave us deaf and blind to the resources of the Christian tradition and to the content of our current experience. Both act as barriers between us and God's presence, power, and purpose. They block the ability of us who call ourselves Christians to mediate the compassion, love, justice, healing, forgiveness, and reconciliation of Jesus Christ for others. They seduce us into believing life will not call into question our most cherished certainties. They obstruct growth in wisdom or understanding.... Because these understandings dominate discussions of values in our culture and in our churches, we are in desperate need of theological reflection. Without theological reflection, faith becomes something that belonged to the forebears of the tradition and currently is protected by the theological experts. Faith is reduced to a possession. Faith serves as a justification for what we already think, religious code language to legitimate whatever psychological, sociological, economic, or political theory that we hold.... Without authentic theological reflection we Christians cannot achieve the personal maturity and integrity appropriate for us.... If authentic theological reflection cannot happen then the tradition's only value is to bolster and baptize social, economic, and political conventions, then it is dead or, worse, demonic.[29]

Seeking God's presence and guidance involves theological reflection or the artful discipline of putting our experience in conversation with the heritage of our Christian tradition. It is not easy, but without theological reflection we often assume our interpretations are absolute, unchanging, and true. Every "certainty" presents this danger—we can miss the gift available to us in our experiences. In lusting after certitude in matters of faith in order to reassure ourselves we are on the *right* path to God, we often miss God's revealing presence on uncertain and ambiguous days. When we attempt to apply absolute rules, we avoid looking deeply at situations and the people involved, taking responsibility for interpreting and acting with hearts of faith, and being responsible carriers of Christian heritage.

Genuine theology is the fruit of a dynamic process of reflection. Without reflection we are tempted to use our theological assumptions to justify what we already believe (reminiscent of the null expectancy factor). Without theological reflection people of faith often struggle with hoped-for personal maturation and living lives of Christian integrity. If something doesn't happen as you prayed it would, without theological reflection we are left "stranded" and confused, asking, "Why didn't God answer my prayer the way I asked him to?" Theological reflection lifts us to new planes of understanding that we don't call the shots and God works in mysterious ways.

Having the ability to reflect on our personal experiences is powerful. Group theological reflection can be even more powerful as we learn from others who are in different places on the journey of faith. Group theological reflection is about creating a context for honest conversation between people's experiences and Christian tradition so faithful, life-giving insights may emerge. The process always encourages change because participants are open to being transformed by God's power and to being instruments in God's kingdom. It impels us, individually and communally, to increased knowledge, greater awareness, growing compassion, and critical thinking about self, family, community, and tradition.

In past generations a person's community and religious tradition expressed essentially the same ideas. That is no longer the case. We live connected to the world yet separated from it. We are capable of watching horrible, life-altering events from all over the world on our television or computer screens while we eat our dinner in the privacy of our homes. Today's challenges demand we reflect on the deeper questions of the meaning and value of life. We must choose to juxtapose precepts of our faith with our culture. Forming faith as we try to make sense of the world is more likely in groups that practice theological reflection.

## Theological Reflection Process

Killen and deBeer outline a basic framework for theological reflection:[30]
1) focus on some aspect of an experience
2) describe the experience to identify the heart of the matter
3) put the heart of the matter into conversation with the wisdom of Christian heritage
4) identify new meanings and truth to take back to daily living

For several years I served as adjunctive faculty at Baptist Theological Seminary at Richmond. Third-year students serving in field placement—often in a local church setting—met regularly to engage the practicum group process. Our objective was to nurture and challenge seminarians' vocational formation and ministerial development by helping them reflect theologically on their practice of ministry. Students wrote reflections, verbatim, and case studies drawn from their field placement experiences. Every week groups of five or six students engaged in the practice of theological reflection.

During a training session for practicum group field supervisors in Toronto, Canada, presenter Janet Clark shared a simple and memorable process of theological reflection called LEARN that I found very useful in my work with students:[31]

*Look* back on a recent experience (dialogue or encounter) in which you personally engaged. Select one that stands out as particularly challenging, thought-provoking, puzzling, or that raised questions and/or dilemmas for you.

*Elaborate.* Describe what happened during the event.
- Answer the basic questions of "who, what, when, where, and how."
- Include your feelings and thoughts.
- How did you respond (be specific)? How did others respond?

*Analyze* the experience or outcomes.
- What key issues seem to be at work in this situation (interpersonal dynamics, dilemmas, value conflicts, sociocultural issues, communication issues, unclear assumptions)?
- What do you think influenced your responses and actions in this situation?
- What seemed to be effective? Ineffective?
- Why is this experience important to you?
- What specific question(s) do you bring for reflection?

*Reflect* theologically on the experience.
- What theological issues or themes are present in this situation?
- What biblical stories, passages, images, metaphors, or principles (not proof texts) seem applicable?

- What learning and insight from your studies/readings are relevant?
- How do you perceive God to be present (or absent) in this situation?

*New* insights for action.
- What insights surfaced from your reflection that you can take with you into similar situations in the future?
- How have you changed?
- What do you want to remember to do (or avoid doing) in the future?
- What is your action plan?

Key to this work with seminary students was realizing that in ministry we are not dealing simply in the realm of measurable competencies. We are developing gifts and callings and working on character formation. Students were given sacred space to ask, "How can I align myself with what God wants for my life?" The goal of good theological reflection was helping students deepen their spiritual lives.

During each class period I learned much from intense theological conversations with the seminarians. I wondered how their experiences and discoveries would influence my own local church ministry. One direct impact was my decision to offer a Wednesday night small group focused on theological reflection in my local church setting. We used no published curricular resource. Instead, participants' experiences determined the content of each session. The process worked beautifully. Participants understood that their own life stories and experiences were the basis for group reflection. Participants shared freely with the group. Conversation was personal and rich. Stories described various personal struggles or dilemmas. Group members developed skill in helping each other process personal experiences in light of Scripture, church tradition, and cultural context. The process helped folks reflect on experiences in light of faith, discern God's presence and power in the midst of the experience, and make sense of their lives with God and people.

Again, I learned much from the small-group experience. I gained personal insight from what happened in people's lives as a result of helping them learning to engage in good theological reflection. After that small group I encouraged every adult Bible study teacher to incorporate some aspect of theological reflection into each lesson plan.

In my opinion theological reflection is helpful, even necessary, for shaping and nurturing faith. The ability to honestly and deeply reflect leads to action and transformation that cannot be accomplished by simply "teaching lessons."

## Notes

[1] Richard Robert Osmer, *Teaching for Faith: A Guide for Teachers of Adult Classes* (Louisville: Westminster John Knox Press, 1992), 15–16.

[2] Ibid., 17.

[3] Ibid., 15.

[4] C. Ellis Nelson, *Where Faith Begins* (Atlanta: John Knox Press, 1967), 11.

[5] Ibid.

[6] David G. Benner, *Spirituality and the Awakening Self: The Sacred Journey of Transformation* (Grand Rapids: Brazos Press, 2012), 59.

[7] Benner, *Spirituality and the Awakening Self*, 156.

[8] Ibid.

[9] Ibid., 161–162.

[10] David L. Watson, *Forming Christian Disciples* (Alpharetta, GA: Discipleship Resources, 1995), 22.

[11] Ibid.

[12] Jim Wallis, *The (Un)Common Good: How the Gospel Brings Hope to a World Divided* (Grand Rapids: Brazos Press, 2014), 48–51.

[13] Glen Harold Stassen, *A Thicker Jesus: Incarnational Discipleship in a Secular Age* (Louisville: Westminster John Knox Press, 2012), 193.

[14] Christopher Maricle, *The Jesus Priorities: 8 Essential Habits* (Nashville: Upper Room Books, 2007), 120.

[15] Drew Smith, *The Real Jesus Isn't the Popular One*, Blog article on EthicsDaily.com, June 30, 2010.

[16] Nicholas Carr, *The Shallowing: What the Internet Is Doing to Our Brains* (New York: W. W. Norton & Co, 2011), 115–116.

[17] Stassen, *A Thicker Jesus*, 18.

[18] Wallis, *The (Un)Common Good*, 160–163.

[19] Ibid.

[20] Adam Hamilton, *Seeing Gray in a World of Black and White: Thoughts on Religion, Morality, and Politics* (Nashville: Abingdon Press, 2008), 6.

[21] Jim Walker, *Dirty Word: The Vulgar, Offensive Language of the Kingdom of God* (Nashville: Discipleship Resources, 2008), 55.

[22] N. T. Wright, *How God Became King: The Forgotten Story of the Gospels* (New York: HarperOne, 2012), 144.

[23] Ibid., 150.

[24] M. Robert Mulholland Jr., *Shaped by the Word: The Power of Scripture in Spiritual Formation* (Nashville: Upper Room Books, 2000), 19.

[25] Ibid., 22.

[26] Eddie Hammett, *Reframing Spiritual Formation: Discipleship in an Unchurched Culture* (Macon, GA: Smyth & Helwys Publishing, 2002), xii.

[27]Patricia O'Connell Killen and John deBeer, *The Art of Theological Reflection* (New York: The Crossroads Publishing Company, 1994), 7–8.

[28]Ibid., 18.

[29]Ibid., 14–15.

[30]Ibid., 119.

[31]Janet L. Clark, *Five Interdisciplinary Tools for Catalyzing Reflection*, ATFE Biennial Consultation, Toronto, Canada, January 21, 2004.

Chapter 15

# Forming Together

The "big idea" that emerged from CBF's 2015 rebranding effort was *Forming Together*. While each individual Christ-follower is formed and shaped by the Spirit, formation is more than a solitary endeavor. Formation happens in the context of Christian community. This conviction challenges current American thinking, which asserts the individual reigns supreme. One heresy circulating right now is the belief that individuals can be faithful Christ-followers while separated from each other. We begin to assume we don't have to sacrifice much, if anything, to follow Jesus. *Forming together* reminds us we are called to rebel against rampant individualism and to choose to live each day by the Jesus ethic. Within Christian community we are shaped and formed in the image of Jesus Christ for the sake of the world. In community we lose our self-centeredness as we learn to imitate Jesus in relationship.

What I describe above is an ideal faith community comprised of mature believers who passionately imitate Christ in order to model for new converts and the world what it means to be Christian. We live in an imperfect world. Our practices often reflect cultural-tribal thinking that leads to selfishness and greed instead of compassion, hospitality, and acceptance. Unfortunately, we still don't get it! Jesus modeled movement toward, not separation from, each other. Community shaped and formed Jesus himself. We, too, are social creatures in need of "God with skin" and interaction with fellow strugglers on the journey toward spiritual enlightenment. "No one is an island, and no one stands alone," or so the song says. Hermits tend to be unhappy people. Life is meant to be lived together. Admittedly, harmony isn't always easy to create, but we are called and designed by God to try. Only in the context of community living can we exercise the tenets of the faith and learn how to lovingly affect each other as we are formed into the likeness of Christ.

In the previous chapter we wrestled with relevant questions about what it means to form faith. Now we focus greater attention on how faith is formed in community: How is our community currently forming faith? What is the nature of the faith we are forming? Is our approach effective, and does it lead to transformation? Does it matter how a congregation goes about the process of shaping and forming faith in Jesus?

Before we interact with these questions, we acknowledge different people are at different stages of growth or development—very much like the seeds tossed onto different types of soil as described by Jesus in Matthew 13:4–9. Many have sought to outline the spiritual journey in terms of stages, though we acknowledge real-life progress is not linear and stages are not sequential.

I appreciate the work of James Fowler. Let's review Fowler's *Stages of Faith.* Theologically grounded and based on extensive research, Fowler's ideas have become mainstream and foundational in understanding *how* communities of faith "form together"—or not!

For Fowler, faith is not something one possesses; rather, it is a *process of becoming.* Faith is more a verb than it is a noun. Though the word *faithing* has recently been included in some dictionaries, we typically substitute the word *believe* to connote active faith. The words really don't mean the same thing. Actions we take to live out our faith and trust in God are not the same as espousing beliefs or doctrine.

Fowler describes how an individual's faith journey moves through six stages.[1] Some people only progress through two or three stages. Each person finds a stage that works (is most meaningful) for him or her. The task for the faith community is to achieve proper balance between respecting where people are on their journeys while encouraging them to explore other stages.

### Stage 1: Intuitive-Projective Faith (The Innocent)

Stage 1 is seen primarily in preschoolers and children ages 3–7, whose understanding of God is learned from parents. Stage 1 is a time of fantasy, imagination, and powerful images that play an important role in a child's first understanding of matters of faith. Faith at this stage places trust in superheroes who can be relied upon to deliver children from scary fantasies.

### Stage 2: Mythic-Literal Faith (The Literalist)

Stage 2 begins around age 6 and usually lasts until age 11 or 12. The child's understanding of faith is essentially a reflection of the beliefs of others—including the influence of adults outside the family. The child's faith begins to broaden, but religious images are understood literally. Strong commitment to justice is evident (i.e., good is rewarded, and bad is punished). Biblical stories and religious tradition are authoritative. Simplicity and security characterize

Stage 2. Adults who adopt a straightforward and literal faith may remain at this stage.

### Stage 3: Synthetic-Conventional Faith (The Loyalist)
Stage 3 typically begins in adolescence and often persists into adulthood. Conformity to a group and approval of peers is important because *faithing* takes place most fully in relationships with peers. Stage 3 faith is often observed among church members who need a common faith identity and a strong sense of community. Frequently, expressions of faith are an extension of beliefs and values held by other church members. For many, this stage offers meaning throughout life.

### Stage 4: Individuative-Reflective Faith (The Critic)
In Stage 4 young adults take charge of their *faithing* as they wrestle with the ultimate meaning of life. This stage includes doubting and sometimes rejecting long-held assumptions, which is an important step for maturing faith. While struggling with difficult questions, people in this stage may become disillusioned with the established or "institutional" church. Unfortunately, some in the church may perceive this tendency as "losing" faith. Stage 4 folks need encouragement in their search to find meaningful answers to faith questions.

### Stage 5: Conjunctive (The Seer)
Stage 5 rarely appears before age 30. Maturity is a key factor in its development. One's faith expression is no longer that of parents, church, or tradition. Stage 5 faith is *owned* faith. Persons in Stage 5 find meaning in cross-cultural experiences. They explore myriad ways to broaden and deepen faith. Some Stage 5 people get more involved in a church community; others find it necessary to explore other contexts to express their faith.

### Stage 6: Universalizing Faith (The Saint)
Stage 6 is the most difficult phase to understand. Beliefs truly become a way of life as the Stage 6 person becomes totally committed to an Ultimate Authority as Jesus expressed in his statement on the cross: "Thy will be done." Stage 6 people include Gandhi, Martin Luther King Jr., Mother Teresa, Dietrich Bonhoeffer, and Thomas Merton. Their faith meant total commitment, even in the face of death. Stage 6 represents the ultimate fulfillment of one's faith journey. Rarely do we find people who are one with themselves and with God.

Though some people resist categorizing different stages of faith and analyzing stages that are seldom fully realized, we certainly recognize and experience the reality that different people are at different stages in their *faithing* journey. To say one has more faith than another is not meant to be judgmental. One person may or may not be more faithful than another. No matter where we are in our faith pilgrimage, faithfulness means engaging the journey in appropriate ways. Most importantly, familiarity with Fowler's stages helps us better understand faith as a verb, a process of becoming, and a journey.

What does this exploration of stages of faith mean for congregations desiring to take seriously the call to "form together"? Consider these possibilities:

- Communities of faith, like individuals, journey through the stages of faith.
- Most congregations express faith at Stage 2 or 3 because congregations reflect their members, who tend to be at Stage 2 or 3.
- Christians at Stage 4 or 5 are often uncomfortable in traditional church because their capacity to explore more deeply and think outside the bounds of current belief or practice are considered "liberal" and are not welcome.
- The task of the faith community is to find balance between accepting and respecting where people are on their faith journeys and encouraging them to explore next stages.
- Homeostasis (what gives balance to the congregation) makes it difficult to move a congregation to explore the next stage. Resistance will be great because the questions being asked change and because faith communities are more comfortable and comforted staying at their current stages.

I mentioned earlier how much I enjoy facilitating adult small-group discussions. Classes that challenge participants to awaken consciousness about their faith pilgrimages are favorites of mine. I will never forget what happened at the end of one twelve-week experience. A senior adult man told me after everyone else had left, "Terry, you have blown away my childhood understanding of so many biblical stories, and I am grateful!" This 70-year-old who had been a Christian all his life was no longer content understanding stories as a Stage 2 believer. The reflection we did together nudged him toward a new stage of faith. Offering deep, more spiritually mature, less prescriptive ideas is one characteristic of forming faith, as opposed to indoctrination, which tells believers exactly what and how to believe.

## The Congregational Container

What can the stages of faith teach us about the process of *forming together* in Christian community? An image that has become helpful to me in considering how we form together is the congregation as a container. What determines the shape, depth, and expandability of a container? Some of the factors that contribute to a congregational container are:

- Denominational affiliation and expectations—how prescriptive are denominational leaders and the resources they produce and recommend (telling people what they must believe and think)?
- Birthing DNA—what happened during the church's birth narrative (for example, being birthed out of conflict) shapes what is acceptable and what isn't.
- The faith stages of the leaders who started the church leave a lasting imprint on the congregational system.
- The spiritual health of congregational leaders, lay and clergy, over the years
- Conflicts, how they were handled, and how they were resolved (or not)
- Capacity of congregational members to stand up to "bad behavior" of "hurt people who hurt people"
- Capacity of the congregation to have conversations around difficult issues

An illustration may be helpful. Several years ago the congregation I served engaged in an intentional discipleship process. A key component of the process was determining the spiritual maturity of the congregation, measured by where members were on their faith journeys. A survey designed for this purpose was given to members during Sunday morning worship. The surveys were compiled to calculate a "maturity level score." The image used to help us interpret our "score" was a baseball diamond. Familiar baseball images made numbers and insights memorable. Members of the congregation were quite surprised to discover the congregation as a whole was just rounding second base. That revelation provided the impetus and gave us the push we needed to consider ways to grow deeper (i.e., begin moving toward third base). Our consciousness was awakened. Tools and the way we were using them were not shaping and nurturing mature faith like we thought they were.

Another key learning from this survey was that congregations tend to struggle with reaching and keeping more mature Christ-followers. Those who are no longer content with "Sunday school questions and answers" will be frustrated when most other members of the congregation remain at Fowler's Stage 2 or 3. The questions folks at Stage 4 or 5 ask are uncomfortable and not appreciated by those at Stage 2 or 3. Thus, the congregational container assumes the shape with which most members are "comfortable."

Stage 2 congregations are committed to moral rules that are interpreted literally. This gives greater clarity about who is right and who is wrong, who is in and who is out, and the good that is rewarded and the bad that is punished, etc. People are defined by their roles and behaviors (according to their own understanding) with little reflection about what influences those behaviors. The danger is that this faith posture can be rules-bound, judgmental, and driven by fear. Fundamentalists, as Gene Wilder described earlier, reflect the mythic-literal stage of faith development, or Stage 2.

Stage 3 congregations are characterized by conformity to the majority position held by the group. Beliefs are defined by authority—typically a religious leader, tradition, or sacred text. Identity is shaped and formed by alignment with core beliefs and perspectives of the community. Critical reflection is discouraged because theological reflection encourages thinking outside the boundaries established by the leaders. The dangers associated with Stage 3 are evident: being so committed to group-think discourages sound judgment or discernment when needed; tribal thinking sends the message that "we have arrived."

Why are so many "congregational containers" described as Stage 2 or 3? In these stages, identity as a Christ-follower is intentionally connected to opinions and expectations of others. Moving toward Stage 4 is uncomfortable because folks must take responsibility for their values, beliefs, and faith frameworks. What was previously accepted as truth is now subject to scrutiny. We begin to wrestle with important questions about the meaning of life. The transitional period can cause disorientation, disillusionment, and cynicism. We begin to realize the world is much more complex than we were led to believe. Unlike Stages 2 and 3, which resist reflection and the transformation it most likely will bring, Stage 4 is defined by capacity to engage in critical reflection on previously unexamined convictions and beliefs. While uncomfortable at times, faith is now owned and internalized with greater opportunity to enrich the life of the individual (personal) and the lives of others (community).

The fact that different people are at different places in their faith development does not mean some have more faith than others. Fowler does not suggest that. Stage 4 believers are not necessarily more faithful than Stage 2 believers.

Each person is at a specific place in the journey of faith (uniquely defined and acted upon) and encounters God in ways appropriate for that stage.

Another concept some will balk at hearing is this: Periods of reflection, questioning, even doubt are necessary for corporate *faithing*. Do not fear hard questions and the search for answers. God honors the struggle. Easy answers may at first seem satisfying, but most of us realize living lives of faith can be very difficult and complicated at times. The Spirit is ever available to open our eyes, ear, minds, and hearts as we "work out our own salvation"—under God individually and in the context of community. Congregations that rejoice in diversity of thought encourage the spiritual growth of all. In *Faith Is a Verb* Kenneth Stokes says it this way:

> In matters of faith, you can give her a creed, a tradition, and a denomination and say, "These are your faith—do not question them!" They are a total package, and her response will be the result of many factors as she matures. She may adhere to your teachings without question or, in later years, she may well reject it all.
>
> Or you can help her to think, and to worship, to study, to pray—all building blocks of faith—but say to her: "These are the basic components of your faith, but you must put them together in those ways that have meaning for you.... Your faith must be your own response to those options you have considered." This alternative is, for me, the ultimate goal of the faithing experience.[2]

The approach Stokes advocates is no "believe anything you want" approach to nurturing faith. Instead, he advocates for congregations that support the questions and struggles of faith. Congregations that encourage growth and maturation respond to tough questions with, "We're glad you are asking these questions. Let's explore them together!"

### Process of Conversion

If conversion is considered a one-time experience of placing faith and trust in Jesus Christ, the gospel is minimized, and capacity to grow and move toward mature faith is shut down. For me, the journey of faith is about the process of being converted—something needed many, many times as we daily seek to become more like Jesus for the sake of the world ("Take up your cross and follow me"). Our faith may be awakened by our experiences, but if we are not careful, we can easily fall back to sleep and return to what is comfortable and known (homeostasis).

A few years ago I attended *ChurchWorks*, a CBF workshop for young clergy. Bill Stanfield, who guides the work of *Metanoia* in South Carolina, talked about the process of conversion and drew it on a white board for us:

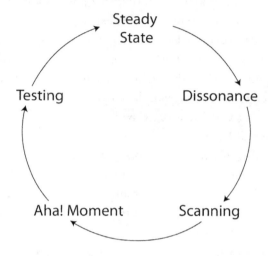

To understand this conversion process, we need to understand the role of dissonance in change or transformation. When we hold two or more ideas, understandings, or beliefs that relate to each other but are inconsistent with each other, we experience discomfort, or dissonance. Research suggests cognitive dissonance can lead to lasting attitude, belief, or behavior change.

In our most honest moments we confess our desire to stay in "steady state" because it is comfortable and easier. When we encounter something that creates dissonance, we want to return to steady state as quickly as possible; we prefer to avoid pain. As long as we are alive, we will experience moments of dissonance; it's a natural part of life. Dissonance comes when our current beliefs or practices don't work anymore as a result of a precipitating event. When we encounter the discomfort of dissonance (for example, we say one thing and do another), we begin searching for new solutions to address the dissonance. This scanning process can be time-consuming and energy-draining. After seeking new understandings or beliefs to address the dissonance, we arrive at an *aha!* moment, that is, an option that helps us find relief from the pain we are experiencing. Then we test this discovery by putting the new understanding into practice. After a period of testing, we become more comfortable and assume a new steady state, and the cycle begins again. Thus, we perpetually engage in the process of conversion.

Moments of dissonance will come no matter how hard we try to avoid them. The question is: How open are we to wrestling with conflicting beliefs or practices? *Faithing* demands we continue the journey and allow the Spirit to awaken consciousness to help us take the next step toward maturation.

Dissonance also occurs when we gain information that is inconsistent with our current beliefs and practices. Jesus frequently used this teaching method. For example, when the woman caught in adultery was brought to him, Jesus refused to see things from the religious leaders' perspective. Instead, he suggested the one without sin cast the first stone. Jesus aroused dissonance when he confronted the leaders' hypocrisy.

Jesus creates dissonance in my favorite parable, the Prodigal Son (or, more accurately, the Loving Father). Religious people believed God loved those who "stayed home and did the right thing" more than the ones who went away and lived differently. Jesus knows both sons in the story are out of fellowship with the father. Upon the younger son's return, the father welcomes him back and throws a big party for him. Shoes are placed on his feet, a ring is put on his finger, and a robe is placed over his filthy attire. Radical and unconditional love for the wayward son creates dissonance and causes hearers to reflect on their own beliefs about who it is God loves and forgives.

Many stories show Jesus arousing dissonance when he provides information that is inconsistent with current beliefs and practices or offers new understanding: talking to a Samaritan woman (something a good Jewish man would never do, especially if he knew how "sinful" she was), placing a child in front of adults to teach (when tradition said children are of little value), eating with tax collectors and sinners (when tradition says stay away from "sinners"), touching leprous persons (when society deemed them unworthy throw-aways), with righteous indignation removing tables from the temple to counter abusive practices targeting the poor (when culture claimed it to be good business practice), and many other examples. Jesus modeled how dissonance confronts our steady state—an essential step in ongoing conversion.

What is the relationship between the *faithing* process we're describing and the process of conversion? I believe they are integrally related. Here's why:

• For ongoing conversion to happen, one must be willing to submit to shaping forces. Every encounter becomes a potential faith-shaping experience.

- When dissonance is encountered, our perspective on faith determines our willingness to deal honestly with pain and change. If faith is reduced to a set of beliefs about God, we are not motivated to pay attention to dissonance when it arises. This hearkens back to the ideas of certitude and unhealthy self-assurance.
- Effectual faith must be lived out in the real world. We can respond to dissonance by digging in our heels and clinging to beliefs and practices that no longer work, or we can be pliable in the hands of the Master Potter, who desires to take our experiences and shape them into something meaningful and life-enriching.
- Faith includes learning to trust God more and more with our lives as we journey through difficult life experiences. Inevitably, our faith is tested and we arrive at new understandings that sustain us on our journey.
- *Faithing* means remaining open to the Spirit's leading. The Spirit uses our experiences and resulting dissonance to transform our lives (i.e. attitudes, beliefs, and behaviors inconsistent with the life and teachings of Jesus).

In the same way dissonance leads to individual transformation, dissonance is a strong force in congregational transformation. Remembering to affirm where people are in their faith journeys while simultaneously awakening consciousness that faith can have greater impact than they think it can factors heavily into congregational transformation.

Congregational leaders are central in this process. Two things really matter if we sincerely desire spiritual change: (1) who the leaders are, and (2) the questions the leaders ask. If a congregation is comfortable with "things as they are," is driven by cultural expectations, or is stuck because of literal thinking and believing, leaders are pressured into preserving current reality. This naturally limits the depth and difficulty of questions leaders are willing to risk, especially if pastors are worried about job security.

Leaders are in the unenviable position of being both comforter and challenger (change agent). Asking powerful questions that expose inconsistencies in congregational life creates anxiety in the system. Leaders play key roles in shaping emotional states of church bodies. Self-defined leaders who clearly articulate what they believe while staying connected to congregants and remaining non-reactive in times of stress can lower collective anxiety. Otherwise, fear and anxiety take the day, and homeostatic forces ("Let's keep things in balance by keeping church the way it is") win out over heretofore untried options. Many excellent books on family systems theory have been written. I commend them to all pastoral leaders.

Of course, pastors are not the only leaders in churches, but pastors carry major responsibility to build a healthy immune system for the congregation. This allows the congregational system to move forward (rather than simply maintaining the status quo). Pastors are leaders among leaders—all of whom have spiritual responsibility for the health and vitality of the body. Healthy leaders constantly assess current cultural understandings of "faithful" or "successful" versus expectations revealed in Jesus' life and ministry. Pastoral leaders must be out "ahead" of the body in order to encourage forward momentum of church members. If vocational pastors aren't themselves growing and evolving in their faith, expecting their members to engage the ongoing conversion process is disingenuous. "Do as I say, not as I do" does not model faithful servant leadership well.

### Role of Crisis in Forming Faith

We typically think of a crisis as a bad thing that immediately puts us in a gloom and doom frame of mind. In reality, a "crisis" can be a turning point. Examples such as the death of a loved one, being fired from a job, getting married, divorcing, child leaving home to attend college, birthing or adopting a baby, etc., often include a period of increased vulnerability and heightened potential for faith formation. Crises or major life transitions become catalysts for rethinking values and meaning—if one engages the process.

A crisis or major life transition presents ripe opportunity for spiritual growth. Difficult life events evoke dissonance and send us searching for new ways of understanding ourselves and our relationship with God.

While writing this book, our family experienced a tragedy of the worst kind. Our daughter's husband of 13 months was killed by a 16-year-old driving a stolen truck on the wrong side of the road while fleeing from police. Our grief is gut-wrenching. No doubt we experienced increased vulnerability—that is, if a person (our son-in-law) doing everything right while driving down the highway still gets killed, similar things could happen to us too. We have spent many hours rethinking our values and what is important to us. We know *why* the accident occurred—a series of very bad decisions that resulted in a beautiful 30-year-old life being snuffed out far too soon. We don't blame God, but many family members, friends, and acquaintances have struggled, asking

"Why did God allow this?" or "Why didn't God protect Josh?" We believe God was where God always is—positioned lovingly with Josh at the moment of his untimely death and solidly in the middle our grief and suffering. Has our faith been affected by this experience? Certainly. What we hope we can do as the months continue is submit to the shaping forces of this horrible life event and trust God to do what God always does—bring something good out of a horrible experience and, eventually, peace of mind.

As long as we live in this flawed and unredeemed world, bad things will happen. The question for us is will we invite the Spirit to change us in positive ways in response to the pain. I think about my friend and colleague Chuck Morris, who served on staff with me at Huguenot Road Baptist Church in Richmond, Virginia. Chuck and Erica's son took his own life during a time of extreme stress in his career. Even as they experienced such devastating and tragic loss, Chuck and Erica modeled faith and trust as they allowed their son's death to shape and form a new ministry for them—serving as counselors and friends to those in similar places of pain and shock. Out of the crisis, life-giving ministry was born.

## Container Controlled Content

In the previous chapter we examined a few ways formation is blocked. Some communities of faith, out of fear, seek to control the content of study materials and limit what can be read or studied. Efforts to monitor the gospel usually result in a reduction of the gospel—making it less than God intends. Allow me to share from my own experience.

Growing up in a conservative SBC congregation, the "rules" for good Christians were very clear:

- Stick with your kind—don't hang out with people who have different values or convictions because they may rub off on you.
- Be very suspicious of anything you read (other than the Bible). In other words, education can ruin you.
- The only trustworthy curriculum resources are produced by the Sunday School Board of the SBC.
- Don't date anyone who is not a Southern Baptist (don't laugh—in those days I would never have dated or married anyone who was not a Southern Baptist, so the indoctrination worked!).
- No drinking or dancing or playing cards (except Rook!).

While these "rules" seem totally ridiculous to me today, the Southern Baptist container shaped and formed me—positively and negatively. I owe a huge debt of gratitude to SBC congregants who loved me, invested in me, and affirmed gifts they saw in me. I am most thankful for my theological education at SBTS, which changed my life in powerful ways. My seminary education made me aware that Christendom is so much bigger than the denomination that formed me. Course work prompted me to read widely and deeply—allowing God's Spirit to continue shaping my mind and my heart. Before long, the "rules" of my childhood were seen as an impediment to richer and deeper faith. Wrestling with my inherited faith helped me to arrive at owned faith—one not defined by a self-limiting container. I came out of the experience of seminary with stronger faith—a faith no longer fearful of education or exposure to new ideas or new authors.

I very much understand why theological education became a lightning rod within the SBC. Theological education did its work—it shaped and formed me and opened my mind to new horizons, giving me permission to cross boundaries established by the denominational institution. For those in the SBC who were clinging to certitude, theological education was threatening. The perceived threat contributed to a different SBC, one that preferred an indoctrination approach over true, honest, and authentic theological education and faith formation.

When denominational entities or congregations attempt to "control" what constituents read or study, shaping and forming of believers becomes prescriptive, and congregational autonomy is violated. How far one can stretch and grow is defined by what is acceptable within the container. Educational and discipleship experiences may be encouraged, but they must happen within rigid guidelines. Otherwise, these entities surmise, folks may begin to "doubt" and entertain other (unsanctioned) ideas about faith.

Journeying alongside diverse theologians and friends stretched (and continues to stretch) my faith and my understandings in profound ways. Deep-thinking professors and congregational practitioners of all kinds, open-minded church members, and dedicated work and ministry colleagues also contributed in subtle and bold ways to my understanding of faith and faith development. I am forever grateful to all.

Finally, I cannot imagine how different my journey of faith and my life would be today had I stayed within the narrower confines of the SBC. I might have missed the richness of great authors who influenced me: Diana Butler

Bass, Richard Foster, Robert Mulholland, Parker Palmer, Richard Rohr, Phyllis Tickle, Dallas Willard, and so many others. I have enjoyed and benefited from reading authors outside the Baptist circle.

If the goal of Christian education in the church is to control content and make sure there is uniformity of belief, then a restrictive container is required. If, however, the goal is to form faith in Jesus Christ for the sake of the world, leaders must turn the reins loose and set the Spirit free to guide the shaping and forming process. We know faith forms in ways that are developmentally appropriate for each age group.

### *Ongoing Conversion Process*

As previously mentioned, certitude about faith matters can short-circuit the conversion process. Probably all of us have been involved in at least one encounter in which incompatible perspectives were voiced. Because each party assumes it possesses the "right" answer, attempts were made to avoid conflict. Rather than engage the process, parties sidestepped the dissonance, and potential spiritual growth was discouraged. Peace and harmony are good things, but when folks are satisfied and believe they have arrived, they become complacent and avoid faith-challenging conversation, thus limiting their own spiritual growth and development.

Congregations are bodies comprised of individuals. The unique blending of personalities, leadership, follow-ship, and interaction certainly make each congregation one-of-a-kind. Though this is true, astute generalizations can be made about most church families. Churches, like individuals, become satisfied and complacent about their role and functioning. Congregational certitude shuts down capacity of the body to fully engage the conversion process.

The chief culprit in congregational tendencies to express certitude is fear. Fear blocks the ability of congregations to ask honest and open questions about matters of faith. If we assume we have the right answer to every question, the Spirit struggles to "teach us a new thing," and congregations become stuck. Fear keeps us in line with what we've decided (or have been told) are expressions of strong faith and belief. When we are too afraid to doubt or ask hard questions and we exert pressure to suppress the questions of others, we live in the land of certitude and false assumptions. Conversion welcomes change and forward momentum. Conversion welcomes winsome curiosity and acknowledgment of God's mystery. In our human finiteness, we can never come close to fully understanding God's mind or how God works in the world. Our best hope for ongoing conversion is to put into practice what we learn about God through Jesus' exemplary life and love.

Another contributor to congregational certitude is reducing the gospel to our final destination: insisting all that occurs in matters of faith is that we get to heaven after our physical condition ends. Some approaches to evangelism (the spreading of the Christian gospel by public preaching or personal witness) provide people only bits and pieces of what it means to commit to the reign of God. If our evangelism approach is primarily focused on whether or not a person goes to heaven when we die, we reduce the gospel to "fire insurance" and establish a poor framework for the ongoing conversion process.

If we oversimplify a life of faith to words and actions that point only to passing through the pearly gates, we miss opportunities to make a difference today. Jesus lived in the present and worked for good in his setting. We are called to embrace and live a faith ethic the moment we accept the gift of relationship with a holy God, not to delay and defer spiritual thoughts and behaviors until the day we physically die and live like the devil in the meantime!

How do we explain our relationship to God? Conversion and salvation are not the same thing. Salvation is relationship based on God's grace, available to us because Jesus was born into the human predicament, lived, died, and rose. Salvation and freedom from the pain of sin and spiritual separation from God are available to us because of Jesus' sacrificial life and love. Frank Stagg says, "Salvation must offer redemption from bondage, forgiveness for guilt, reconciliation for estrangement, renewal for the marred image of God."[4]

The church today must think critically and theologically about conversion. Conversion is the human response to God's offer of salvation. Gordon Smith in *Beginning Well* says, "It is most helpful to think of authentic Christian conversion as a cluster of seven distinct elements—if we expect conversion to reflect the full expectation of the New Testament rather than the minimalism of wondering if we will go to heaven.... Conversion is best seen as a protracted experience that involves seven distinct elements or events," which Smith stresses are not stages or steps in conversion but elements of conversion experienced uniquely by each person on the journey of faith:[5]

1. Belief: the *intellectual* component. This component involves belief in Christ, belief in good news, and trusting in God's grace. One's mind is illumined, leading to change.

2. Repentance: the *penitential* component. In Christian conversion a person is confronted with sin. Repentance is not simply feeling sorry for wrong thinking and doing. Repentance is radical rejection of the human tendency to live in rebellion against God's precepts. Repentance is rooted in the awareness that we are flawed and in need of God's grace.

3. Trust and assurance of forgiveness: the *emotional* or *affective* component. Christian conversion has a distinctly emotional element that is experienced uniquely by each individual. Smith suggests the emotional component includes assurance of forgiveness, trust in God, and joy of life in Christ.

4. Commitment, allegiance, and devotion: the *volitional* component. In Christian conversion our fundamental loyalties change; we resolve to live in obedience to Christ. We no longer live for ourselves alone but for kingdom purposes in the world.

5. Water baptism: the *sacramental* component. New Testament writings suggest baptism is an integral component of coming to Christ and engaging in Christian community. Some traditions call baptism a sacrament; Baptists refer to believer's baptism as an act of obedience to Jesus' command. This external ritual affirms the change taking place inside.

6. Reception of the gift of the Holy Spirit: the *charismatic* component. Christian conversion includes the appropriation of the Holy Spirit. The pressing question in the New Testament is not "Have you been born again?" but "Have you received the Spirit?" (Acts 2:38).

7. Incorporation into Christian community: the *corporate* component. Our conversion is incomplete until we are incorporated into a community of faith. We are not designed to live in isolation from the people of God.

The goal of familiarizing ourselves with these elements of conversion is to help the church reclaim the whole of New Testament teaching about conversion, repent from myopic thinking about a "good conversion," come to grips with radical individualism that has overtaken the church, and awaken consciousness about the complex nature of conversion. If we take seriously the call to focus and make headway on all seven components, we foster conversion that leads to spiritual maturity.

Also instructive is considering what many see as shifting paradigms for conversion:[6]

| Old Paradigm | Contemporary Paradigm |
| --- | --- |
| Conversion occurs suddenly | Conversion occurs gradually |
| Conversion is more emotional than rational | Conversion is rational more than emotional |
| External forces act on a passive agent | Convert is an active, seeking agent |
| Dramatic transformation of self | Gradual self-realization |
| Behavior change comes from belief change | Belief change flows out of behavior |
| Conversion is a one-time experience | Conversion is not permanent, occurs frequently |
| Conversion typically occurs in adolescence | Conversion typically occurs in young adulthood |
| Good example is Paul's conversion | No one experience is typical |

We confess the church is lacking in spiritual depth and spiritual vitality. When the church is weak, she struggles to impact the community and the culture in which she resides. A good conversion provides solid foundation for transformation of community and culture. Smith says, "Conversion is the prerequisite for transformation."[7]

### Continuing Conversion of the Church

From its inception the church has found ways to reduce the gospel from its original intent, and any reduction ends up being a distortion. An example is how we constantly declare that our way of understanding the gospel is the final version of Christian truth, like we in our finiteness can understand the infinite nature of God. Because it became preoccupied with its place among other religions, the early church lost its focus on its commitment to the reign of God. The gospel was weakened by shifting attention from a "movement of God" to "institutional thinking and acting in the world." The meaning of salvation was diminished from meaning a total commitment of life to Christ to an emphasis on individual salvation and concern for the afterlife. This tendency toward distorting God's original design for the church demands a continual conversion of the church.

I appreciate the work of Darrell Guder and other authors who help us rethink the mission of God. They remind the church that emphasis must be placed on the *missio Dei* (God's mission). The church does not have a mission; the church acts upon God's mission and mandate. This reminder helps the church get its eyes off itself and onto the object of God's mission—the needy world. In recent years this movement became known as the missional church and helped reconnect the "benefits of salvation" with the "call to join God on mission in the world"—a more holistic understanding of conversion.

The mission of God focuses on both the inward experience of salvation AND the primary role of Christianity to promote the social gospel or apply Christian ethics to social problems. Theologically, the social gospel seeks to realize the Lord's Prayer (Matt 6:10) "*Thy* kingdom come, *Thy* will be done on earth as it is in heaven." Promoting justice is central to the reign of God. Guder describes this outward experience like this:

> In Jesus' outreach to the poor, the disenfranchised, and the marginalized, he demonstrated that God's justice requires a complete reordering of any and every society. He demonstrated the divinely mandated "preferential option" for the poor, the young, the weak, and the helpless. Jesus trained his followers to form their communities under principles of just order that differed radically from both Jewish and Hellenistic patterns of the first century.[8]

"Christianity without discipleship is Christianity without Christ," declared Dietrich Bonhoeffer. Christianity demands allegiance to Jesus Christ and submission to the lordship of Jesus Christ. What if the church's long-held assumptions about how to be and do church have been embraced for so long that we are unable to consider the implications of Jesus' lordship over all of life? What if the culture has so convinced us what is really important is getting our beliefs right that we lose the biblical mandate for obedient discipleship? What if our watered-down version of the gospel causes what we deem "Christian" to be un-Christ-like?

We must not compartmentalize our faith. We cannot say Jesus will be Lord in one area of life but not in another. There is no realm of life, no business, no politic in which the lordship of Christ is excluded. We cannot look at Jesus' teachings about loving enemies, sharing our provisions, or practicing forgiveness and see them as optional. If we do, we reduce the gospel to "beliefs" about who Jesus is and debates about who is in and who is out. We must not focus on getting our beliefs and preferences affirmed by the church and ignore the importance of the kingdom of God. Kingdom of God fundamentals speak truth into all of life, including governmental action and leadership decisions that impact the common good.

The reason we spent time examining "forming faith in the person of Jesus Christ" in the previous chapters is because it is so hard to do! We live in a broken world. Watch the evening news! Every day you will hear about nation fighting nation; radical groups rising up and committing atrocities; teens, adults, even children shot in drug deals gone bad; murder in cities across America and the world; families in crisis; rampant divorce rates; politicians fighting over ideologies while avoiding discussions on the real problems and possible solutions. Humans can become prideful, ambitious, lustful, greedy, and self-seeking—exactly the opposite of what Jesus taught and modeled. We live in a culture that prefers the "fallen" qualities over Christian ethics (i.e., Jesus' way).

Has Western Christianity perverted the gospel by believing Jesus is made in our limited image? Do we somehow believe this approach will make Jesus more "respectable" and more attractive to the broader culture? Have churches in the United States been complicit in forming cataracts over the spiritual vision necessary to see the world as Jesus sees it?

When my dad began to struggle to see, his vision became so impaired that he could not see clearly enough to drive safely. Something had to be done. He went to the doctor and was diagnosed with cataracts—cloudiness of the lenses of the eyes, which obstructs vision. Dad's cataracts had to be removed in order to bring back quality vision. Dad was very grateful for restored vision, clarity of sight, and permission to drive again!

Could it be the lenses of the Western church are cloudy and blocking the clarity of God's mission in the world? What if we are so preconditioned by our culture that we no longer possess spiritual insight and wisdom in order to ask questions that challenge the status quo?

We remember Baptists began out of a position of weakness. Those with clear vision, asking good questions, challenged the relationship between church and state and moved the cause along. Baptists were persecuted for their willingness to fight for convictional beliefs. The "down" position of early Baptists drove the types of questions they asked. Even as Baptists immigrated to America seeking freedom of and from religion, persecution continued.

Many years ago when Baptists gathered in Augusta, Georgia, to form the SBC, questions being asked were quite different than those of earlier Baptists. Operating from a position of wealth and power (i.e., the ones who owned slaves), questions no longer focused on what benefited the common good. Questions focused on how wealthy landowners could use biblical texts to justify slavery. Sadly, many Baptist preachers assisted in the unholy effort.

By the time the Southern Baptist controversy (outlined in Part 2 of this book) began, Baptists were a dominant force in the South—operating from a position of power because of sheer numbers, amongst other things. From that "up" position, Southern Baptists sought to use power for political purposes—forfeiting cherished Baptist tenets—and, if necessary, to impose the will of a denomination on an entire country.

Our position determines the questions we ask of Scripture. The questions we ask of God while sitting in an ivory tower (blessed with resources, power, and choices) are very different from the ones we ask if we reside in slave quarters or toil in sweatshops or live on the streets. Our history and our social position drive how we see God and others.

As Baptists in America moved from being an oppressed minority to a majority in power and status, a cataract formed. The questions we considered urgent and important changed.

The truth is local congregations have practiced a particular type of Christianity for so long that members no longer ask hard questions that invite transformation. For example, I worked with one church body dead-set on firing its pastor who had served the church for fewer than two years. The initial experience of the pastor was very positive, but before long the tide turned. Why? The pastor began leading the church to focus on the needs of people in its community. The chair of deacons confronted the pastor and told him in no uncertain terms, "That's not the kind of church we are. We exist to offer worship services and Sunday school and care for each other." A cataract had formed over this congregation's vision—that is, the congregation's vision was no longer in alignment with God's mission. Congregation leaders no longer saw with kingdom lenses from a kingdom perspective; they no longer heard the call of Jesus to serve the least of these; and they no longer tolerated a leader who saw things differently—even if it was Christ-like!

Jesus' foremost command is clear—love God, love neighbor. Love always includes action. Jesus commanded loving enemies, sharing our provisions with those in need, practicing forgiveness, and extending grace. Certainly, the church possesses answers for our troubled world, but the church often offers an ineffectual status quo or (God forbid!) solutions in direct opposition to what Jesus taught. Current practices that comply with cultural expectations won't cut it. Only authentic discipleship buffets us against the impact of greed and power. Only as we return to the source of our faith can the church effectively address our compartmentalized faith and make Jesus Lord of all.

### Key Understandings

Before we look at what is and isn't happening with faith formation in local congregations, let's hear from faith formation expert John Westerhoff, whose understanding of the differences between instruction, education, and formation is helpful:[9]

*Instruction* aids persons to acquire that knowledge and those abilities useful for responsible personal and communal Christian life in church and society. For example, through instructional processes persons acquire knowledge of the content of Scripture as well as the ability to comprehend its meaning and interpret its implications for daily life and work. Instruction alone, however, can produce a person who knows all about Christianity but who does not intend to be Christian. Nevertheless, without the benefit of instruction, persons may not know what faithfulness is, what it implies, or how to decide what is faithful.

*Education* aids persons to reflect critically on their behavior and experiences in the light of the gospel so they might discern if they are being faithful and when they might need to change their behavior. For example, through critical reflection on the ways in which we live together as families, congregations, or schools, we can reform them to be more faithful. Christians, therefore, need to make education a natural way of life and not just a program, as they engage in critical reflection on every aspect of their lives.

*Formation* aids persons to acquire Christian faith (understood as a particular perception of life and our lives), Christian character (understood as identity and appropriate behavioral dispositions), and Christian consciousness (understood as that interior subjective awareness or temperament that predisposes persons to particular experiences). For example,

Christian formation is the participation in and the practice of the Christian life of faith. We do that by identifying with a community, observing how persons in it live, and imitating them. Instruction informs us in terms of knowledge and skills believed by the community to be important for communal life.

Education "reforms" us by aiding us to discover dissonance between how we are living and how we are called to live. And formation both confirms (nurtures) and transforms (converts) us through a process best understood as apprenticeship. Formation is related to a natural process called enculturation; when enculturation becomes intentional it is called formation. Education is necessary for faithful formation, and instruction is important for faithful education, but formation is foundational because it is the primary means by which Christians are shaped in mind, affections, and behaviors.

These distinctions are vitally important as we consider what is happening in congregations today. A holistic approach to Christian growth and maturation demands we pay attention to all three dimensions of Christian education.

### Current State of Christian Education in Congregations

What is the state of Christian education in Baptist congregations today? How much attention is given to instructional methods, education that reforms, and formation that shapes Christian character? How much thought is given to the kind of faith being shaped and formed? How do we measure success?

I suspect approaches to Christian education are as diverse as our congregations. Many years ago a myth was perpetuated: "If church members attend Bible study and worship on Sunday mornings, discipleship training on Sunday evenings, and give a tithe to the church, they have done what is necessary to nurture a faith relationship with Jesus Christ." This myth is still alive and well in many churches! Is it possible this widely held but false idea has resulted in low expectations for individual and corporate transformation? This reduction (oversimplification) of the gospel has yielded faith communities that may enjoy good fellowship but do not embrace and exercise a transformational approach to faith development that results in tangible expressions of mature Christianity.

I wonder how much of what is considered Christian education in Baptist congregations is informed more by culture and tradition (i.e., we've always done it this way) than sound theology and good educational philosophy? Following are a few of my observations after serving as educator in three Baptist churches, from participating in educational experiences in many congregations, and from facilitating leadership conferences:

- Many teachers assume the educational methods used in school classrooms work effectively in church classrooms. They are unaware faith is more caught (modeled) than taught (didactic/instructive method).
- In most classes the teacher assumes full responsibility for what happens in the teaching/learning process.
- Educational focus is on teaching instead of learning (teacher vs. learner is central to the experience).
- Very little engagement of the student
- The best learning—discovery learning—is not practiced; instead, the teacher spoon-feeds the students what s/he has learned.
- PRAXIS (process through which we learn, do something about what we've learned in the real world, and then reflect on the experience) is not a regular part of most congregational educational experiences.
- Reflection on life experiences in light of Scripture and tradition is not a regular practice in most classes.
- Spiritual disciplines, other than prayer and Bible study, are not practiced in the classroom.
- The teacher believes his/her primary function is "teaching lessons."
- Many teachers are unaware of the role of the faith community in nurturing faith.
- Teachers and students do *not* come to Bible study expecting to be shaped or transformed (in fact, the word *change* is probably a dirty word in many congregations).

Primary responsibility for Christian education is usually given to the Sunday school. I'm a strong advocate for Sunday morning Bible study classes, but 50 minutes (or less) of "Bible instruction" is not going to accomplish the task of forming people. At best, we can hope for good fellowship, pastoral care, and some basic instruction. Sunday school was never intended to be the only Christian education process. We need a broader understanding—the firmly held conviction that every aspect of church educates all the time. Everything the congregation does has potential to shape and form faith. The whole of life provides contexts for education, not just specific times on Sunday morning.

As a result of our commitment to traditional approaches in Christian education (primarily Sunday school), we ignored the need for ongoing conversion; we neglected the gap between belief and practice; we failed to take advantage of potential for the Christian community to nurture faith; and we gave Christ-followers permission to relinquish responsibility for their growth and maturation to teachers/preachers. In other words, we settled for what made people "comfortable" so they would keep coming. We fostered an environment that reinforced what people already believed rather than one that inspired perpetual curiosity and openness to change.

What is the byproduct of this long-standing, deeply rooted pattern? Dr. Israel Galindo calls the byproduct the "null expectancy factor," meaning people do not participate in the life of a congregation *expecting* to be transformed by God's Spirit. Instead, people are taught to be well-behaved church members, not disciples who emulate Jesus. There must be a better, more effective way!

### *Learning a Better Way*

I am an avid college football fan. As a proud alumnus of the University of Alabama, I root for the Crimson Tide, but I also enjoy observing other teams for the fun of it.

Recently, while watching an Alabama football game, a commentator, an Alabama graduate who played football under Nick Saban, was asked what it was like to play for a strict disciplinarian like Saban. The commentator recalled how focused and organized the coach was in his own personal life. Saban approached every game the same way—whether playing for the national championship or against an SEC foe or other opponent. The part of the conversation that caught my attention was this statement from the commentator: "While Coach is strict about the process he uses to teach the game of football, he is always willing to change—even when it goes against how he prefers to play the game." The example he gave related to offensive strategy. For years, Alabama was committed to running the football in most situations, scoring a few points, and keeping the opponent from scoring at all! With the advent of new, high-powered, spread offenses, Saban had to adapt—both on offense and defense. The change in Alabama's strategy has been so dramatic, it is no longer surprising to see an Alabama offense score 40-plus points in a game (and sometimes give up 40-plus points in a game).

Coach Saban's style worked brilliantly for many years (don't mess with a winning formula, right?), and more than likely Saban would not have changed his modus operandi unless he had been pushed to do so. How does this illustration relate to Christian education in the local church? The success of the original Sunday school model was undeniable, but times change, which demands evaluation and adaptability. The key is to stick to the overall goal while remaining responsive to new ideas regarding the process.

Some have called the long-standing approach to Christian education practiced in many congregations *programmed piety*—an approach that clearly is showing cracks. At the 2008 CBF General Assembly in Memphis, Dr. Tim Brock pointed to the following as evidence that the programmed piety approach no longer works:[10]

- Attendance in Sunday school, in many churches the primary setting for studying the Bible, has for years waned. Brock predicts Sunday school as we know it today will no longer exist in 50 years.

- Most congregations no long offer discipleship training. Many congregations offer short-term studies, but many of these are superficial at best.

- Participation in Woman's Missionary Union has declined, and seismic shifts in mission support have occurred. In many congregations "women's ministries" have supplanted WMU.

- Shifts in worship styles have moved congregations away from graded choir programs to praise choruses.

- Many churches no longer offer Sunday evening worship.

- Many churches no longer hold revival or renewal services.

These ways of practicing piety that were birthed primarily in rural contexts no longer work in suburban and urban congregational settings. Brock contends,

> The "programmed piety" approach to faith maturity was based on the premise "knowledge" defined in terms of biblical facts and sets of theological statements, is the primary foundation for Christian formation. The program was based on these assumptions:
> - We can find specific answers to all questions of faith if we study the scriptures and agree on their interpretation and application.

- We can maintain theological orthodoxy if we claim basic Baptist principles and then apply these principles in matters of interpretation, ethics, and informed behavior.
- We are in "right relationship" with others only when we share a common set of biblical and theological assumptions about matters of faith.[11]

Undeniably, Baptist congregations benefited greatly from Sunday schools for many decades. Sunday schools emphasized learning and memorizing scripture, inspired church growth, created systems through which members received care and ministry, and fostered fellowship (the primary reason most people participate). I personally witnessed extremely effective classes in which participants were challenged to grow in faith and practice ministry. At its worst, however, the Sunday school approach was blind to injustice, promoted a nationalistic agenda, and sometimes encouraged intolerance. Many folks became disenchanted with the local church when these overt "Sunday school values" clashed with what Jesus taught and practiced. According to Cassandra Carkuff Williams in *Learning the Way,*

> Effective formation of disciples depends largely on the Christian community's capacity to communicate, clearly and with integrity, the presence of Jesus in its internal life and in its relationships with the world. I have identified responsiveness, gratitude, grace, communion, and witness as marks of authentic Christian community.... These marks serve as indicators of our potential to nurture committed disciples. Only if we acknowledge that our communities do not always successfully practice the presence of Jesus will we be able to turn to the work of becoming effective learners and teachers of discipleship.[12]

I was greatly encouraged when Willow Creek Church came clean about their educational resources' ineffectiveness in producing spiritually mature Christians. This honest confession led them to much-needed critical reflection about what they were producing and why those resources did not accomplish their intended purpose.

Likewise, congregations need to "come clean" about the ineffectiveness of their educational systems. Is the approach producing the desired outcome— Christ-followers who pattern their attitudes and actions after Jesus? Israel Galindo and Marty Canaday say it well:

The unspoken truth of Christian education today is that the educational practices of the past have not served us well in shaping persons in "Christlikeness" because they run counter to the way people need to be educated in faith. A better way to facilitate the process of Christian education is congruent with how Christian faith is actually formed in the context of a community of faith.[13]

It's time for congregations to invest time and energy in addressing what faith is, what faith is not, and how faith is best shaped and formed in community. Only then will our churches discover what it means to become authentic Christian communities. Williams' five marks of Christian community[14] listed below are a good place to start in assessing whether or not current practices align with those evident in the earliest Christian communities. They can help us experience and embody the presence of Jesus today:

- Responsiveness—readiness to change to meet new needs in new times while preserving the message and work of Jesus
- Gratitude—lived response to the love God offers us in Jesus
- Grace—God's attitude toward us revealed in loving actions
- Communion—fruit of the Spirit we hold in common with others in community
- Witness—prophetic presence through which the kingdom is made known in the world

### A Holistic Approach

The word *forming* reminds us conversion is not a one-time or a solo experience but something that happens over and over as we live and serve together in faith communities and the world. This "big idea" also takes seriously that individuals and communities of faith are formed over time, so it matters *how* we engage the process. Forming also reminds me that everything a congregation does for God's kingdom has faith-influencing potential. Our faith is shaped and molded as we worship together, learn together, serve together, advocate together, share faith stories together, discuss and disagree together, think deeply and grow more mature together, even fellowship together.

The church is always in the process of dying to old forms and birthing new ones. That means the church must always be in the process of re-formation. Phyllis Tickle says the church goes through a major reformation every

500 years or so. She refers to this major shift as a time to clean out the attic, that is, determine what needs to be kept and what needs to be tossed.

When our thinking is clear, we confess the church *must* continually change. Each generation embarks on a journey to discover how the gospel speaks into the current context. We cannot demand the church remain static (secure and predictable) while the world moves on and challenges intensify. Methodologies that worked well in the past are no longer effective. Congregations dare not sit around dreaming of the "glory days" when pews were packed and everyone seemed to be "on the same page." Instead, it behooves the church to invest time and energy discerning what faithfulness means now. Our God is dynamic and speaks to all of life at all times. Removing our own "cataracts" and faith-limiting, growth-smothering shackles is necessary if the church desires to be prophetic and relevant. Do not fear change! Embrace it! Eagerly engage in a revisioning process and listen for Spirit promptings. God will blow new life into our faith communities if we say "yes" to the directions in which God is pointing.

Observe the pace of change in the world today. Recall big companies that did not survive because they could not adapt quickly enough. Many congregations face the same fate if they continue to use the same "measures of success" that served them well 50 years ago.

While on earth Jesus journeyed in the company of his disciples. He called them and others to join him in his work. I'm sure we all agree Jesus' priorities are still appropriate for today's faith communities. By looking at Jesus' life and mission, we discover Jesus' intentions for faith communities today.

Baptists are a busy, even hyperkinetic lot. We usually define our success by how many ministries we offer and how active members are. Our worth is determined by how many times we say "yes" to the nominating committee's call to serve. Certainly, love is a verb, and we are called to be Jesus' hands and feet in the world. However, everything we do must be grounded in sound, solid theology or understanding of God. We know that best by studying the life and motives of Jesus. Jesus was a busy man, but Jesus also took time to "be" or center himself in the loving company of God the Father. He retreated so he could pray away from the demanding crowds of people who waited for impressive, awe-inspiring miracles (action). Jesus needed time to regroup, refuel, and renew. We need time for that too as we emulate Jesus' methods and ministries. Loving and caring for ourselves makes loving neighbor more likely. Jesus even teaches it: "The second is this: 'Love your neighbor as yourself.' There is no commandment greater than these" (Mark 12:31). We minister best when we know why we minister. Doing for doing's sake begins to drain us, even causes deep resentment in our souls.

The church I served in northern Virginia took a large group of youth and adults to Vermont on mission every summer. A requirement for being on the team was weekly preparation meetings for the work ahead. In addition to familiarity with teaching materials, team members established theological foundation for our mission efforts. We not only discussed the "how" of our upcoming trip but the "why" or theological underpinnings. When we returned from Montpelier, we spent time in theological reflection, holding our expectations up to our actual experiences and our faith understandings of what happened in our own lives and the lives of those to whom we ministered. Being and doing worked hand in hand.

Earlier we looked at Maricle's understanding of Jesus' priorities both in thought and deed. Maricle also offers the following habits of faith communities that enable Christ-followers to embody Jesus' priorities:[15]

*Healing for All:* Christ-followers treat all with compassion. Christian congregations discover needs within their local community and work proactively to collaborate with others to meet needs in Jesus' name. Leaders of congregations know the members and personally invite them to offer their gifts and skills to provide healing.

*Excluding No One:* Jesus modeled the practice of welcoming strangers for his disciples to follow. This practice means going far beyond simply having greeters at the door of the sanctuary on Sunday mornings. The body of Christ must welcome others as Christ welcomes us. This is a natural byproduct of the first part of the Great Commandment—love your neighbor. How well congregants do this is evidence of the depth of their discipleship.

*Focusing the Money on the Mission:* This one is a challenge for individuals as well as congregations. The church knows its mission, but often the mission of God takes a back seat to structures and infrastructures, especially buildings, "maintenance." When most all of a congregation's resources go into fixed expenses and care for buildings, few financial resources are directed toward missions and community needs. When a congregation has clarity about its mission (i.e., God's mission), decisions about allocating resources become much easier.

*Finding Greatness in One Another.* Maricle says it well: "The humility modeled by Jesus does not require us to pretend we are less than other people. This humility requires us to acknowledge each person is created in God's image, endowed by God with gifts, created by God in love, and so each person is worthy of our love. Christian humility asks we find the talents in ourselves to serve those worthy (and all are worthy) of God's love." Together we can do so much more than we can accomplish alone—another plug for partnering together. When all parts of the body of Christ serve out of the gifts entrusted to them by the Spirit, there is synergy and power, people are mobilized to live the gospel, and much is accomplished for the kingdom.

## Nurturing a "Forming Together" Culture

Thus far in this section of the book, we have explored the concepts of "forming" and "forming together." We made the case for formation as opposed to indoctrination, and we outlined a number of barriers to making the shift to formation in the local church. Now we suggest practical handles to help congregations more effectively shape and form faith.

### Study the life and ministry of Jesus in earnest.
Surely this practical suggestion is evident and what we eagerly long to do. While all Scripture is profitable and worthy of our time and study, Christ-followers long to invest time learning about the life of the One we emulate. The goal is to spend time exegeting or interpreting Jesus to discover insight for living the disciple life.

### Leave room for God's mystery.
We need to be honest about God. Acting as if we know everything about God or understand exactly what God desires in every situation puts God in a box; we insist upon our limited human understanding within our often flawed parameters. God cannot be subdued in a container constructed by humans. We yearn to remain open to where God's Spirit leads. Honesty demands we leave room for the mystery of God. We seek to know as best we possibly can this side of heaven who God is and what God expects by looking at Jesus while remembering God is also *Other*, a designation that defies definition.

### Educate about interpreting Scripture.
Congregations have responsibility to educate followers in how to rightly inter-pret the Bible. The old adage "The Bible says it, and that settles it" reinforces

the myth that Scripture doesn't have to be interpreted. We seek to understand the language of the Bible, the context into which it was written, and how the text speaks to and guides us today.

I believe the framers of the 1963 *Baptist Faith and Message* got it right with this statement regarding Scripture: "The criterion by which the Bible is to be interpreted is Jesus Christ." Also apropos are statements in the prelude: "Baptists are a people who profess a living faith. This faith is rooted and grounded in Jesus Christ…. Therefore, the sole authority for faith and practice among Baptists is Jesus Christ whose will is revealed in Holy Scriptures…. A living faith must experience a growing understanding of truth and must be continually interpreted and related to the needs of each new generation."

In light of these statements, our goal must be to understand Scripture the way Jesus did and to interpret it in light of Jesus' life and ministry. Jesus was not a literalist. Instead, he was guided by the Spirit and used Scripture to explain his points. He frequently said, "The Law says, but I say…" Jesus trusted his own experience. Jesus understood the power of story. His parables conveyed meaning in ways his listeners could relate to because the images and characters were familiar to them. Parables contain truth even when the stories themselves are sometimes hard to accept. Jesus was not concerned about "fairness" but about deep spiritual insight that changed hearts, minds, attitudes, and relationships. Jesus knew "what comes out of a person's heart—evil thoughts, murder, adultery, sexual immorality, theft, false witness, slander—is what defiles a person" (Matt 15:19), not to mention fear, anger, jealousy, judgment, gossip, and so many other unvirtuous feelings and behaviors.

The Bible is a living document that reveals the living God. Our understanding of God grows as we interpret it in our context and apply its truths to our lives. Jesus interpreted texts available to him in dynamic ways pointing to the renewal of all things. People marveled at Jesus' authority. Jesus used Scripture as a living document, not a dead book of out-of-date, irrelevant rules.

**Return to the classic spiritual practices for reading Scripture.**
In the "forming" chapter, we noted one of the barriers to formation is how we read Scripture. What we need is an approach to Scripture that helps us overcome obstacles and makes us available for an encounter with God. We need an approach that keeps us from reading desires and wants into the text. We need practices that focus on inner transformation.

Robert Mulholland outlines classic practices in the article "Spiritual Reading of Scripture" in *Weavings*. Mulholland insists these practices "pry us open to the recreating love of God" and lead to inner transformation. The classic disciplines have proven the test of time. They are referred to as "spiritual reading" or *lectio divina*. Here are the movements as outlined by Mulholland:[16]

*Silencio*: Despite our best intent, we rarely come to the reading of Scripture with total openness and receptivity to God. "Time must be given to silence the grasping, controlling, manipulative dynamics of our being." We need silence to relinquish our lives to God's control. The goal of this silence is to, as Wesley said, "know the whole will of God, with a fixed resolution to do it." Silence helps us release our will to God's will even before we know where it will take us. I would call that faith.

*Lectio*: If we begin the process of being open to God in silence, how we read Scripture will be different. Instead of trying to control the text with our minds, we approach the reading as an address from God. We may actually say, "Lord, what are you saying to me?" So in *lectio* we stay intentionally open and listen for God in, through, and around our encounter with the text. *Lectio* demands attentiveness to God.

*Meditatio*: In meditation we examine ourselves in response to God's address to us. Meditation helps us discover the gaps in our lives—where our lives are out of alignment with God's intent. *Meditatio* allows God to address where we are comfortable (our pattern for staying broken) and should not be.

*Oratio*: After we hear from God, we then address God. "*Oratio* is the pouring out of ourselves to God in response to God's address to us." More than what we typically call prayer, *oratio* is the deep cry of our hearts to God because we have been awakened to our brokenness, we need to surrender our disobedience to God, or we need to reach a new level of commitment to God. This is an honest expression of our thoughts, feelings, and desires to God.

*Contemplatio*: At this point in the reading, we have heard God's address to us, wrestled with it, responded to it, and now we simply wait in stillness before God. The purpose of contemplation is to help us be pliable in God's hands. The change that needs to happen in our lives won't happen because of our effort—it's God's work. We wait actively, and we yield to God's transforming presence in our daily living.

*Incarnatio*: When contemplation is carried into our lives, it becomes incarnation. The way we live begins to be shaped by openness and obedience to God. We are a witness to God's transforming presence in our lives and in the world. When this happens, Mulholland says, "The Bible becomes the word of God—the profound and mysterious reality which has transformed numberless women and men across the centuries and makes them agents of healing love in a broken world that is once again incarnated."

*Lectio divina* can free us from our broken or limited perspectives and keep us from projecting our brokenness or our broken understandings of God on the world. The journey begins with heart hunger for God's transforming love to penetrate our lives. If the members of our churches begin to appropriate this truth, our congregational systems could become houses of transforming love and grace intent upon shining light into the darkness.

### Consider following the liturgical calendar.
Many CBF churches faithfully follow the liturgical calendar, and their pastors preach from the lectionary texts. Many have yet to experience the formative power of this practice. The main reason to follow this cycle is to get into the rhythm and flow of the Christian story, to experience it, to learn it, to relive it through the telling and the doing. The church calendar helps Christ-followers bring their faith into everyday lives. This practice brings freshness, provides a well-rounded scriptural approach, deepens our understanding of God and his work in the world and in our lives and the faith formation potential of any who interact with the message. Studying the strong and foundational stories of faith and the men and women God used for his purposes encourages us to be men and women on mission for God.

For congregations not yet ready to embrace the church year, begin by taking an Advent journey. Most are willing to take a journey that prepares the members of the congregation for the birth of Christ. Once that pattern is established and folks see the value of this intentional focus, then begin taking a Lenten journey.

### Be willing to experiment.
Patterned ways of praying and reading Scripture can become routine and weaken their impact. We need to experiment with innovative ways to read Scripture and different ways of praying to open new formation pathways. We need not fear taking risks. Those possessing the gifts of leadership, discernment,

risk-taking, openness to new, creative ideas must be encouraged to exercise their gifts. Do not punish those who challenge us to discover novel ways of expressing and growing our faith. Alternatively, ideas may be seasonal. What may have passed away because of a community's unique mix of gifts may in the future become viable again. Remaining fluid, open, and responsive to the Spirit's leading in matters of faith practice is an absolute necessity for serious followers of the Way.

Examples of experimenting include: walking a labyrinth, silent retreats, ecumenical faith gatherings, listening to a wide variety of Christian music (including Celtic, Taize, jazz-inspired), participating in the Academy for Spiritual Formation, Examen, *lectio divina*, fasting, using the imagination to read Scripture, etc.

### Build capacity to say "yes...and."

CBF Executive Director Suzii Paynter awakened CBF consciousness regarding the power of "and," symbolized by the ampersand (&). Paynter believes CBF built its identity on "and" because Christianity is an ampersand (inclusive) endeavor. Through the CBF branding campaign, we discovered what we already knew—CBF is a both/and kind of enterprise. We are diverse in theology and practice, and we are a woven together in a denomi-network.

Why do congregations need to build capacity to say *yes...and*? This practice empowers congregations to reject dualism (see earlier discussion) and the self-serving nature of certitude. *Yes...and* enables congregations to ask good questions instead of believing they always have the one-and-only right answer. *Yes...and* builds capacity to see and evaluate with God's eyes. *Yes...and* keeps us from creating disciples in our image and from manipulating the Bible to serve our prideful purposes.

In her sermon at the 2015 CBF General Assembly, Suzii Paynter used the words of Richard Rohr to beckon us with the voice of Christ to the shining word "and":[17]

> **And** teaches us to say yes.
> **And** allows us to be both/and.
> **And** keeps us from either/or.
> **And** teaches us to be patient and long-suffering.
> **And** is willing to wait for insight and integration.
> **And** keeps us from dualistic thinking.
> **And** allows us to live the always and perfect now.

**And** keeps us inclusive and compassionate toward everything.

**And** demands that our contemplation become action.

**And** insists that our action is also contemplative.

**And** helps heal our racism, our sexism, our privilege or classism.

**And** keeps us from the false choice of liberal or conservative.

**And** allows us to critique both sides of things.

**And** allows us to enjoy both sides of things.

**And** is far beyond one political party.

**And** helps us face the dark side of our own fears.

**And** allows us to ask for forgiveness and apologize.

**And** is the mystery of paradox in all things.

**And** is the way of mercy.

**And** makes daily, practical love possible.

**And** does not trust love that is not also justice.

**And** does not trust justice if it is not also love.

**And** is far beyond my religious tribe versus your religious tribe.

**And** allows us to be both distinct and yet united.

**And** is the very mystery of the triune God—the very mystery of our God.

*Yes...and* is a gift to CBF. It enables us to be inclusive instead of exclusive. It keeps the Fellowship focused on love and grace and the common good. *Yes...and* enables us to build beloved community.

### Cultivate capacity to say "no."

As we established earlier, we live in a fast-paced world. We are too busy, and we perversely take pride in that fact. Our culture rewards a "can-do" spirit. We want to be the ones who spin many plates without dropping any. We wear multitasking as a badge of honor. We incorrectly assume this is what God expects from us.

The time is long past for churches to help people learn the spiritual discipline of saying "no." Churches and church leaders must become life-management advocates. Often in church life we value most those who always say "yes" to our requests. We look down on those who have capacity to self-define by setting limits—seeing them as somehow less spiritual. Church leaders sometimes exercise a subtle form of judgment (whether expressed inside our heads or spoken aloud) when church members make the decision to allow another to experience the blessing of ministry or to take a much-needed pause from a long-performed ministry. This is wrong and must change. The church cannot afford to be complicit in wearing people out and robbing them of much-needed rest and re-creation. A better approach is for churches and their leaders to help members discern where the Spirit can best put their gifts to work in light of life demands made upon them. In some cases, timing is everything. Patience is a virtue. Remember human coercion, impatience, and judgment can push people away from faith communities rather than winsomely coaxing them toward a loving, accepting body of believers and meaningful, life-changing ministry.

The truth is Christ-followers need to build capacity to say "no" to some things in order to give priority to more important things. God modeled and commanded Sabbath rest, but sometimes church is the hardest place to find time and space for communion with God. Wouldn't it be lovely, even godly, if the church was a permission-giving body that helped people unplug?

Barbara Brown Taylor was willing to share her Sabbath vision in *An Altar in the World*. We do well to consider her advice and her practice:

> At least one day in every seven, pull off the road and park the car in the garage. Close the door to the toolshed and turn off the computer. Stay home not because you are sick but because you are well. Talk someone you love into being well with you. Take a nap, a walk, an hour for lunch. Test the premise that you are worth more than what you can produce—that even if you spent one whole day being good for nothing you would still be precious in God's sight—and when you get anxious because you are convinced this is not so, remember your own conviction is not required. This is a commandment. Your worth has already been established, even when you are not working. The purpose of the commandment is to woo you to the same truth.[18]

Give opportunity for honest dialogue about cultural messages regarding the link between productivity and value. The time has come for the church to take the lead in communicating the counter-cultural truth of God's Sabbath command. Sabbath rest is essential because everyone needs unscheduled time and relaxed space to cultivate a relationship with God and others.

Likely, churches must change their scorecards in order to foster Sabbath. If we define church success by how many activities are offered and how often people show up at the church building, congregations will believe it "right" to intensify people's busy schedules. If, however, we begin to measure faithfulness by how many lives are touched for good and for God by congregants in a given week, freedom to exercise discipleship "as we go" through our lives (no trip to the church building required) expands.

An important step toward fostering Sabbath is for church bodies to establish sabbatical policies for their clergy. The demands of ministry are emotionally, spiritually, and physically draining. Setting aside periods of time for clergy to rest and re-create is a good investment in vocational ministers and in the congregations they serve. The policy also sets a good example for congregants as they wrestle with their own time- and energy-management challenges. Let CBF know if it can help your church set up a sabbatical policy.

### Address formation barriers.

In Chapter 15 we fleshed out a number of barriers or impediments to spiritual formation in the church. Though we in no way desire to be prescriptive by telling you how to assess or address these barriers in your context, we do encourage congregational leaders to discern which of the barriers is blocking formation so they may address them proactively. This work will, of course, be difficult because congregants have been shaped and formed (i.e., conditioned to think or not think of them at all!) about these issues and practices in certain ways. To challenge presuppositions may cause conflict, which means this effort requires much discernment, courageous leadership, and willingness to be prophetic by speaking truth into the congregational system.

### Focus on creating beloved community.

Again we look to the life of Christ for our inspiration and instruction. Jesus himself modeled how to live in community with those around him. He enjoyed sweet communion with his family (though, admittedly, we yearn for more detail about his younger years and daily life with Mary, Joseph, and his siblings). Jesus lived in a crossroads town. Nazareth interacted with travelers and influences from many places. I would venture to say Jesus observed much about human nature and relationships in the streets of his hometown. Life in his home "church" added more understanding as he observed and conversed with temple leaders and worshipers. By the time he embarked on his public earthly ministry, Jesus had many years of watching and experiencing community. Beloved community means we are together for the purposes of worship, learning and study, and ministry in Jesus' name. We choose togetherness for God's kingdom work. Will we always agree? No. Will we be unanimous in every decision? No, but we can express unity under God while exercising patience, openness to Spirit nudges, a Christ ethic, and stop assuming our personal interpretation of "God's will" is the right and perfect one. God's will is much broader and more dynamic than we can imagine. Let love reign, get self out of the way, and be much farther along the road toward creating beloved community.

### Engage in hands-on mission projects.

Most of our CBF churches understand God uses mission projects to shape, form, and mature disciples and prepare them for even greater service. Unfortunately, some congregations still measure success and faithfulness by what happens inside the church building (offering Sunday school, providing worship services, and taking care of one another). Of course, none of those should be discouraged, but setting our sights beyond the four walls of the church structure keeps us from "navel-gazing" and reminds us that though we aren't of this world, we do live in it. A myopic vision of what your church is called to be and do limits understanding of the church's purpose in God's kingdom.

Mission engagement changes the lives of those we serve. One mission trip to Mississippi following Hurricane Katrina stands out in my memory. The team's project was to rebuild the flooded house of a woman and her children. The young mother had no other choice but to return to her house, knowing it would flood again. I'll never forget the day we had just finished hanging sheetrock on the walls when she walked into the house. She declared, "I could move in now! The house looks much better than it ever has." Quality of life was definitely improved for this woman and her family, and it happened in similar ways every time I engaged in a mission effort that met specific needs.

Mission engagement also changes participants. Missioners return from mission projects different people than when they left. Working with vulnerable populations exposes the ills and excesses of our society—consumerism, materialism, and individualism, among others. When done well, mission efforts provide intercultural experiences and candid engagement with people in need. Reentry back home is eye-opening. Participants often testify that being on mission and making a difference in the lives of others "changed their lives." Providing time for team members to reflect on the experience can lead to transformation.

Mission engagement also changes congregations. Congregations that frequently send folks on mission at home or abroad reap significant benefits. Over time, congregations change, priorities shift, and ministries of mercy and justice emerge. Congregational witness is strengthened and empowered. Failure to prioritize mission engagement inhibits spiritual vitality of the congregation as well as the congregation's capacity to make disciples.

People grow in faith, love, and compassion as they practice expressing Christ's compassion with neighbors. In fact, Robert Schnase says, "Risk-Taking Mission and Service is one of the fundamental activities of church life that is so critical that failure to practice it in some form results in a deterioration of the church's vitality and ability to make disciples of Jesus Christ."[19]

### Give opportunity for congregants to tell faith stories.

When members hear testimonies from missioners, listeners get excited. Spiritual vitality of a congregation is enriched when mission participants tell how God worked in their lives as a result of helping others. More than a traditional testimony of faith, these stories highlight ways in which congregants discern direction and consent to invest their lives in missions and ministries. I observed firsthand the power of consistently enlisting Christ-followers to talk openly about their faith pilgrimage. Congregants long to hear how God is alive and active within the lives of fellow strugglers. Testimonies are appropriate in the context of worship and are also meaningful in Bible study classes or small groups. Now is the time to change the focus of testimonies from "this is how I became a Christian" to "this is how God is at work in my life today."

### Study current books/resources together.

Another excellent way to awaken congregational consciousness is to study challenging books together. Monte Vista Baptist Church in Maryville, Tennessee, made this a regular practice. The pastoral staff selected a "discipleship-focused" book for adult members to discuss in Bible study classes. The pastor preached and taught based on assigned readings from the book. This approach stimulated conversation everywhere in the life of the congregation. The community mediates faith formation through this kind of group effort.

A similar approach is for a church staff to write discipleship resources designed specifically for the context. We did this several times while I served Huguenot Road Baptist Church. Adult and youth units studied prepared lessons aimed at specific needs in the life of the congregation, the pastor preached to the lessons from his unique perspective as pastor, and the pastor frequently facilitated Wednesday evening conversations around what was studied and preached the previous Sunday. Every time we undertook this type of experience, a boost in the vitality of the congregation was palpable.

### Provide spiritual retreat opportunities.

We talked earlier about how difficult it is for God to get our attention because of busyness and distractions. Sensitive congregations periodically offer opportunities for folks to get away for spiritual renewal and refreshment. Getaways need not be elaborate; just offer a change of pace and venue. My experience has shown God awakens consciousness and more likely captures our attention during dedicated time away with other disciples. Designated occasions allow the Spirit to reveal gaps in discipleship. Many congregations regularly take youth away for faith development. Adults need the same rare opportunities to focus on their faith.

### Emphasize holistic biblical stewardship.

Stewardship is at the heart of Christian discipleship. One cannot be a Christian and ignore scriptural teachings regarding management of life. One way to elevate formation is to become more intentional about stewardship—the care, conduct, and control of all of life for God.

In the local church context "stewardship" is considered to be the annual month-long emphasis on tithing to support the ministries of the local church (which is understood to be an extension of God). Jesus spoke often about money and the change of heart necessary to put our relationship with our finances in proper perspective.

Though the word *stewardship* originally meant the office of a steward or manager of a large household, over the centuries its definition broadened to include oversight of a wide variety of organizations and entities. The idea of careful, responsible management is extremely positive and is the aspect of Christian *stewardship* we see throughout Scripture.

From Genesis to Revelation inspired writers offer instruction that helps us shape and form a godly theology for all resources, including the environment. Stewardship is so much more than local church fundraising. God entrusts *all* aspects of his creation and natural resources to our guardianship. Stewardship is a theological principle that encompasses all of life and is an important part of what we do between birth and death—the Dash.

We are challenged to understand stewardship differently when we become Christians. Because we commit our lives to Christ and make him Lord of our lives, we give God "ownership" of our lives: our time, our talents, and our possessions. Until we are willing to acknowledge God's reign in our lives, we cannot fully understand the concept of biblical stewardship. How we manage all the resources God entrusts to us reveals how we understand God's leadership. If we believe God is in charge of our lives and we do, then we want to consult God through prayer and study regarding stewardship issues.

Christians try to find middle ground when it comes to the resources God entrusts to us. We want to fit into our culture while at the same time be faithful to God. We rationalize and think we can keep certain parts of our lives (like our checkbooks, our time, our skills, our witness, etc.) free from God's oversight. The reality is if Christ is Lord of our lives, Christ directs all aspects of our lives. God calls us to be responsible and accountable.

Christian understanding of stewardship flies in the face of today's consumer culture, which insists, "What I have is mine, and I can do with it what I please." The Bible teaches that God is owner of everything and that we manage what God has given to our care. You didn't "build it" by yourself and in your own strength and wisdom. Rather, "all good gifts come from God" (Jas 1:17) A stewardship ethic connects with every facet of our lives—our gifts, our talents, our skills, our relationships, our time, our money, our possessions, our health, our energy, our passion—everything that God devised and created. Do not fear the subject of biblical stewardship. Celebrate the fact that God trusts us and believes us worthy, capable, and dedicated to the care of all God has made.

The first step is to acknowledge God's ownership of *all that I am or ever hope to be*. The second step is to examine ways God calls *me* to be accountable. It's one thing to say I belong to God; it's another to embrace and act upon my role in God's protection of all things:

- I'm responsible to nourish my relationship with Christ (consent to be shaped and formed).
- I'm responsible for how I use "my" time.
- I'm responsible to invest life to meet needs of hurting people.
- I'm responsible to care for God's world (ecology).
- I'm responsible to use the gifts (talents) God has given me to glorify God.
- I'm responsible to share financial resources I have been empowered to earn with those whose daily needs go unmet.
- I'm responsible to invest my financial resources to meet the needs of the church at home and abroad.

- I'm responsible for the water I drink, the food I eat, and the air I breathe.
- I'm responsible for fostering healthy relationships (at home, at work, etc.)

What happens when Christians understand the spiritual truth that God owns everything, trusts us to care for what has been created, and holds us accountable for how we manage what has been given for our safekeeping? When we recognize God is owner, we are freed from worry, our values align with God's, and we understand our responsibility to use what belongs to God for God's glory.

Jesus showed us how to establish priorities. He modeled how to live a God-centered life of service and sacrifice, and he taught us to "seek first the kingdom." Jesus' parable about the talents (Matt 25:14–30; Luke 19:12–28) gives us keen insight into Jesus' understanding of stewardship. Those who wisely invest what God has given are called "faithful." Clear understanding of biblical teachings regarding our stewardship helps us along our path toward faithfulness to God in all of life.

## Express radical hospitality within the community.

Over the years I've noticed that some congregations possess the "hospitality gene" while for others hospitality does not come naturally. Members of hospitality-expressing churches know how to offer warmth and kindness both within the congregation and to strangers. Hospitality is an important theological issue. Scripture is clear we are to be the hospitable presence of Jesus to all we meet. Capacity to offer welcome and helpfulness is a sign we are mindful of the love and kindness Christ shows us. The hospitality we extend is a reflection of Christ's hospitality.

Fred Craddock relates a story about a small rural congregation in Appalachia. The tradition of the church was to conduct an annual baptismal service on Easter Sunday evening. After candidates were baptized by immersion in the river, they came to the shore, where the congregation sang before eating supper together. After the newly baptized changed clothes, they stood around a campfire to get warm. The rest of the congregation then formed a larger circle around them. One member of the church had the honor of introducing the newly baptized members to the church family. Then an incredible gesture of hospitality and love began. One by one, members from the outer circle offered hospitality to the new members:

"My name is…and if you ever need somebody to do washing or ironing…"

"My name is…and if you ever need anybody to chop wood…"

"My name is…and if you ever need anybody to repair your car…"

"My name is…and if you ever need anybody to sit with the sick…"

"My name is…and if you ever need a car to go to town…"[20]

This ritual continued until all members voiced their commitments to the new members. The church body's willingness to offer self and reflect Christ is a beautiful example of authentic and tangible hospitality. Hospitality shaped and formed in the image of Jesus proved the members of a tightly knit community of faith in rural Appalachia "got it." They knew what it meant to show love and live out "partnering together to renew lives and God's world."

Hospitality comes naturally for some. These individuals may even have the spiritual gift of hospitality. For most of us, hospitality must be experienced and learned by doing—like an apprenticeship. We experience others' courtesy, friendliness, and generosity and sense neighborliness between ourselves and others. Hospitality is a spiritual discipline that must be practiced until it becomes part of who we are, individually and collectively, as the body of Christ.

### Stop having business meetings; practice discernment.

For many Baptists, to suggest congregations stop holding business meetings is like saying you are no longer Baptist! I'm not suggesting churches discontinue gathering to make decisions, but I do think we can transform congregational decision-making into more than asking members to show up for a vote. Voting on matters of importance to a church body inevitably results in an "us vs. them" mentality. I believe there is a better way: teach members of your church to engage in the process of spiritual discernment and how to listen for God's voice in each other.

Webster defines *discern* "to detect with the eyes, discriminate, to come to know or recognize mentally." Spiritual discernment is calling on the Holy Spirit to lead or give direction on a matter. Discernment is how the Spirit shows church people what God wants them to be and do. Though we may spend a few moments in prayer prior to the start of a business meeting, if we are not careful, the focus soon shifts to what *we* want instead of striving to discern God's direction.

Here are important questions to consider when discerning important matters:

- Is the action governed by love?
- Will the action center us on Jesus and his teachings?
- Will moving in this direction help us fulfill God's unique calling for this congregation?
- Will this decision build up the church and its members (promote unity)?
- Will this decision help enrich the spiritual vitality of the congregation?
- Who will benefit from this decision (members of the church or people in the community)?

I encourage you to practice spiritual discernment. Doing so helps us rediscover why the church exists, help us reorder and reprioritize our life together as God's people, and helps us renew our decision to collaborate with God in kingdom ministry. The hymn writer says it well,

> *More of Jesus let me learn*
> *More of His holy will discern;*
> *Spirit of God, my teacher be*
> *Showing the things of Christ to me.*

**Learn to listen to one another and move through conflict.**
Can we truly build loving communities of faith if we can't (or won't) engage in honest dialogue? Listening is an art form, and congregations do well to foster safe environments in which people are invited to discuss important matters of life and faith. Without this capacity our congregations remain stuck, which limits God's kingdom impact. Congregants may need a refresher course on how to listen respectfully and how to speak in non-judgmental, conversation-encouraging ways. Today's cultural climate has unleashed an angry, either-or style of communicating that must not be adopted by the church. Believers are aware of a better model (Jesus) and are called to practice civilized, loving dialogue with all people. The assignment isn't easy, but even our name—"little Christs"—demands noble effort in this arena of community living.

How many times have I heard people say, "We can't talk about that in our church because people will get mad and leave!"? To be honest, tactful timing for difficult conversation is important, but to completely avoid controversial conversations out of fear is not characteristic of how God functions. Honest, trusting relationships in the church bond us to one another. Without this kind of foundation, our interactions will remain superficial and lack substance and depth. If our faith communities are "known by their love," we can learn to work through our differences without fear of alienation and division.

One author sees it this way in *The Church as Movement*: "Conversing with others with reconciling intent is the most powerful way for a community to discover God's Spirit in its midst.... We are not a community if we can't move into conflict and move through it while maintaining our loyal love for one another.... Dialogue, seeking conversation in times of conflict, creates thick community."[21]

Key points in this quotation are instructive. First, the statement assumes reconciling intent. The goal of having conversations is to lean into the reconciling power of Christ's love and grace. Second, conversing enables us to see God's Spirit at work in our midst. We are divided in many ways; only God's Spirit can draw us together and keep us together. Third, we don't have genuine community if we can't engage in conversation (including on potentially conflictual subjects) and walk away still loving one another. Fourth, the goal of this conversing is to create thick community, one that is resilient and able to withstand the slings and arrows of life and the pressures of a fallen world. We all need places to be real and transparent without fear of judgment, ostracism, or ridicule. Church needs to be a safe place where we can ask tough questions and express fear and doubt, still certain of our place in the family of faith we call church.

### Equip teachers/leaders to understand the nature of faith.

Responsibility for creating an environment conducive to learning falls upon the leader-facilitator. If leaders are open and vulnerable, learners are usually willing to be the same. We are fellow strugglers on the faith journey. When we recognize our shared challenges, the load is lightened for us all. Leaders who adopt a facilitator mindset are just that—conversation and discussion prompters or facilitators—not the only ones with the answers. Each participant brings spiritual insight to bear on the collective study experience.

To a large extent, learners themselves determine what and how much they learn. Their own personal preparedness, developmental stage, past and current life situations and challenges, relationships and life experiences, personal history and heritage all influence what they hear, accept, and appropriate into their lives. Astute leader-teachers recognize these factors and adroitly guide conversations that are meaningful for each at his/her place in the process.

In some congregations the goal of the teaching process is to provide information. Certainly, people of faith need to know Bible stories and faith practices to grow and mature. Simply knowing information does not assure impact upon learners' lives. Knowing information and doctrine is not adequate for faith development. We must take the next step and discover together what Scripture means and how it will impact our choices and how we engage the world. We acknowledge teaching for transformation will not always ensure change happens, but teachers and facilitators of our education classes must understand the nature of the faith we seek to form and know the distinction between "teaching lessons to give information" and "discovery learning" that encourages reflection that leads to active faith. To be effectual, our teaching must help participants begin to reinterpret their personal narratives (who I am) in light of the story of the trustworthy God found in Scripture and Christian tradition.

**Assess the faith-forming potential of each ministry.**
One thing became clear to me as a congregational educator—churches establish patterned ways of creating and sustaining community. These patterns get unofficially codified and are "the way it is supposed to be." Making changes or even challenging assumptions is fraught with difficulty. I felt the best way to guide congregations I served was to ask good questions about the kind of community we were shaping and the role of each ministry in helping make it reality. Intentionality in the educational/discipleship process was essential. That meant finding clarity about the purpose and objectives of each ministry. We assessed and evaluated each ministry in light of its capacity to grow and nurture faith in Jesus Christ. Here are examples of some hard questions with which we wrestled:

Worship:
• What is the faith-forming potential of worship?
• How can we craft worship experiences to nudge the faith of congregants?
• What is the role of proclamation in nurturing faith?
• What is the role of prayer, reading Scripture, and silence in nurturing faith?
• How does the theology of the hymnody shape and encourage faith?
• How does the language we use "shape" understanding of God?

Sunday school:

- What is the purpose of Sunday school (Bible study)? How effectively are our classes accomplishing the purpose?
- Are participants coming to Bible study to nurture a deeper relationship with Jesus, or are they coming for fellowship only?
- What can we accomplish through these classes (given the time constraints) to form faith in Jesus?
- What kind of curricular resources are we using? Is the approach didactic in nature (focused on teaching content), or does it focus on asking good questions that prompt participants to reflect and discover for themselves (discovery learning and theological reflection)?

Small groups:
- What do we seek to accomplish through small groups that cannot be expected from a Sunday school class?
- What is the role of intimacy in a small-group experience?
- Are open-ended resources being used (expect engagement with content, no Sunday school answers)?
- Is there evidence participants are maturing in their faith?

Mission projects:
- Why is it important to awaken consciousness about needs within the community?
- How is faith nurtured by engagement in mission projects?
- How does risk-taking form our faith?
- How does loving those who don't love you back nurture your faith?
- What is the role of reflecting on the mission experience (how are we different, or in what ways did we experience God?)?

Retreats:
- What is the value of "going away" with other Christ-followers for concentrated time to focus on God?
- What is unique about a retreat experience that fosters attentiveness to God?
- How does the bonding experience of a retreat contribute to one's discipleship?

Substantive conversations about what we hope to accomplish through each ministry is crucial to evaluating, finding clarity, and discovering gaps between current reality and what is necessary for effective faith formation. Be aware you may meet with resistance to this intentional, time-consuming endeavor, but be assured the resulting insight is worth the effort.

**Pay attention to essential layers of community.**

In addition to thinking strategically about the faith-forming potential of every congregational ministry, assessing different options for building community is helpful. In *The Church as Movement: Starting and Sustaining Missional-Incarnational Communities,* J.R. Woodward and Dan White identify four kinds of space in which people find a sense of belonging: intimate, personal, social, and public. Giving serious thought to how a congregation is making space in each of these layers of community is pivotal.[22]

### *Public Space: 70-plus people*

We typically think of public worship when we think of public space. People come to this space to observe without being accountable and to remain, to a degree, anonymous. One cannot expect emotional needs to be met in this arena; however, this space is vital for public proclamation of the good news. Ideas and concepts can be shared openly and efficiently.

### *Social Space: 20–50 people*

Social space provides ripe opportunity for community formation and incarnational mission. This space is small enough to foster authentic relationships but large enough to mobilize people for mission. People are available to one another but will not necessarily experience vulnerability and accountability. A sense of extended family and relational connections are key in social spaces.

### *Personal Space: 5–12 people*

Personal space is the right size space for discipleship to occur. People journey side-by-side no longer focused only on ideas but reflecting on their lives in light of their faith. Expectations are high in personal spaces. People are expected to follow through on commitments. This is where we learn to imitate Jesus.

### *Intimate Space: 2–4 people*

Vulnerability and deep intimacy characterize intimate space. Participants can "tell the truth" about what is really happening in their lives without feeling ashamed. This type of intimacy grows over time through deep sharing.

We need congregational leaders who are thinking strategically about the different size groups needed to build authentic, beloved community. Knowing what can be accomplished and what cannot at each level of community is important. I suspect these community spaces make sense to us: public spaces are worship spaces; social spaces accommodate planned activity and/or intentional mission groups; personal spaces serve Bible study (Sunday school) well; and intimate spaces encourage a form of mentoring.

A key conviction for thinking holistically about faith formation is this truth: every ministry and activity of the church, properly understood, can shape and form faith in Jesus. We cannot assign this responsibility to the educational ministry of the church alone. Every aspect of congregational life is formative. We must pay attention to everything we teach—the explicit curriculum, the implicit approach (how things are done), and the null curriculum (what we leave out). If we fail to recognize the formational influence of all facets of church life, we may inadvertently end up teaching a gospel that is inconsistent with the life and teachings of Jesus.

### Consider CBF's Dawnings: welcoming a new day in your church missional journey.

I intentionally saved this way to nurture a forming together culture for last because I strongly believe in the process. Dawnings is a process that can help your church see the world and your ministry within it with renewed clarity and purpose. Rather than offering a new "program," Dawnings helps your congregation develop skills that can transform how your church focuses its ministry and missions efforts. When your church participates in Dawnings, you learn to engage in three important ongoing practices: visioning, forming, and engaging.

Unlike a traditional strategic planning process in which congregants dream about what they can do for God and the kingdom, Dawnings teaches congregational leaders how to discern God's vision, to form people who will faithfully go where God leads, and to engage in meaningful ministries that impact lives. Dawnings is not a program to follow. Rather, each congregation engages in spiritual practices that awaken consciousness about God's mission and the church's role in it. Through Dawnings a congregation learns to journey with God instead of engaging in expected ways of being and doing church.

One of the wonderful aspects of Dawnings is that your pastor/leader is assigned a coach. Given the difficulty of navigating change in congregational life, a coach is vital to the process. The coach's primary responsibilities are to ask good and powerful questions and bring a measure of objectivity to the process. Each congregation takes its own journey and determines where the winds of God's Spirit are blowing. The coach supports and encourages the journey.

Dawnings has great potential to nudge your congregation toward spiritual vitality and deeper faith formation. Go to CBF's website (www.cbf.net) to read stories of transformed lives and congregations.

**Add your ideas about nurturing a faith-forming culture here.**

I shared a number of ideas for cultivating a congregational culture that shapes and forms faith. I confess my limited perspective and encourage you to add to the list. Most importantly, find the gaps that are blocking formation in your context, and address them.

### Chapter Conclusion

CBF's "big idea"—forming together—is a big deal. Forming constantly reminds us of the ongoing nature of God's shaping forces upon our lives. The goal of this shaping process is to enable us to become more like Jesus. Forming happens best in the context of Christian community as our ideas and understandings bump into those of other Christ-followers. Together, we listen and discern what God desires from folks who gather within a congregation. Together, we mold our individual gifts and passions into a unified effort to transform the world.

### Notes

[1]James W. Fowler, *Stages of Faith: The Psychology of Human Development and the Quest for Meaning* (New York: HarperSanFrancisco, 1981), 117–211.

[2]Kenneth Stokes, *Faith Is a Verb: Dynamics of Adult Faith Development* (Mystic, CT: Twenty-Third Publications, 1989), 33.

[3]Bill Stanfield, *Process of Conversion,* presented at CBF ChurchWorks, 2014, source unknown.

[4]Frank Stagg, *New Testament Theology* (Nashville: Broadman Press, 1962), 11–13, 80.

[5]Gordon T. Smith, *Beginning Well: Christian Conversion and Authentic Transformation* (Downers Grove, IL: InterVarsity Press, 2001), 138.

[6]James T. Richardson, found in "The Nature of Spiritual Transformation" by Arthur Schwartz, 2000.

[7]Smith, *Beginning Well,* 155.

[8]Darrell L. Guder, *The Continuing Conversion of the Church* (Grand Rapids: Eerdmans Publishing, 2000), 123.

[9]Israel Galindo blog from John Westerhoff, "Fashioning Christians in Our Day," in *Schooling Christians: "Holy Experiments" in American Education*, ed. Stanley Hauerwas & John H. Westerhoff III (Grand Rapids: Eerdmans Publishing, 1992), 262–281.

[10]Timothy W. Brock, *Being Transformed and Transformative: An Approach to Personal Spiritual Formation for Christian Educators*, presented at The Spiritual Formation Network in conjunction with the CBF General Assembly in Memphis, TN, June 12, 2008.

[11]Ibid.

[12]Cassandra Carkuff Williams, *Learning the Way: Reclaiming Wisdom from the Earliest Christian Communities* (Herndon, VA: Alban Institute, 2009), 101.

[13]Israel Galindo and Marty Canaday, *Planning for Christian Education Formation: A Community of Faith Approach* (St. Louis: Chalice Press, 2010), 6.

[14]Williams, *Learning the Way*, 101.

[15]Christopher Maricle, *The Jesus Priorities: 8 Essential Habits* (Nashville: Upper Room Books, 2007), 121, 127.

[16]Robert Mulholland, "Spiritual Reading of Scripture," *Weavings* 3/6 (November/December 1988): 29–32.

[17]Suzii Paynter, "'And' plus 'And' plus 'And'", *fellowship!* 24/5, August/September 2015, 3.

[18]Barbara Brown Taylor, *An Altar in the World: A Geography of Faith* (New York: HarperOne, 2009), 139.

[19]Robert Schnase, *Five Practices of Fruitful Congregations* (Nashville: Abingdon Press, 2007), 83.

[20]Fred Craddock, *Craddock Stories* (Danvers, MA: Chalice Press, 2001), 151–152.

[21]J. R. Woodward and Dan White Jr., *The Church as Movement: Starting and Sustaining Missional-incarnational Communities* (Downers Grove, IL: InterVarsity Press, 2016), 188.

[22]Ibid., 157–160.

### Chapter 16

# Partner in Renewing God's World

## *Focusing on God's Mission*

In the past several years a strong focus on the missional church emerged. Confusion about what it means for the church to become more missional (including some discomfort with the word *missional*) was apparent, but one thing this emphasis has accomplished well is to remind us about God's mission in the world, the *Missio Dei*—in Latin meaning "the mission of God" or "the sending of God." By nature God is a sending God. The missional church focus awakened us to the reality that the mission is not the church's mission but God's mission. The church exists because God has a mission. Jesus was sent by God into the world to accomplish God's mission, and we the church are privileged to participate in that most important work initiated by Jesus. Jesus began the movement, and we are called and commissioned to continue it.

Collaborating with churches engaged in a process (similar to Dawnings) to discover what God desires the church to be and do has been my privilege on several occasions. Key for a congregational spiritual journey is coming to grips with what God is up to in the world (the end game) and the role a congregation plays in helping God accomplish God's purposes in the world (the process). The seriousness with which a congregation engages this endeavor greatly affects the outcome. Only when we identify what God desires to accomplish in the world through us can we effectively discern our role as disciples of Jesus. Discernment is slow and deliberate work—something not appreciated in our fast-paced, success-oriented world where we want easy answers fast!

There is a big difference between congregational members sitting around and "dreaming up what they will do for God" versus "listening and discerning direction from God." This is difficult work because our institutional understandings of what church is about will be challenged. If congregational members believe the church exists to make them comfortable and meet their individual needs, the mission of God will be reduced to "it's all about me," and congregational resources will be directed toward keeping members happy. If members awaken to the reality that God loves and cares about *all* people everywhere and recognize their role in communicating that, congregations will become more other-directed, and resources will be channeled accordingly.

So what is God's mission? What does God seek to accomplish in the world? What is the trajectory of God's action in the world? Ask these questions in our congregations today and you will likely hear many different answers. Scripture is a good place to search for assistance. The Bible, however, is not a flat book—some passages carry more weight than others and help us identify God's mission in the world. The Sermon on the Mount is a good example. CBF focuses on several key passages that draw us together and inspire our cooperation and collaboration: the Great Commandment (love God, love neighbor), the Great Commission (go and make disciples of all nations), Jesus' mission statement (care for the poor, needy, and marginalized), and the command to love justice and do mercy (Mic 6:8). Taken together, these passages provide keen insight into what God cares about and what God calls us to care about and act upon.

We identify God's love in action in the Old Testament. The good news is the reality of God's love seen in frequent gracious acts by God—even when Israel rebels and chooses different paths than the ones God commands. God's compassion means God never gives up on God's people. Israel's response to God's gracious and patient love is to love God back.

God's compassion inspires God's mission. God is determined to heal and restore broken creation. God blessed Israel so Israel would bless the world. God called Israel to be on mission by extending that same grace and patience to the world.

In the New Testament we read how God sent Jesus to live with people in order to inspire us to repent and embrace active faith. Living together raises loving God and loving neighbor to the highest command. Jesus taught his disciples how God's compassion is meant for all people in the world—especially those on the fringes of society. Jesus came to proclaim the kingdom of God—a present reality in him and a future reality for his follower-disciples. Jesus' perspective on God's kingdom (God's will and purposes realized) fueled his ministry, and that perspective drives the ministry of Christ-followers today.

If we keep Jesus' identity and mission front and center in our minds, we remember who we are in the world and what we are called to be and do. These realizations are inextricably linked. Our assignment is to engage the world so it knows God is love, not to cocoon ourselves behind the four walls of our church structures. Brian McLaren says it this way: Christians are to "enjoy and engage the world as followers and agents of Jesus.... Jesus' followers are not to be isolated avoiders.... They're to be in the world, into it—sent into it, in fact—with it, engaged, alive, passionate—not out of it."[1]

Jesus fully engaged the world—making a difference in the lives of those he touched. He told relatable stories to help religious folks of the day wake up to their isolationism. Remember the story about the man on his way to Jericho who was beaten and left on the side of the road? Two religious leaders avoided the injured man, choosing isolation over engagement because of cultural norms and fear. Jesus condemns their actions then elevates the behavior of one (a half-breed Samaritan) who stopped and showed compassion. Instead of hiding and withdrawing within our congregations, we must remember Jesus' identity and appropriate Jesus' mission. That way we stay spiritually alive. That way our lives have purpose. That way we make a difference in the world.

### Renewing God's World

CBF was birthed because leaders within the SBC blatantly disregarded deeply held Baptist convictions. Preserving historic Baptist freedoms was ample reason to respond to God's call to leave our denominational moorings. We acknowledge other deep convictions and reasons to separate, however. Though moderates stayed with the SBC for a long time, trying to hold on to foundational Baptist tenets, moderates also knew reforms were needed to bring the new CBF denomi-network into alignment with biblical imperatives. We knew we needed to expand our understanding of God's salvation (it's not just "fire insurance"), focus on God's call to men and women into vocational ministry, emphasize social justice, heal from the arrogance of certitude and choose to exercise the humility Jesus modeled, embrace ecumenical kingdom ministry, initiate a global mission enterprise not limited to church-planting and evangelism, and more.

We acknowledge the truth of a slogan often associated with the Protestant Reformation: *ecclesia reformata, semper reformanda* ("the church reformed, always reforming"). The origins of the phrase are unknown, but its meaning rings true: Until we are perfectly conformed to the likeness of Christ, the church keeps reforming, better yet re-forming. The church must stay constantly alert to discerning the Spirit's direction, express openness to new ways of being and doing church, and remain pliable in God's hands. There's always room for improvement.

I'm writing this section of the book during Advent. We believe Jesus came to bring hope, peace, joy and love. Jesus' light dispels darkness, and 1 John reminds us that "darkness can't overcome light." Even though Jesus dwelt on earth, all is not well. Evil persists. Daily, we witness atrocities. News reports reveal power gone awry, wars and rumors of war, people killing each other, leaders destroying their own people, politicians denying the common good, the list goes on and on.

After "Jesus moved into the neighborhood" (John 1:14 MSG), he commissioned his followers to govern all of life and every relationship with love. As a good Jew, Jesus daily recited the *Shema*: "Hear, O Israel, the Lord our God, the Lord is one. Love the Lord your God with all your heart, with all your soul, with all your mind, and with all your strength." This practice undoubtedly shaped Jesus' spiritual understanding. When an expert in the Law asked Jesus about the most important commandment, Jesus naturally responded with the *Shema*, but he didn't stop there. Jesus borrowed language from Leviticus 19:18 and added a second command: "Love your neighbor as yourself."

Scot McKnight calls what Jesus declared to be the most important the *Jesus Creed.* Hear his words:

> Right here we discover the *Jesus Creed* for spiritual formation. As Thomas à Kempis puts it, Jesus "put a whole dictionary into just one dictum." Everything about spiritual formation for Jesus is shaped by his version of the *Shema*. For Jesus, love of God and love of others is core. Love, an almost indefinable word, includes unconditional regard for a person that prompts and shapes behaviors in order to help that person to become what God desires. Love, when working properly, is both emotion and will, affection and action.[2]

Little courage was required for Jesus to quote the passage from Deuteronomy. However, incredible courage was needed to add to the sacred *Shema*. What Jesus adds was not unknown to those hearing his words, and he was not criticizing Judaism. According to McKnight, "Making the love of others part of his own version of the *Shema* shows that he (Jesus) sees love of others as central to spiritual formation."[3]

Jesus highlights his addition to the *Shema* in the upper room with his disciples: "I give you a new commandment, that you love one another. Just as I have loved you, you also should love one another. By this everyone will know that you are my disciples if you have love for one another" (John 13:34–35 NRSV). Jesus makes love the litmus test for authentic discipleship.

While acknowledging how easy it is to recite these two most important commands—love God, love neighbor—we must confess how difficult they are to absorb and apply. Key to assimilating the *Jesus Creed* is understanding this elemental truth—God loves us! A good Jew would not pronounce the name of God—YHWYH—connoting the distance between humans and God. Jesus, however, began most of his prayers with *Abba* Father. McKnight contends, "What Jesus wants to evoke with the name *Abba* is God's unconditional, unlimited, and unwavering love for his people. In this name for God we stand face-to-face with the very premise of spiritual formation: God loves us and we are his children."[4] We, in response, love God and others.

We confess how difficult it is to feel love for others, let alone actively work for their good. We find it much easier to love God, who loves us unconditionally. People annoy us; their habits are irritating, and we dislike, even abhor, their behaviors. People frequently disappoint. Are we really supposed to love them like God loves us?

Like God, Jesus is all-knowing and knew we would struggle with his addition to the *Shema*. To explain this kind of love, Jesus told the parable of the Prodigal Son. In my favorite parable (which is why you are encountering it a second time in this book), a son asked his father for his share of the estate so he could leave home and have some "fun." Such a request was a cultural no-no! A son always waited until the father's death before receiving his inheritance. In a way the son was saying to his father, "You are already dead to me." Though the request was unorthodox and hurt him, the father granted the younger son's wish (free will), whereupon the thrill-seeking son went away and wasted his funds on wild living. Soon the son is destitute. He dropped so low, he was willing to feed pigs (something a good Jew would never do) and was so hungry he even considered eating the pigs' slop himself. Finally, the rebellious one comes to his senses and says, "I'll return home and become a servant to my father. At least I'll have food to eat." When the son comes within sight of the house, his dad is waiting for him. The father welcomes his wayward son home, bestows gifts of son-ship on him, and throws a big party.

This response to a child who disgraced the family was not typical. Scholars tell us a disobedient son would have been shamed by elders in the town square by breaking a pot at his feet in an act of banishment. In Jesus' parable, however, the father runs to the son and offers objects of acceptance and forgiveness, something very unexpected and counter-cultural.

This parable is so very powerful because it intimates why Jesus eats and parties with sinners. *Abba* Father celebrates reunions with returning sons and daughters. Jesus embodies the unconditional love of the father and came to show us what God's love looks like. Jesus came to teach us how to love those we label unlovable.

Because the word *love* is used in so many different ways, we need a clearer understanding of its meaning. The apostle Paul helps us with his brilliant insight in 1 Corinthians 13. Paul offers a number of descriptors to move us closer to this mystery he calls love: "Love is patient; love is kind; love is not envious or boastful or arogant or rude. It does not insist on its own way; it is not irritable or resentful; it does not rejoice in wrongdoing, but rejoices in the truth. It bears all things, believes all things, hopes all things, endures all things. Love never ends" (NRSV).

Richard Rohr writes that divine love is "an absolute open-heartedness. When you're in that space, your energy flows outward and even expands. When you're not in that space, your energy sucks in. It's all about who did me wrong and why I don't like those people and how my aunt never talks to me and why so-and-so is a jerk.... You have to deliberately, consciously choose to love and not hate. Because people haven't been taught that, we have even decent people in our country, in political parties, and even in leadership positions in our churches who are much more at home with hate than they are with love. And they do not even know it."[5]

We cannot keep our hearts open to God and our neighbors in our own strength. Too many voices in our culture tell us to judge, hate, and fear the other. Without spiritual practices that shape and form us to be like Jesus, our hearts stay closed to our neighbor.

Jesus came to earth to show us what God is like—to communicate how God loves all equally (breaks down barriers that divide) and to embody the love and compassion of God. Jesus came to confer or invoke divine favor upon us. We confess we fall far short in embodying these ideals. All of us who claim the name "little Christ" have a role to play in renewing and re-forming the world to make it more like God's vision for creation. We, too, must "move into the neighborhood" as ambassadors for Jesus to make a difference by loving and serving. To get there requires spiritual practices that nurture compassion.

## *Birthing Compassion*

"Be compassionate, just as your Father is compassionate" (Luke 6:36). I wonder how seriously we people of faith take these words of Jesus. Certainly we acknowledge too many bombs; too many wars; too many lonely, sick, suffering, grieving, defeated, and depressed people everywhere. Perhaps our survival depends on our ability to cultivate compassion.

Sue Monk Kidd recalled an experience she had when she was twelve years old. Under duress, Sue went along to a nursing home with a group of youth from her church. With a bouquet of crepe-paper flowers in her hand, she approached an elderly woman. Everything about this lady saddened Sue. Sue woodenly thrust the bouquet at the resident. The old woman looked at Sue in a way that pierced Sue's bone marrow. Then the woman spoke these words: "You didn't want to come, did you, child?"

Sue was stunned by the plain-spoken words. "Oh yes, I wanted to come," Sue protested. The lady smiled at her and responded, "It's okay; you can't force the heart." Sue tried hard to forget the uncomfortable nursing home encounter. Not until many years later did Sue discover the truth in the lady's words:

> You can't force the heart. Genuine compassion cannot be imposed from without. It doesn't happen simply by hearing a sermon on love or being sent on a loving mission.... The point is, you don't arbitrarily make up your mind to be compassionate so much as you choose to follow a journey that transforms your heart into a compassionate space.... God is the life of us all and we are one in God together.... Our lives are irrevocably bound up with one another.[6]

Compassion literally means with (*com*) suffering (*passion*). Compassion connotes suffering with another or experiencing another's grief or pain or as Sue Monk Kidd says, "lifting our finger to the world's teary face."[7] While compassion cannot be forced, it can "become a womb where compassion is gestated and birthed." The journey of "birthing God" naturally leads to our neighbor.

We discovered the truth of birthing compassion while living next door to an Indian pharmacist and his beautiful wife. Sethu and Valli (and their children) were more than neighbors; they became like family to us the more we learned about them. Valli, who is a wonderful cook, frequently brought over unique fare she prepared for Hindu festivals. I'll never forget the first time we invited this younger couple over for dinner. Conversation was rich as we discussed life, children, work, house and garden, even politics. We also enjoyed open conversation about their Hindu faith and our Christian beliefs. Toward the end of the meal, Sethu told us it was the first (and only) time they had been invited into an American home. Many months later, we felt honored and humbled to be included in a very special mother's blessing ceremony prior to the birth of Sethu and Valli's second child. Love and compassion were birthed through community and understanding. In the words of another, "we recognized our own humanity in the face of our neighbors—it was then we recognized the face of God."

Diana Butler Bass insists, "Compassion is the whole purpose of any sort of spirituality or morality or ethics. When religion fails at compassion, it fails at its own test. To neglect loving your neighbor—to lack compassion—that is the problem underlying all other human problems."[8] My challenge to people of faith is to be practitioners of compassion. Our world needs more love, more understanding, and more compassion. We move closer to solving humanity's problems if we follow Jesus' model of openness to the lovely and the unlovely, the known and the unknown alike. Put aside preconceived notions. and do what Jesus did—saw, listened, touched, understood, and loved. In this way we gladden the heart of our Creator, whom we exist to please.

### Reconciliation and Transformation

The apostle Paul frequently expounded on the concept of reconciliation. We admit today's feeble attempts at reconciliation do not come close to capturing the power and scope of *reconciliation* as it is portrayed in the Gospels. John de Gruchy, a South African theologian, offers this explanation of reconciliation:

> The Greek words translated by 'reconciliation' or 'reconcile' only occur 15 times in the New Testament, and almost only in the Pauline letters. All of them are compounds of the Greek alloso, 'to exhange.' The words thus carry with them the sense of exchanging places with the 'other', and therefore being in solidarity with rather than against 'the other.' Reconciliation literally has do to with the way in which God relates to us, the human 'other', and in turn with our relationship to the 'other', whether understood as an individual or a group of people. It has to do with the process of overcoming alienation through

identification and in solidarity with 'the other', thus making peace and restoring relationships.[9]

This author's experience with dehumanizing apartheid in South Africa shaped his understanding of reconciliation that then helped inspire the movement to overthrow a carefully crafted and controlled culture of white supremacy. Apartheid was a poisoned way of life. De Gruchy and other South Africans worked to appropriate this understanding of reconciliation because they shared an African worldview called *ubuntu*, roughly translated "human kindness." Anglican Bishop Desmond Tutu defines *ubuntu* in this way:

> [*Ubuntu*] is to say, "My humanity is caught up, is inextricably bound up, in yours." We belong in a bundle of life. We say, "A person is a person through other persons." It is not, "I think therefore I am." It says rather: "I am human because I belong, I participate, I share."[10]

In the Anglican Bishop Tutu's understanding, God has, through reconciliation in Christ, showed humanity that "we belong in a bundle of life together." We are caught in God's community, restored to it. It's as if God says, "My being is caught up in your being and yours in mine." God's reconciling action is fundamentally a relational process, and we are healed by our own trust in its reality.

A few years ago the focus of Tennessee CBF's General Assembly was on reconciliation and repair. Our keynote speaker was Andy Watts, Christian ethics and New Testament professor at Belmont University. During his presentation Watts noted,

> *Reconciliation* is not merely an action, but a new way of being in relationship with the other, believers to each other, believers and non-believers, individuals and groups, human and animal kin, the environment and the economy, the city and the country. The requirement of these relationships is mutual dignity, voice, and authority. We are literally to exchange ourselves for others and vice versa…or, as Jesus says, *to love neighbors as ourselves*. The actual contours of the relationship will emerge after solidarity is established. This seems to be the meaning of Paul's term "ministries of reconciliation" in 2 Corinthians. Yet, this kind of reconciliation is scarce in our world. Transformative

action has heavy demands, and Jesus makes this evidently clear. They lead to individual and communal dissonance.[11]

Reconciliation requires transformative action. What is the difference between a *transformational* (of, pertaining to, or leading to transformation) and *transformative* (that which causes transformation) presence? Watts contends both are relational terms describing kinds of relationships. He describes the difference in this way: "The term *transformational* conveys the idea of 'changing a condition' while the term *transformative* hints at 'discovering and participating in something new.'"[12]

The CBF has significant experience in transformative ministries. Much of what we do through Together for Hope and global missions seeks to improve the life conditions of God's people who live in poverty by addressing social, political, and economic challenges.

Another vehicle for CBF's ministry efforts in social, political, and economic realms is *advocacy*. Advocacy is the act or process of supporting a cause or proposal. The first known use of the word advocacy comes from the 15th century. It is not a new concept. Advocacy does, however, look different in today's context. CBF has identified pockets in our society that need the assistance of advocates. Advocacy work is essential to heightening public awareness to ways to make the world a better place for the abused, disenfranchised, and suffering.

Just as formation is a relational enterprise and is transformative work, advocacy, too, is transformative work. Jesus engaged in transformative action. If we hope to be shaped and formed in the image of Jesus, we must engage in transformative action.

One goal of our faith journey is transformation of the world. This happens best in community. The CBF community has delved deeply and reflected long about how best to be part of God's transformative work. After much prayer, planning, and practice, CBF has chosen to intentionally partner with others to renew God's world. We recognize the good kingdom work being done by other faith groups and sense God's delight in our decision to join forces with other faithful God-fearers in serving the least of these. As I've heard it said, "There's no need to reinvent the wheel," which certainly encourages better use of the resources of all involved. Linking arms with those already doing good advocacy work is efficient, strategic, cooperative, impactful, and faithful.

## Partnering to Expand Our Horizons

CBF affirms this key motivation for partnering together: acknowledgement of contributions made and resources produced by other Christian groups; partnering expands our horizons. Cross-pollination of ideas and methods is desirable and much needed. Remaining isolated and insulated and standing apart from other believers as in "we only read what is produced by 'our' publishing house or is vetted by our denominational leaders" smacks of religious arrogance. Denying that God is capable of "doing a good thing" in myriad and diverse ways and by a variety of people and entities is short-sighted and slows down God's movement.

Reading widely and deeply is so very important. The Spirit uses authors of many stripes and traditions to awaken consciousness, to help us wrestle with questions we prefer to ignore, to challenge our assumptions, to show us our blind spots, and to highlight cultural patterns that are not in alignment with the Jesus Way.

Brian McLaren declares that for the future to be bright, denominations must "view themselves not as narrowing alleys but as portals into the widest sense of the Christian tradition."[13] As participation in congregational life wanes, we are compelled to focus on what draws believers together—the person of Jesus Christ—not the nuanced beliefs and practices that formerly divided us. People today are not drawn to isolationist Christianity. They see value in other patterns and practices. Many have adopted broader understanding and reject the "our way is the only way" mentality. Believers want expanding connections that enrich life and ministry. I believe these open-minded thought processes are blessed by God and remind us of Jesus' open-armed reception to all people he encountered. Jesus' strongest criticism targeted those who were dogmatic in their understanding. Let us not be among those for whom Jesus voiced his harshest commentary.

## Partnership—A Guiding Value for CBF

Partnership is a core organizational value for the Fellowship. From the time of our founding, CBF has operated with a "partnering paradigm." By working with other mission and ministry organizations, we more effectively accomplish our common goal of equipping individuals and churches in service to Christ. Throughout the years a rich network of relationships has developed, allowing CBF and partners to deepen their impact beyond what is possible in isolation.

Formal partnerships are established through written agreement. Such agreements articulate the expectations of each partner, clearly define methods of cooperation and outcomes to be achieved, and ensure the relationship is ultimately mutually beneficial. All partnerships must be built upon trust and open communication between partners and CBF staff.

CBF maintains a diverse network of partner relationships. Each partner makes a unique contribution that strengthens the broader mission effort of the Fellowship. Since the term *partnership* has been applied to a wide variety of relationships, it defies precise definition. CBF evaluates all partnerships and seeks to develop models for partnering that reflect more accurately the nature and goal of each relationship. Following are the foundational principles guiding establishment of CBF partnerships:

- must be voluntary
- are born out of desire to achieve a goal that cannot be achieved alone
- are based on mutual trust and respect
- require persistence, patience, and planning
- function most effectively when accountability is built into the relationship

### State and regional organizations

CBF's most direct partners are state and regional organizations. These entities are one step closer to the churches served by CBF. State and regional coordinators gather with CBF Global leaders three times per year. This group, called the Movement Leadership Team (MLT), developed to determine how best to collaborate and coordinate, cast vision and direction for CBF, share information, learn from one another, and foster collegial fellowship.

State and regional coordinators are viewed as integral to the work of the CBF and collaborate with one another and CBF staff to enrich and inform the work of the Fellowship. More specifically, the MLT exists to:

- *Steward:* As the only identifiable leadership group in the CBF community without time-limited rotating terms, stewards CBF's identity and brand within and beyond the Fellowship
- *Strategize:* From its unique position relating to national and state/regional councils and boards, develops and implements strategy to accomplish the goals of the Fellowship

- *Share*: Serves as a forum for communication, collaboration, dialogue, asset-sharing, network development, and fellowship-building across the Fellowship
- *Speak*: From its unique perspective as connectors between regional constituents and CBF's global presence, speaks to the Fellowship on matters affecting our shared mission and ministry

State and regional leadership constantly explores ways to enrich the work of the whole Fellowship. Here are a few of the ways collaboration has occurred between states/regions and CBF Global in the past few years:

- Branding: crafting new logos for states and regions under the CBF house brand.
- Sabbatical fund: encouraging congregations to create a sabbatical policy and contribute money to a fund that enables staff ministers to have resources for a sabbatical
- Travel fund: providing resources to enable folks who need financial assistance in order to serve within the CBF organizational structure
- Raisers edge: participating with a number of states and regions in CBF's data management system in order to share data
- 25th anniversary celebration: strategizing ways to encourage individuals and congregations to participate in CBF's 25th anniversary fundraising campaign
- Nominations: providing state and regional leadership with the names of potential leaders to serve on CBF councils, Governing Board, and Nominating Committee

As one who has served as coordinator for two different states, I attest to the value of the work accomplished between CBF and states/regions. The goal of our collaboration is to create symbiosis. CBF Global initiatives shape how states and regions do their work, and state and regional leadership helps shape and interpret those initiatives. A beautiful example is Dawnings. CBF Global designed this wonderful process for congregations. Congregational leaders in the states and regions implement the process, learn lessons from the journey, and assist CBF Global in reshaping the process to make it even more effective. The pastors of these congregations often help provide leadership for Dawnings training.

## Current CBF partner organizations

CBF is constantly considering new partners and new ways of being faithful in partnership with others. Here is a listing of partners at the time this was written: Baptist Center for Ethics, Baptist History and Heritage Society, Baptist Joint Committee, Baptist News Global, Baptists Today, Baptist Women in Ministry, Baptist World Alliance, Bread for the World, CBF Foundation, Center for Congregational Health, Center for Family and Community (Diana Garland School of Social Work), CBF Church Benefits, Center for Healthy Churches, Christian Churches Together, FaithLab, Global Women, New Baptist Covenant, North American Baptist Fellowship, Operation Inasmuch, Passport, Samaritan Ministry, and Together for Hope.

I can personally attest to the powerful impact of partnerships. I provide a few examples from my time as a field coordinator. The Tennessee CBF Coordinating Council made the decision to partner with Together for Hope in Arkansas. This ministry site in Helena, Arkansas, is geographically convenient to CBF churches in Memphis, Tennessee. What began as an informational conversation with leaders of the ministry quickly turned into a meaningful partnership. Tennessee CBF connected churches in Memphis with the work in Helena. A symbiotic relationship between the churches in Memphis and Together for Hope soon developed—people from Memphis traveled to Helena to serve, and people from Helena traveled to Memphis to deepen relationships and give back. Second Baptist Church in Memphis even engaged students from Helena in its annual pumpkin ministry. Tennessee CBF took on ministry projects like securing the top 100 most-recommended children's books for a literacy bus. Together for Hope's commitment to childhood literacy inspired us and gave us opportunities to have kingdom impact.

Tennessee CBF also partnered with Kentucky Baptist Fellowship's signature ministry, *Extreme Build*, in McCreary County. This project is known as a "miracle of partnerships" because many groups work together to build a home for a needy family in one week every summer. Lives have been transformed by this mission effort.

Tennessee CBF is a front-line partner with Samaritan Ministry in Knoxville. This hands-on HIV/AIDS ministry makes a difference in the lives of those affected. Led capably by Wayne Smith, Samaritan Ministry is a compassionate spiritual presence and advocate for those dealing with the physical, emotional, and social stigma of HIV/AIDS. Besides financial support, Tennessee CBF provides assistance at educational seminars and ministry conferences. Wayne's dream is that groups similar to Samaritan Ministry will form everywhere in the world in order to address the human toll resulting from HIV/AIDS.

Since coming to serve CBF of Virginia, I have enjoyed working closely with Baptist Theological Seminary at Richmond, a CBF partner school. CBF of Virginia and Baptist Theological Seminary are finding ways to collaborate that are mutually edifying. This past year we launched CBF Virginia's sponsorship of a Pastors' School. By working together both entities are stronger.

These types of stories exist because of CBF's strong commitment to partnership and collaboration. These stories are frequently featured in *fellowship!* magazine.

## Partnering in theological education

Theological education has been an integral part of CBF life from its inception. While CBF owns no seminaries or divinity schools, CBF partners with the following academic institutions to encourage and ensure sound theological education for clergy, chaplains, pastoral counselors, missionaries, and other ministry leaders: Baptist Theological Seminary at Richmond, Baptist University of the Americas, Baptist Seminary of Kentucky, Brite Divinity School, Campbell University School of Divinity, Candler School of Theology at Emory University, Central Baptist Theological Seminary, Duke University Divinity School, Gardner-Webb School of Divinity, International Baptist Theological Seminary, Logsdon School of Theology at Hardin-Simmons University, Lutheran Theological Southern Seminary at Lenoir-Rhyne University, McAfee School of Theology at Mercer University, Truett Seminary at Baylor University, and Wake Forest University School of Divinity.

Every Baptist congregation has a vested interest in theological education. "Where will we find the next pastor for our church?" is heard frequently. This network of divinity schools creates a pool of trained clergy to serve within congregations and in other ministry roles.

## Ways CBF Partners to Renew God's World

Space does not allow me to share all the ways folks within the CBF network are working together with others to renew God's world, but here are a few examples:

- CBF partners with New Baptist Covenant to awaken consciousness regarding racial issues and to promote covenants of action between African-American and Anglo-American congregations. This important work is breaking down walls that divide, encouraging relationships with people different from us, and modeling for the world the power of cooperation, collaboration, and reconciliation.

- CBF partners with Baptist Joint Committee to advocate for and promote religious freedom for all. Like early Baptists, we work for the freedom of others (believers or non-believers) with the same passion we invest in our own freedom.

- CBF partners with states and regions to provide Together for Hope sites in the poorest counties in America. This work highlights critical concerns within communities and partners with other helping agencies to address food insecurity, literacy needs, and systemic issues fostering generational poverty.

- CBF partners with Baptist Women in Ministry to prophetically proclaim God calls all—women and men—to all roles of leadership within the church.

- CBF partners with Passport to ensure quality discipleship/ministry experiences for students and children.

- CBF partners with the Center for Congregational Health and the Center for Healthy Churches to make resources available to congregations in their times of need. Both of these entities help congregations find clarity around who they are, the focus of their ministries, and the types of leaders they need.

- CBF partners with Baptist World Alliance in its efforts to unify the worldwide community of Baptists.

- CBF partners with federal and state agencies, congregations, and regional networks to respond to disasters like hurricanes, tornadoes, earthquakes, flooding, wildfires, etc. We also partner with excellent Southern Baptist "first responders." CBF sees its role as a present help until cleanup and recovery are complete.

- CBF endorses chaplains and pastoral counselors to address real needs in people's lives.

- CBF partners with college students to form faith and shape vocation through Student.Go, Student.Church, and SelahVie.

- CBF's Young Baptist Ecosystem partners with young adults across the country to call out and empower the next generation of leaders.

- CBF partners with people of all ages among us who have the gift of prophecy to start new and innovative congregations.

The list of partners and ways they collaborate to renew God's world is lengthy.

We need look no further than the global mission enterprise of CBF to hear myriad stories about how CBF partners with others to renew God's world. Here are just a few examples of transformation taking place because of CBF Global Missions:

- In southern Kentucky, where poverty abounds, CBF field personnel Scarlette Jasper partners to renew God's world through education, housing assistance, and developing the assets of local residents. Jasper bears witness to Jesus Christ as she strives to repair lives broken by poverty.

- In Fredericksburg, Virginia, Sue and Greg Smith work with Latino immigrants. They engage in hands-on ministries themselves (finding jobs, getting children in school, navigating life in English, etc.), and they partner with other agencies and organizations to advocate for these newcomers to America.

- Ben and Lenora Newell approach their ministry in Texas with a "business as mission" model. This is an economic missional strategy that encourages Christians to use their business expertise to increase God's influence. Creating jobs in poor communities utilizes a comprehensive approach to economic development.

- Missy Ward Angalla advocates for struggling women from many different countries who are displaced due to war, famine, and economic collapse.

- Eddie and Cindy Ruble serve in Malaysia. They are committed to education and interact with local educators to train teachers. Cindy has become an expert in education and engagement to stop human trafficking.

- Following the devastating earthquake in Haiti, CBF focused its mission efforts on rebuilding houses and churches, providing medical assistance, and empowering people. CBF partners with 14 agencies in Haiti to provide relief. CBF field personnel Jenny Jenkins leads efforts in medical assistance and health intervention.

- Through the South Africa Ministry Network, several CBF congregations work together with trusted partners in South Africa to promote meaningful short-term mission projects, not mission tourism. This partnership is redefining what it means to participate in short-term missions. The pressing question becomes, "How can we make a real difference in the places we partner as well as learn from our South African friends?" The goal becomes taking part in renewing God's world rather than trying to "fix" anything.

We could fill volumes with stories about the effectiveness and kingdom impact of partnerships. The call to "form together" and "renew God's world" is too big for lone rangers. The idea of cross-organizational partnership holds great promise. Others benefit from what we bring to the partnership; we benefit from the skills and knowledge our partners bring to the relationship. Together we are stronger, and the impact is greater.

### Notes

[1] Brian D. McLaren and Tony Campolo, *Adventures in Missing the Point: How the Culture-controlled Church Neutered the Gospel* (El Cajon, CA: EmergentYS Books, 2003), 123.

[2] Scot McKnight, *The Jesus Creed: Loving God, Loving Others* (Brewster, MA: Paraclete Press, 2004), 8–9.

[3] Ibid.

[4] Ibid., 25.

[5] Richard Rohr, *Love Never Fails, Center for Action and Contemplation*, December 29, 2016.

[6] Sue Monk Kidd, "Birthing Compassion," *Weavings* 5/6 (November/December 1990): 20.

[7] Ibid.

[8] Diana Butler Bass, *Grounded: Finding God in the World—a Spiritual Revolution* (New York: HarperOne, 2015), 259.

[9] Andy Watts, *Prepare to Repair: Becoming a Fellowship of Reconciliation*, presentation during Tennessee CBF General Assembly, 2013, 4–5.

[10] Desmond Tutu, *No Future Without Forgiveness* (New York: Image Doubleday, 1999), 31.

[11] Watts, *Prepare to Repair*, 5.

[12] Ibid., 2.

[13] Brian McLaren, "Denominations do invaluable things" (interview by Faith & Leadership, January 18, 2010).

# Epilogue

This book's call to reclaim our Baptist heritage, to reflect on the first 25 years of the CBF, and to unpack the meaning of "forming together" and "partnering to renew God's world" comes to a close—for now. CBF has persevered and continues in its conscientious effort to stand up for historic Baptist principles. Of even greater importance is CBF's dedication to re-formation. Baptist principles are powerful and necessary, but they are always subservient to forming authentic Christian disciples intent upon being the ongoing presence of Jesus. Superficial community will not get the job done. We need transformed human beings engaged in relationships through which the very nature of God is revealed to the world. The apostle Paul describes the type of community in which the fruit of the Spirit is evident in the lives of participants: "But the fruit of the Spirit is love, joy, peace, forbearance, kindness, goodness, faithfulness, gentleness, and self-control" (Gal 5:22–23 NIV).

In the words of Cassandra Carkuff Williams, "Christian discipleship both creates and is created by Jesus-centered community, which, in turn, makes Jesus known to the world through the quality of its interior life and the power of its external mission.... Effective formation depends largely on the Christian community's ability to communicate, clearly and with integrity, the presence of Jesus within the life of the congregation and through the community's relationships with the world around it."[1]

The earliest Christian communities showed remarkable capacity to adapt to changing circumstances. That flexibility empowered the spread of the gospel everywhere. Many would say the Christian church in America today is struggling because it has lost ability to adapt to changing circumstances. Declining attendance and shrinking budgets are forcing us to ask hard questions about our purpose and the path forward.

Congregations that exist primarily to meet the needs of members will likely die. Certainly, caring for one another in community is vitally important, but a spiritually vibrant faith fellowship must experience and live out the presence of Jesus beyond the immediate group and patterns. A Christian faith community is tethered to Jesus and the Jesus way of living. Again I quote

Williams: "Much like those earliest disciples, we walk a previously untrod-den path into unfamiliar territory. To navigate it faithfully, we must be firmly grounded in the foundations of our faith, yet free enough to respond to the ever-changing terrain. We must hold on to what is essential, while having the courage to adapt to a new day. Our *roots* must be deep and our branches flex-ible, for without rootedness, we cease to be *Christian* disciples, and without responsiveness, we cease to the Christian *disciples*."[2]

We live in a day when many see tradition and specific ways of being and doing church as absolutely authoritative. When that is the case, we lose sight of the need to be constantly shaped and formed in the image of Jesus Christ for the sake of the world. A loyal soldier sits on the shoulders of many in our congregations. The loyal soldier's job is to make certain "things stay the same" and that we don't allow too much change into the congregational system. Faithfulness to Jesus may require dismissing the loyal soldier whose job it is to preserve the institution and the status quo, thank him for his service, and embrace the process of listening and discerning where Jesus wants us to go and who Jesus wants us to become.

We live in troubling times. Theologian Harvey Cox calls this the Age of the Spirit. He writes, "Faith is resurgent, while dogma is dying. The spiritual, communal, and justice-seeking dimensions of Christianity are now its lead-ing edge.... A religion based on subscribing to mandatory beliefs is no longer viable."[3] A spiritual revolution or reformation is underway. Richard Rohr describes it this way: "There is a broad awareness that Jesus was clearly teach-ing non-violence, simplicity of lifestyle, peacemaking, love of creation, and dying to the ego for both individuals and groups by offering a radical social critique to the systems of domination, power, and money. There's a growing recognition that Jesus was concerned about the transformation of real persons and human society here on earth. Christianity is meant to be a loving *way of life now*, not just a *system of beliefs and requirements* that people hope will earn them a later reward in heaven."[4]

Many within CBF recognize the necessity of this re-formation of Christianity and the Baptist expression within it. We understand the disciple-ship call to be formed and re-formed, not for our own edification, but for the needs of the world. This re-formation demands a Jesus ethic that focuses on civic responsibility and the common good—not "self-seeking consumerism that erodes neighborhoods, churches, and cooperative action for the common good."[5] Called to embody Jesus, this type of re-formation moves churches to action as incarnational witnesses for Jesus Christ.

"Business as usual" won't accomplish the lofty goal of becoming like Jesus in thought, word, and deed. Think about the conversion and transformation of Saul. He became a new person and experienced a "dramatic re-formation of attitudes, values, character, and behavior."[6] Saul didn't just change religions or adopt new beliefs. Paul began to see with different eyes, moving not only from physical blindness to sight but from certitude to a new vision from God: "New life began to surge through parts of his self that had shriveled under the weight of hate and murderous zeal. Love began to seep into his soul.... He didn't simply switch causes and retain the same self: his mind and his heart were transformed, his spirit realigned, and his life reorganized."[7]

I believe God is birthing new and more faithful ways to follow Jesus. These new approaches might look radically different from what we've previously experienced—do not let that be scary or threatening. God is always doing a new thing! Jen Hatmaker wrote this incredible description of what God is up to these days:

> Something marvelous and powerful is happening in the church. The Bride is awakening and the Spirit is rushing. It is everywhere. This movement is not contained within a denomination or demographic, not limited to a region or country. It's sweeping up mothers and pastors and teenagers and whole congregations. A stream became a current, and it is turning into a raging flood. It is daily gathering conspirators and defectors from the American Dream. It is cresting with the language of the gospel: the weak made strong, the poor made rich, the proud made humble.
>
> The body of Christ is mobilizing in unprecedented numbers. Jesus is staging a massive movement to bind up the brokenhearted and proclaim freedom for captives. The trumpet is blowing. We are on the cusp, on the side of the Hero. So while we're mistakenly warring with ourselves, Jesus is waging war on injustice and calling us to join Him.[8]

Sisters and brothers in Christ, now is the time to join this powerful movement of God—this re-formation of the church. May we all consent to be shaped and molded by God's Spirit! Be who God created you to be. Do the reflective work. Stay open to new understandings and directions. Align yourself with God's big dreams for your life. Engage the world God loves. Be salt and light. Pepper the world with grace. Awaken to God's vision for creation. See through Jesus' eyes, love with God's heart, move with the Spirit's purpose—God's ways change everything!

CBF is compelled by Christ's love to put faith into action through global missions, local ministries, and sustainable partnerships. We seek deeper obedience to God as we move forward together. God doesn't expect perfection in our actions but perfection of our intent. To that end, we invite you to journey with us on this exciting spiritual movement inspired by love, grace, compassion, and justice—for all!

I leave you with these words of encouragement from the apostle Paul:

"So here's what I want you to do, God helping you: Take your everyday, ordinary life—your sleeping, eating, going-to-work, and walking-around life—and place it before God as an offering. Embracing what God does for you is the best thing you can do for him. Don't become so well-adjusted to your culture that you fit into it without even thinking. Instead, fix your attention on God. You'll be changed from the inside out. Readily recognize what he wants from you, and quickly respond to it. Unlike the culture around you, always dragging you down to its level of immaturity, God brings the best out of you, develops well-formed maturity in you" (Rom 12:1-2 MSG).

### Notes

[1]Cassandra Carkuff Williams, "Christian Discipleship, Christian Community: Deep Roots and Flexible Branches," *The Christian Citizen* 2 (2011): 16.

[2]Ibid., 17.

[3]Harvey Cox, *The Future of Faith: The Rise and Fall of Beliefs and the Age of the Spirit* (New York: HarperOne, 2009), 5–6.

[4]Richard Rohr, *A New Reformation, Center for Action and Contemplation*, January 3, 2017.

[5]Harold Glen Stassen, *A Thicker Jesus: Incarnational Discipleship in a Secular Age* (Louisville: Westminster John Knox Press, 2012), 6.

[6]David G. Benner, *Spirituality and the Awakening Self: The Sacred Journey of Transformation* (Grand Rapids: Brazos Press, 2012), 3.

[7]Ibid.

[8]Jen Hatmaker, *An Experimental Mutiny Against Excess* (Nashville: B&H Publishing Group, 2012); found in "A Guide to Prayer for All God's People," 89.

# Questions for Your Reflection

### Part 1

1. Why is knowing our Baptist history and heritage important?

2. What did you learn to help you better understand diversity within the Baptist family?

3. Look again at each chapter in Part 1, and identify characteristics of each tradition with which you most identify. Which characteristics are most offensive to you?

4. How has each of the traditions shaped the congregation of which you are a part? Articulate values and convictions flowing from each tradition that inform the practices of your congregation.

### Part 2

1. Reflect on Shurden's comment, "Fundamentalists want you to interpret the Bible in one way—their way. They do not want you to have freedom to interpret it your way, even if you do believe the Bible is the sufficient, certain, and authoritative Word of God."

2. Do you see diversity as an asset or liability?

3. What is the difference between indoctrination and theological education?

4. What happens to theological education if those guiding it believe they alone possess the "truth"? How do they account for the mystery of God (that which humans cannot know)?

### Part 3

1. As you read about the values and convictions that shaped and formed CBF, what stands out as most important to you?
2. Look at the various identity statements that have guided the Fellowship over the past 25 years. How do you see CBF growing and evolving?

3. Reflect on the ministry of our three Executive Coordinators. What stands out about the "unique gifts" each brought to the Fellowship?

4. Read Chapter 14 again. Which of these "lessons learned" resonate most with you? What would you add to the list?

5. How might you use content from Marion Aldridge's "elevator speech" to tell others about CBF?

### Part 4

1. What was your understanding of CBF's "big idea" (*forming together*) before reading this book? How has your awareness changed?

2. How could deeper insight into "forming faith" change your appreciation for nurturing a relationship with Jesus Christ?

3. Unpack your understanding of the difference between "educating for a belief system about Jesus" versus "forming faith in the person of Jesus Christ."

4. What are the pitfalls of doing discipleship "our way" instead of Jesus' way?

5. How would your life be different if you adopted and lived by Jesus' mission statement?

6. How has your comprehension of what Jesus taught in the Sermon on the Mount changed? What will be necessary to live in alignment with Jesus' expectations?

7. Why is studying Jesus' life and ministry important? To what degree do you allow how Jesus lived to guide your life?

8. Respond to Maricle's 8 Essential Habits. What insights do you gain from reflecting on how Jesus spent his time?

9. Which of the barriers to nurturing a "forming together" culture cause you the most discomfort? Do you see these barriers at work within your congregation?

10. Spend some time reflecting on the section about certitude. How is certitude a barrier to faith? Would you agree certitude might be the opposite of faith?

11. If theological reflection were incorporated into all aspects of congregational life, how would members and the body itself change? What happens if we fail to encourage reflection?

12. How does the verb *faithing* change your understanding of faith?

13. Discuss different approaches to forming faith: "These are your faith—do not question them" versus "These are basic building blocks of faith but you must put them together in ways that have meaning for you."

14. What in your faith journey leads you to understand conversion as a process (as opposed to a one-time experience)?

15. Who controls the content of your "congregational container" (i.e., who determines what is acceptable and how far the container may expand?)?

16. Why must the church be continually converted?

17. Evaluate efforts to "form faith in Jesus" in your congregation. Where are the gaps?

18. Respond to the suggestions about how to nurture a "forming together" culture.

19. How might focusing a congregation's attention on God's mission (what God is up to in the world throughout time) influence how time and energy is invested?

20. What is the role of the "Jesus Creed" in spiritual formation? Why is this so important?

21. Can we really call ourselves *Christian* if we are not intentional about "birthing compassion"?

22. How has your understanding of "reconciliation, transforming, and transformative" changed? What are the implications of these understandings for your congregation? For CBF?

23. Why do you believe "partnering" is woven into CBF's DNA?

24. With whom is your congregation partnering (in your local community, in your state, in the United States, around the globe) to renew God's world?

# A Historical Timeline

### By Aaron D. Weaver

**Editor's Note:** The following is a brief timeline of significant events from the history of the Cooperative Baptist Fellowship. This timeline was first published in *CBF at 25: Stories of the Cooperative Baptist Fellowship* (Nurturing Faith Publishing, 2016).

## 1990

- Baptist Cooperative Missions Program (BCMP; forerunner of the CBF) chartered as a nonprofit corporation in Georgia on August 1 with Duke McCall as incorporator and a 17-member board of directors
- August 23–25 meeting of moderate Baptists in Atlanta (Consultation of Concerned Baptists) convened by Baptists Committed with Jimmy Allen as convener; 70-member Interim Steering Committee forms, chaired by Daniel Vestal, to receive and distribute funds through the BCMP and develop a detailed plan and distribution formula for the alternative mechanism for funding missions of Southern Baptist agencies and institutions, as well as non-SBC entities
- CBF of Florida forms in November at Bayshore Baptist Church in Tampa (incorporated May 1991)

## 1991

- 70-member Interim Steering Committee meets in January, agrees on name "The Baptist Fellowship" for recommendation to a planned convocation in Atlanta May 9–11
- CBF of Arkansas forms March 21–22 at Lakeshore Drive Baptist Church in Little Rock; originally the Arkansas Fellowship of Concerned Baptists; incorporated as CBF of Arkansas on March 5, 1994

- Kentucky Baptist Fellowship forms March 19 at St. Matthews Baptist Church in Louisville
- Interim Steering Committee approves proposal in March to establish an ongoing relationship with *SBC Today* (now *Baptists Today*) for news coverage of "The Fellowship"
- First employee, Sandra Davey, hired on April 15
- CBF born May 9–11 in Atlanta at "Convocation of the Baptist Fellowship"; adoption of constitution, bylaws, and organizational name "Cooperative Baptist Fellowship"; John Hewett elected as first Moderator as well as 79-member Coordinating Council; adoption of Fellowship's founding document, "An Address to the Public," and a three-track funding mechanism with a proposed budget of $545,000; more than 5,000 in attendance
- Convocation attendees adopt giving plans for 1992, which include funding for new seminaries George W. Truett Theological Seminary at Baylor University (begins classes in fall 1994) and Baptist Theological Seminary at Richmond (begins classes in fall 1991)
- Baptist Fellowship of Missouri (BFM; now CBF Heartland) incorporates June 16 and a board of directors selected; September 15, 1990, meeting at Little Bonne Femme Baptist Church in Columbia, Missouri, instrumental in birthing BFM
- CBF of South Carolina forms October 1 at St. Andrews Baptist Church in Columbia
- Midwest region CBF (formed/renamed as North Central region in 2000) holds first meeting October 11–12 at New Christian Valley Baptist Church in South Holland, Illinois; bylaws adopted June 1992
- CBF provides financial support via designated contributions to Associated Baptist Press (founded July 17, 1990; now Baptist News Global) and the Baptist Joint Committee on Public Affairs (founded 1936; now Baptist Joint Committee for Religious Liberty)

## 1992

- CBF Coordinating Council votes to expand its missions program and hire specific missionaries in Europe who no longer want to work for the Foreign Mission Board of the SBC

- CBF begins sending funds to the Baptist Theological Seminary in Rüschlikon, Switzerland, including scholarships to students, and sends funds to the new Baptist Center for Ethics (formed in July 1991 and led by Robert Parham)
- Cecil Sherman becomes first CBF Coordinator on April 1
- BCMP merges into CBF on April 1
- Southern Baptist Women in Ministry (renamed as Baptist Women in Ministry in 1993) holds its annual gathering in conjunction with the CBF General Assembly in Fort Worth, Texas
- 6,000 people attend the General Assembly in Fort Worth, April 30–May 2; attendees affirm guiding statement on global missions and welcome first four CBF "missioners" (called "missionaries" beginning in 1993): John David and JoAnn Hopper and Charles "T" and Kathy Thomas (all recently resigned Southern Baptist missionaries)
- General Assembly attendees pass statement on racial reconciliation, confessing their complicity in "sin of racism in our own heritage" and pledging to work to address the "critical needs of all people of color" (resolutions on human sexuality and ecology were referred to the Ethics and Public Policy Ministry Group)
- General Assembly revises giving plans to devote more money for Fellowship ministries and decrease funding for SBC entities; attendees receive greetings via telegram from Billy Graham
- Inaugural CBF Offering for Global Missions is received with the theme "Keeping the Promises" and raises nearly $2 million
- CBF state leaders organize network at September 9–10 meeting; 22 people representing 16 CBF state and regions participate
- Election of Patricia Ayres as CBF Moderator, the first female and layperson in this position
- Baptists in Texas form steering committee that meets informally (later known as CBF of Texas and legally incorporated July 3, 2002); part-time coordinator hired in 1994 and full-time coordinator named in 2000
- CBF West forms at Nineteenth Avenue Baptist Church in San Francisco, California (incorporated in 1997)
- CBF of Oklahoma forms February 29 at First Baptist Church of Norman, Oklahoma (officially incorporated March 26)

- Tennessee CBF forms July 24 at Woodmont Baptist Church in Nashville
- Fellowship provides relief beginning August 27 to south Florida following Hurricane Andrew, marking its first disaster response effort
- CBF of Mississippi forms October 16 at Edison-Walthall Hotel in Jackson
- CBF of Virginia forms in November at First Baptist Church in Virginia Beach
- CBF of Georgia forms November 9 at First Baptist Church of Christ in Macon
- Scholarships awarded to 19 Baptist students at eight theological schools, including students at Baptist Theological Seminary at Richmond for the 1992–1993 academic year as well as students at the Baptist Studies Program of Candler School of Theology (Emory University) and the Baptist House of Studies of Duke Divinity School (Duke University)
- CBF and the Alliance of Baptists hold dialogue session September 9 and issue a joint statement stating plans not to merge

**1993**
- Keith Parks hired as first CBF Global Missions Coordinator, begins January 18
- Baptist Fellowship of the Northeast forms January 30 at Greenwich Baptist Church in Greenwich, Connecticut
- CBF of Louisiana forms in May
- Former president Jimmy Carter gives keynote address at General Assembly in Birmingham, Alabama, challenging attendees to embrace racial reconciliation, women in ministry, and the world's poor; Assembly adopts new constitution due to sunset clause in 1991 constitution; new constitution limits membership to contributing Baptist individuals and churches (rather than anyone in attendance) and prohibits introduction of resolutions and similar motions from the floor of an Assembly business session
- CBF produces first missions resource, titled "Doing Missions in a World without Borders"
- Fellowship commissions at General Assembly first missionaries who were not former employees of the Foreign Mission Board: Bert and Debbie Ayers (Albania); six additional new missionaries commissioned

in September: David and Tracy Bengtson (Miami), Allen and Verr Dean Williams (Czech Republic), and Stanley and Kay Parks (Indonesia)

- Fellowship continues to award scholarships to students pursuing theological education at numerous non-SBC schools for 1993–1994 academic year

- First CBF missions education study series created for children, youth, and adults in December, adapted from *Formations* curriculum of Smyth & Helwys Publishing, Inc.

- CBF begins partnership with Seeds of Hope, Inc., a Waco, Texas-based ministry providing hunger publications and resources for churches and individuals

**1994**

- CBF of North Carolina forms January 21 at First Baptist Church in Winston-Salem

- CBF Foundation created in February to provide investment and endowment services for CBF supporters and churches; Ruben Swint named as first president

- Alabama CBF forms May 6

- SBC votes in June to refuse to channel contributions to its agencies and institutions through CBF (in 1993 CBF sent just over $2 million to support SBC missions); CBF officers vote July 6 to replace Fellowship's three giving plans with a single plan that supports only Fellowship causes and its partners

- Ethics and Public Policy Ministry Group of CBF partners with Bread for the World, supporting its "Covenant Church" program, where congregations agree through worship and study to understand the causes and solutions to global hunger

- Mid-Atlantic CBF incorporates August 16 and holds second annual General Assembly at Woodbrook Baptist Church in Baltimore, Maryland, on October 22

- Earl and Jane Martin become CBF's first emeritus missionaries after three decades of mission service in east Africa, Rwanda, and Baptist Theological Seminary in Rüschlikon, Switzerland

## 1995

- CBF Coordinating Council adopts a formal mission statement in February, highlighting the Fellowship's goals to "network, empower and mobilize Baptist Christians and churches for effective missions and ministry in the name of Christ"

- CBF Coordinating Council votes to give $50,000 to support capital needs of Central Baptist Theological Seminary, a new partner with historic ties to American Baptist Churches USA

- CBF announces in March the move of its retirement and insurance plans for employees and missionaries from the Southern Baptist Annuity Board to the Minister and Missionaries Benefit Board of American Baptist Churches USA

- CBF Global Missions expands with the appointment of two-year missionaries to service alongside career missionaries (later renamed/formalized as Global Service Corps program)

- CBF's 100th missionary is appointed

- Woman's Missionary Union announces July 12 it will produce missions education supplements for CBF to be sent to churches wishing to study the work of CBF missionaries

- CBF Global Missions gives $100,000 grant to First Baptist Church in Abilene, Texas, to help build a hospitality house for the visiting families of inmates at two area prisons

- American Baptist Churches USA host CBF leaders at American Baptist Assembly at Green Lake, Wisconsin, for first joint gathering.

- CBF Coordinating Council approves agreement to purchase tract of Atlanta property from Mercer University and enters into a five-year rental agreement for its headquarters to be housed in what will become the building for Mercer's McAfee School of Theology on the Atlanta campus (giving Mercer $2 million to build its theology school)

## 1996

- CBF launches website: *www.cbfonline.org*

- CBF Global Missions initiates Envoy program to spread a network of secularly employed Christians around the globe

Reclaiming & Re-Forming Baptist Identity

- Attendees to General Assembly in Richmond, Virginia, vote for CBF to remain a network of individuals and churches rather than become a convention/denomination

- Cecil Sherman retires, becomes visiting professor at Baptist Theological Seminary at Richmond; Tommy Boland selected to serve as Interim CBF Coordinator from June through December

- Daniel Vestal selected in December to succeed Cecil Sherman as CBF Executive Coordinator

## 1997

- CBF makes first venture into China in July/August, sending a volunteer team to help Chinese English teachers develop better conversational skills

- Student scholarships for theological education are renamed as "Leadership Scholarships" beginning with the 1997–1998 academic year to foster a stronger connection between student scholars and the Fellowship, including funds to participate in CBF events such as General Assembly

- CBF Albania missions team evacuated during Albanian rebellion of 1997, a violent uprising marked by disorder and anarchy in which the government is overthrown and 2,000 people are killed; CBF missionary Debbie Ayers suffers a head wound from a stray bullet during the evacuation

- Upon the recommendation of a study committee, CBF declares itself a "religious endorsing body" for the purpose of endorsing chaplains and pastoral counselors

- New Global Missions initiative launches for local churches in June called "Adopt-A-People" to assist CBF-related churches to become directly involved in "World A" missions by identifying and "adopting" an unreached people group

- Passport Camps (formed in 1993) uses its summer mission offering collected from teen campers to fund the construction of 10 huts in Thailand to assist the work of CBF field personnel

## 1998

- Fellowship endorses first five chaplains and pastoral counselors and later in the year endorses its first military chaplains; CBF recognized in summer by Department of Defense as an endorsing body

- CBF recognized by the United Nations as a non-governmental organization, allowing the Fellowship to participate directly in UN processes
- Presidents and deans of CBF-related theological schools gather for third annual retreat and vote to become a consortium of schools partnering with CBF
- First student at Campbell University Divinity School (founded in 1996) to be awarded a CBF Leadership Scholarship

## 1999

- Keith Parks retires as Global Missions Coordinator; Barbara and Gary Baldridge appointed in October as Co-Coordinators of CBF Global Missions
- Fellowship begins ministry in November to plant new churches with matching grant from Georgia-based Venture Ministries and with support of Atlanta's Dunwoody Baptist Church
- CBF begins officially providing reference and referral services for churches and ministers

## 2000

- First CBF Young Leaders retreat held in spring
- Donna Forrester becomes first ordained woman to serve as CBF Moderator
- CBF Coordinating Council adopts during its fall meeting an administrative policy on homosexual behavior related to personnel and funding, stating, "we believe the foundation of a Christian sexual ethic is faithfulness in marriage between a man and a woman and celibacy in singleness"
- Church Benefits Board incorporates in September to provide benefits to Fellowship staff, field personnel, ministers, and partner organizations; Gary Skeen, CBF's Coordinator of Finance and Administration, named as founding president

## 2001

- CBF holds inaugural True Survivor conference for Christian educators (now known as ChurchWorks)
- 10th anniversary celebration of the Fellowship at three-day General Assembly in June at the Georgia World Congress Center in Atlanta

includes "Decade of Promise" banquet and keynote address from former president Jimmy Carter

- Together for Hope—CBF's rural poverty initiative and 20-year commitment to offer funding and resources to people in and around 20 of the poorest counties in the United States—is launched

- CBF responds to 9/11 terrorist attacks in Washington, DC, and New York City; allocates emergency relief funds to field personnel and Metro Baptist Church in NYC

- CBF joins with World Vision to provide emergency relief ministries for Afghan refugees facing conflict and drought following the U.S. invasion of Afghanistan in October; CBF contributes $100,000

- CBF becomes partner with Samaritan Ministry, a ministry of Central Baptist Church of Bearden in Knoxville, Tennessee, founded in 1996 by Wayne Smith to serve people affected by HIV/AIDS

## 2002

- "It's Time" is theme of General Assembly in Fort Worth, Texas, where CBF Executive Coordinator Daniel Vestal casts his vision for churches to represent Christ in the world; book published by Vestal titled *It's Time!: An Urgent Call to Christian Mission*

- CBF Global Missions begins commissioning "field personnel" rather than "missionaries," adopting new language due to the growing negative connotation of "missionary" in many parts of the world and to allow commissioned individuals to enter certain areas where they might not otherwise be welcomed

- CBF Coordinating Council adopts statement during its fall meeting, defining the Fellowship as a "Baptist association of churches and individuals" separate from the SBC, but declines to call itself a convention or denomination; statement made in response to request by the Membership Committee of the Baptist World Alliance to demonstrate that CBF was not an "integral part" of any Baptist World Alliance member, specifically the SBC

- CBF launches Student.Go, a student missions initiative to send undergraduates and graduates to serve alongside CBF field personnel and partners around the world

- CBF begins partnership with Center for Family and Community Ministries of Baylor University School of Social Work (founded in 1998); center tasked to provide congregational assessments using the church census for leadership planning, workshops on family, and internship opportunities for social workers who are Cooperative Baptists

## 2003

- Fellowship forms partnership agreement with Hispanic Baptist Theological School (now known as Baptist University of the Americas)
- Lilly Endowment awards CBF $2 million to participate in a national program called "Sustaining Pastoral Excellence," part of an effort to maintain excellence in the nation's pastoral leaders; grant helps fund Fellowship's Initiative for Ministerial Excellence, which includes peer learning groups, sabbatical study, and a residency program for prospective ministers studying at CBF-partner theological schools
- Baptist World Alliance votes to extend membership to CBF on July 11
- CBF continues relief efforts in war-torn Iraq, distributing food, clothes, shoes, hygiene kits to an estimated 20,000 Iraqi families

## 2004

- CBF and Passport Camps co-sponsor Antiphony, a retreat for college students and seminarians which was the Fellowship's first national event for young adults
- Formation at Clemson University of the first Cooperative Student Fellowship
- CBF participates in its first meeting of the North American Baptist Fellowship as a member of the Baptist World Alliance; 16 member bodies of the North American Baptist Fellowship represent 17 million Baptists
- CBF and Lutheran Theological Southern Seminary in Columbia, South Carolina, create partnership to develop Baptist studies program under leadership of Rev. Dr. Virginia Barfield (a Cooperative Baptist) to offer opportunities for Baptist students to take specialized courses in Baptist history and theology and also to provide continuing education for Baptist ministerial staff members and laity in the state
- CBF partners with Center for Congregational Health (formed 1992) for the center to provide consultation to CBF churches in areas including

strategic planning, interim ministry, conflict management, staff relationships, and leadership

## 2005

- Jack Snell, CBF's Associate Missions Coordinator, named as Interim Global Missions Coordinator following the February resignation of Barbara Baldridge and December 2004 retirement of Gary Baldridge
- CBF launches response to southeast Asia tsunami, contributing and raising more than $2.5 million for relief and development projects
- CBF responds to Hurricane Katrina, and over next five years donates more than $1.5 million to long-term recovery work
- Attendees at General Assembly in Grapevine, Texas, give $45,000 in support of first Jimmy and Rosalynn Carter Offering for Religious Liberty and Human Rights
- Joy Yee assumes CBF Moderator duties at conclusion of General Assembly, becoming Fellowship's first female senior pastor and first Asian American to hold the position

## 2006

- Rob Nash selected to serve as Global Missions Coordinator at June meeting of CBF Coordinating Council
- HIV/AIDS summit held on eve of General Assembly in Atlanta
- Emmanuel McCall assumes duties as CBF Moderator, first African American to hold this position
- CBF becomes founding participant in the ecumenical organization Christian Churches Together
- CBF receives second major Lilly Endowment grant to continue and expand its Initiative for Ministerial Excellence to offer sabbatical grants and support to peer learning groups as well as a ministerial residency program
- Faith in 3D student conference is held at Walt Disney World Resort in Orlando, Florida—a partnership of CBF, Passport Camps, Presbyterian Church USA, and the Episcopal Church

- CBF offers missional ministry grants to encourage Fellowship churches in their missional journeys; eligible churches complete *It's Time: A Journey Toward Missional Faithfulness*

- CBF Coordinating Council votes in October to approve four schools as "identity partners" to receive institutional funding, scholarships and initiative support: Mercer University's McAfee School of Theology, Baptist Theological Seminary at Richmond, Campbell University Divinity School, and Baylor University's George W. Truett Theological Seminary; and nine schools as "leadership partners" whose students apply for CBF Leadership Scholarships: M. Christopher White School of Divinity at Gardner-Webb University, Central Baptist Theological Seminary, Logsdon School of Theology at Hardin-Simmons University, Baptist House of Studies at Duke Divinity School, Baptist Studies Program at Candler School of Theology, Wake Forest University School of Divinity, the Baptist Studies Program at Brite Divinity School of Texas Christian University, Baptist Seminary of Kentucky, and the Baptist Studies Program at Lutheran Theological Seminary; Baptist University of the Americas and International Baptist Theological Seminary named as global partners

- CBF age-graded missions education resources *Form*, *Spark*, *Ignite*, and *Affect* are introduced

- CBF partner Baptist History & Heritage Society publishes "Beginnings of the Cooperative Baptist Fellowship" booklet by Pam Durso

## 2007

- Historic joint gathering of CBF with American Baptist Churches USA in Washington, DC, in conjunction with the CBF General Assembly and ABC-USA Biennial Summit

- General Assembly adopts UN Millennium Development Goals, which aim to eradicate extreme poverty and hunger, achieve universal primary education, promote gender equality and empower women, reduce child mortality, improve maternal health, combat HIV/AIDS, malaria and other diseases, ensure environmental sustainability, and promote global partnerships for development

- CBF and ABC-USA jointly commission Marcia and Duane Binkley and Nancy and Steve James to serve as co-appointed field personnel in the United States (with Karen refugees and Haiti, respectively)

- Leaders of 30 Baptist organizations, including CBF, announce plans for a "Celebration of a New Baptist Covenant"

## 2008

- "Celebration of a New Baptist Covenant" meeting held in Atlanta, where more than 15,000 Baptists gather as part of an effort to unite Baptists in North America around the Luke 4 mandate to "bring good news to the poor, proclaim release to the captives and recovery of sight to the blind, to let the oppressed go free, and to proclaim the year of the Lord's favor"
- Eight historic Baptist colleges and universities announce they will offer undergraduate tuition scholarships for the children of CBF field personnel (Mercer University made a similar commitment in 2007)
- On the seventh anniversary of the 9/11 attacks, CBF co-sponsors national summit on torture on the Atlanta campus of Mercer University

## 2009

- Rob Sellers, a professor at Logsdon School of Theology of Hardin-Simmons University, represents CBF at a historic Baptist-Muslim dialogue comprised of a diverse group of Baptist and Muslim leaders at Andover Newton Theological School near Boston, Massachusetts, on January 9–11
- CBF develops partnership with Japan Baptist Convention to send field personnel to the country; Carson and Laura Foushee appointed in 2013 as first CBF field personnel to Japan

## 2010

- CBF creates Collegiate Congregational Internship program (now known as Student.Church), offering grants to churches to fund summer internship positions for 97 students in its inaugural year
- Voluntary Organizations Active in Disaster recognizes CBF as a disaster response organization
- Cooperative Baptists donate more than $1.2 million to Haitian earthquake relief efforts; CBF signs three-year agreement with Convention Baptiste d'Haiti for earthquake recovery, including development strategy, medical ministry, and micro-enterprise; CBF helps start Haiti Housing Network, a joint collaboration with partners Conscience International, Fuller Center for Housing, and the Baptist General Convention of Texas

- Christy McMillin-Goodwin becomes first person elected as CBF Moderator to have graduated from a CBF-partner seminary (Baptist Theological Seminary at Richmond)
- CBF Moderator Hal Bass appoints 14-member task force (known as 2012 Task Force) to conduct two-year study of the Fellowship's mission and organizational future
- General Assembly workshop titled "A Family Conversation About Same-Sex Orientation" at General Assembly explores what it means to be the presence of Christ among persons of same-sex orientation
- CBF holds inaugural Selah Vie retreat, a yearly end-of-summer gathering for student participants of Student.Go, Collegiate Congregational Internship Program, as well as other young Baptists
- Founding CBF Coordinator Cecil Sherman dies April 17
- CBF Executive Coordinator Daniel Vestal and Baugh Foundation president Babs Baugh convene "Fellowship Baptist Movement" retreat April 27–29 at Callaway Gardens in Pine Mountain, Georgia, for leaders from CBF-related organizations to reflect on the past and look to the future
- Advisory Council of CBF, on behalf of Coordinating Council, adopts statement on September 10 condemning a plan by a Florida church to burn the Quran on September 11 and encouraging prayers for peace and understanding among all religions

## 2011

- Fellowship celebrates 20th anniversary at General Assembly in Tampa, featuring banquet with keynote address by Molly Marshall, president of Central Baptist Theological Seminary
- CBF of the Bahamas forms October 23 in partnership with CBF of Florida; installation of first national coordinator, John McIntosh, and first national administrator, Preston Cooper

## 2012

- Rob Nash resigns as Global Missions Coordinator in June to return to academia as Associate Dean at Mercer University's McAfee School of Theology; Jim A. Smith named as Interim Global Missions Coordinator (Smith and his wife, Becky, were among the first field personnel appointed by the Fellowship in 1993)

- CBF hosts "CBF Day" during spring at Wake Forest University School of Divinity, Campbell University Divinity School, and the M. Christopher White School of Divinity of Gardner-Webb University to celebrate their partnership and shared dedication to theological education ("CBF Day" is an annual day-long event on campuses of CBF-partner theology schools started several years prior to celebrate the partnership in training women and men for vocational ministry)

- CBF co-sponsors with Mercer University "A [Baptist] Conference on Sexuality and Covenant," held April 19–21 at First Baptist Church of Decatur, Georgia, to provide Baptists with an opportunity for honest, compassionate and prayerful dialogue around matters and questions of sexuality

- General Assembly adopts 2012 Task Force Report; Fellowship staff and leaders begin planning for implementation of recommendations

- CBF announces first two annual "Vestal Scholars," named in honor of Daniel and Earlene Vestal, at General Assembly in Fort Worth, Texas; Daniel Vestal retires June 30 as CBF Executive Coordinator after 15 years of service in the position; Fellowship leader and former CBF Moderator Pat Anderson begins as CBF Interim Executive Coordinator on July 1

- Dawnings, CBF's initiative for congregational renewal, launches with several churches taking part in pilot process focused on visioning, forming and engaging

- CBF Fellows program starts with support of a Lilly Endowment grant to provide encouragement and support for ministers in their first call after seminary graduation; Terry Hamrick directs the first cohort of 25 Fellows

## 2013

- CBF Coordinating Council selects Suzii Paynter as Executive Coordinator; begins March 1

- 2012 Task Force recommendations implemented, including new CBF governance structure with creation of a Missions Council, Ministries Council, Governing Board, and Nominating Committee

- General Assembly approves new CBF constitution and bylaws; organization of state and regional leaders called the Movement Leadership Team further formalized

- CBF launches formal advocacy efforts; Stephen Reeves of Texas Baptist Christian Life Commission hired to coordinate advocacy work

## 2014

- CBF forms partnership in February with the Baptist World Alliance for international religious liberty and global advocacy efforts at the UN
- CBF partners with Wilshire Baptist Church in Dallas, Texas, to create a three-year pilot project focused on congregational advocacy to help congregations discern how they might become effective advocates within their communities
- Steven Porter, a professor at Baylor University's George W. Truett Theological Seminary, named as Global Missions Coordinator
- Kasey Jones begins duties as CBF Moderator, becoming the first African-American woman to hold the position
- Longest-serving CBF staff member, Clarissa Strickland, retires June 30 after 23 years of service
- Suzii Paynter meets with President Obama and a small group of faith leaders in the Oval Office at the White House to discuss immigration reform
- CBF and CBF of Florida sponsor in November the first "Academy for Spiritual Formation" for pastors in Cuba, a five-day enrichment event of The Upper Room, the ecumenical division of the United Methodist General Board of Discipleship

## 2015

- CBF Global Missions begins strategic planning for the 21st century
- First inaugural CBF Seminarian Retreat—students and faculty from all 14 U.S.-based partner seminaries and divinity schools participate
- CBF Advocacy helps start and joins Faith for Just Lending, a coalition of faith organizations aiming to combat predatory lending
- CBF joins BReAD (Baptist Relief and Development Network) to improve collaboration among Baptist groups involved in international relief and development work; CBF takes part in BReAD's response to April earthquakes in Nepal
- CBF launches Sabbatical Initiative in June to invest in the health of ministers and local congregations through making saving funds easier for

churches, providing grants and encouraging significant sabbatical experiences; initiative is a multiple-organization endeavor also including CBF Foundation, CBF Church Benefits, and CBF state and regional organizations

- CBF Executive Coordinator Suzii Paynter gives August commencement address at CBF partner Baptist Seminary of Kentucky (formed in 2002) as seminary celebrates receiving accreditation from Association of Theological Schools

- CBF Executive Coordinator Suzii Paynter participates in events surrounding the visit of Pope Francis to the United States

- CBF renews and expands partnership in November with Global Women, an organization addressing women's issues around the world such as clean water, maternal health, and sex trafficking awareness and prevention

- CBF receives significant grant from the Lilly Endowment as part of its "National Initiative to Address Economic Challenges Facing Pastoral Leaders"; grant awarded to initiate education and financial initiatives for pastoral leaders of the Fellowship

## 2016

- CBF announces in January a comprehensive plan for Global Missions, doubling down on its commitment to the long-term presence of field personnel through new sustainable funding model that consolidates field personnel under a single employment category with equitable funding

- CBF Council on Endorsement on March 5 selects Erin Lysse, a chaplain in Winston-Salem, North Carolina, as the 1,000th CBF-endorsed chaplain or pastoral counselor

- CBF turns 25 on May 11; celebrates 25th anniversary at General Assembly, June 20–24 in Greensboro, where a $12 million endowment campaign was launched to support the long-term presence of CBF field personnel, to help form healthy congregations, and to nurture young Baptists

- CBF contributes funds in June to support the safe passage of Syrian refugees to Belgium as part of its multifaceted and sustained response to the Syrian refugee crisis, popularly described as "the biggest humanitarian emergency of our era." CBF's response began in 2013 with field personnel and ministry partners in Lebanon and Syria, and by June 2016 was led by mission workers in five countries in Europe and the Middle East

- CBF partners with faith-based ministries to provide support to area congregational leaders on rapid crisis response in the aftermath of the June 12 mass shooting at Pulse, a LGBT nightclub in Orlando, Florida, where 49 people were killed and 53 others wounded

- CBF Executive Coordinator announces June 21 the launch of the Illumination Project, a process of discernment and accompaniment involving Fellowship congregational leaders to build and strengthen CBF unity through cooperation; CBF Moderator Doug Dortch names a five-member committee to guide the work of the Illumination Project in its first implementation focused on matters of human sexuality

- CBF Governing Board approves the creation June 22 of the Clergy Sexual Misconduct Task Force, an effort born from a partnership between CBF and Baptist Women in Ministry to focus on the prevention of clergy sexual misconduct

- CBF Governing Board adopts a statement on June 24 in response to the June 12 mass shooting at Pulse nightclub in Orlando, Florida: "Admittedly and sadly, the Church has said to be tacitly complicit in the Orlando attack because some Christians have either spoken in hateful ways about LGBTQ persons or have remained silent when other people spewed hate. No more. We stand united in our belief that every person is created in God's image and endowed with a sacred dignity that cannot be taken away."

- CBF forms partnership with the National Baptist Convention of America International, Inc. (NBCA) on October 5 to "build an authentic and Christ-like community through shared work" at Simmons College of Kentucky in Louisville, a historically black college and location of the NBCA headquarters

**Terry Maples** serves as Field Coordinator for Cooperative Baptist Fellowship Virginia, after almost six years in a similar role with Tennessee CBF. He spent 27 years guiding faith formation and discipleship for three congregations in Florida and Virginia including almost twenty years at Huguenot Road Baptist Church in Richmond, Virginia.

Terry has written articles, studies, and lesson plans addressing issues of faith and practice. He enjoys coaching pastors and churches, and has extensive experience leading discipleship conferences and stewardship campaigns.

Terry received the Virginia Baptist Christian Educator of the Year Award in 2000. He earned a Master of Divinity in Religious Education degree from Southern Baptist Theological Seminary and an accounting degree from the University of Alabama.

In addition to his deep passion for nurturing congregational spiritual vitality, Terry enjoys hiking, reading, listening to music, watching college football, and putting his many manual skills to good use. He has been married to Joan for 37 years; they have two grown children.


**Dr. Gene Wilder** served as pastor of churches throughout the Southeastern U.S. for more than 40 years. In 2016 he was Interim Field Coordinator for the Tennessee Cooperative Baptist Fellowship.

A graduate of Carson Newman University, Southwestern Baptist Theological Seminary and Southern Baptist Theological Seminary, he has been published in several journals and newspapers. He is the author two books and has been a contributing author for several others.

Dr. Wilder was honored with the "Golden Pen Award" from Macon News in Macon, Georgia, and on two occasions received first place awards by the Georgia Press Association.

He and his wife, Pat, have two adult children and three adorable granddaughters. They live in Jefferson City, Tennessee, where in retirement Gene continues to write, read, travel, play golf and hike in the Smoky Mountains.

For more information or to contact him, visit *gene-wilder.com*.

CPSIA information can be obtained
at www.ICGtesting.com
Printed in the USA
JSHW011728270819
1226JS00006BA/35